THE POLTAVA AFFAIR

THE POLTAVA AFFAIR

A Russian Warning: An American Tragedy

GLENN B. INFIELD

Macmillan Publishing Co., Inc.
NEW YORK

Macmillan Publishing Co., Inc.
Collier-Macmillan Canada Ltd.

Library of Congress Catalog Card Number: 72-93628

First Printing

Printed in the United States of America

For Dad

Contents

Acknowledgments

This book has had many contributors for whose advice, help, and patience I would like to express my gratitude and thanks. Since the book deals with three distinct areas of "Operation Frantic"—diplomatic, political and military—I owe a debt to many individuals in each of these areas who provided their diaries, recollections, and reports. Former Ambassador W. Averell Harriman's hospitality at his Georgetown home where he provided invaluable information on the complicated diplomatic negotiations that were conducted with the Russians during this period was greatly appreciated. General John R. Deane, who, as head of the U.S. Military Mission to Moscow, worked very closely with W. Averell Harriman during this period, was very cooperative, as were Generals Edmund W. Hill, William L. Ritchie, and Robert L. Walsh, each of whom commanded the Eastern Command of the USSTAF with headquarters at Poltava at various times during "Operation Frantic." General Walsh graciously permitted use of his fact book, which is now deposited at the United States Air Force Academy, Colorado. General Ira Eaker, who led the first mission of "Operation Frantic" and did much of the planning for the unique United States-Soviet Union collaboration attempt, not only provided a great deal of material for the book but provided office facilities in Washington, D.C., while the material was studied.

In Germany, Franz-Josef Giehl interviewed for me many former Luftwaffe pilots who had opposed the American aircraft and crews during "Operation Frantic" and also did detailed research at the German Air Force Archives at Frieburg for my benefit. Colonel Wilhelm Antrup of the Luftwaffe, one of the group commanders who led his aircraft on the very successful bombing mission to

Poltava on the night of June 21, 1944, wrote his account of the operation for use in the book, for which I am grateful.

Marguerite K. Kennedy, Chief of the Archives Branch, Historical Research Division, Maxwell Air Force Base, Alabama, and her staff helped me search the hundreds of reports, narratives, and histories available on "Operation Frantic" at the archives and declassified much of the still-secret material so that it could be used in this book. At the U.S. Air Force Museum, Royal D. Frey, Chief of the Research Division, made available his files despite an impending visit by President Richard M. Nixon to dedicate the museum's new home.

After the planning was completed and the complex negotiations had ended, the dangerous missions had to be flown by the same aircrews that had been opposing the Luftwaffe from bases in Italy and England for months. To obtain the details of the "Operation Frantic" flight operations I had the complete cooperation of fliers such as General Thomas S. Jeffrey, Colonel S. L. Sluder, Colonel James S. Stewart, and U.S. Army Air Force members John Mitchell, Ron Brown, Leroy Nitschke, Sidney Cheney, John Komar, Garry Fry, Ernie McDowell, Don MacDonald, Barrie Davis, Roy Hogg, Robert Sitterly, Ted Harris, Henry Walden, Ken Leininger, and many, many others.

As always, Colonel Gerald Holland, Chief of the Magazine and Book Branch, U.S. Air Force headquarters, guided me to many sources of information and materials that I would otherwise not have obtained.

Last, but certainly not least, I acknowledge the indispensable reading of the manuscript and suggestions that I have come to expect and very much need from my wife, Peggy.

Prologue

During the years 1943-44, when the United States and the Soviet Union were supposedly firm allies, the Soviet Union gave the United States a very distinct warning signal. This warning signal was clear and obvious, but it was ignored by most political, diplomatic, and military leaders of the United States. The signal came during a secret attempt at military collaboration code-named "Operation Frantic." Had these leaders been listening, they would have realized that Soviet Russia had a deep mistrust of the United States and had no intention of collaborating during or after World War II except in those instances in which the Soviet Union would benefit. If our leaders had understood the signal, it is probable that the Soviet Union would not have emerged from World War II in possession of half of Europe.

"Operation Frantic" was the code name for shuttle bombing by American heavy bombers using Russian bases. It was well known to Allied intelligence officers that the Germans were re-locating many of their factories further east out of range of American and British heavy bombers operating out of bases in Great Britain and Italy. It seemed reasonable to American military leaders that American heavy bombers could strike these targets from bases in Russia. Furthermore, such missions would force the Germans to deploy many of their fighter units from the western front to the eastern front, thereby spreading their defenses thinner. Since the early days of the war, U.S. Army Air Force (USAAF) leaders had been attracted by the idea that shuttle bombing between widely separated bases might pay large dividends. In 1943, with the Allied invasion across the English Channel imminent, the value of deflecting German attention to the east became even greater, and United States military leaders believed that the time was right to press the Soviet Union for the use of air bases that American bombers could use as eastern terminals for bombing missions originating in Italy or Great Britain. But perhaps of greatest importance was the desire of the United States to demonstrate how eager it was to help the Russians on the eastern front and to cooperate with them in every way. Since relations with the Soviet Union prior to this time had been difficult, it was thought that the shuttle missions might improve understanding between the two countries.

During the early years of World War II, the lack of cooperation by the Soviet Union had shocked both the United States and Great Britain. They had assumed that all three countries were allies against a common enemy, and that the success of one was the success of all three. But American leaders soon discovered that every aspect of the relationship, no matter how small or how large, was the subject of protracted and difficult negotiation. Even in the matter of Lend-Lease, without which the Soviet Union could not have withstood the Nazi onslaught, the relationship was not an equitable one. Instead, the Soviet Union constantly demanded more materiel, or different types of equipment, and faster delivery; and when these conditions were not met immediately, the United States was accused of acting in bad faith. However, as long as Lend-Lease was needed by the Soviet Union, Soviet leaders were forced to make some concessions to keep the flow of materiel coming to their country from the United States. One of those concessions was the agreement to collaborate in "Operation Frantic."

But Stalin and his military and political associates, while seeming to say yes to the shuttle mission plan, placed almost endless obstacles in the path of the USAAF. After months of stalling, Foreign Minister V. M. Molotov approved the operation "in principle," a phrase that was misunderstood by American negotiators. "Approved in principle" was one thing; action toward the culmination of the objective was another thing entirely. Weeks passed before any definite steps were taken by the Soviet Union to implement "Operation Frantic." At the Tehran conference in December 1943, Ambassador W. Averell Harriman and Colonel Elliott Roosevelt discussed the proposal at length with Stalin himself and Stalin seemed to approve the plan. But again no moves were taken to provide the necessary air bases. Finally, in February 1944, Harriman had another talk with Stalin in Moscow and, after detailed questioning by the Russians, Stalin agreed to have Molotov and Red Army representatives meet with Harriman and General John R. Deane, who was in command of the newly created U.S. Military Mission in Moscow to coordinate U.S.-U.S.S.R. land, sea, and air activities.

The meeting between the Soviet and American representatives was held on February 5, 1944, in the Kremlin. Harriman and Deane presented their case for "Operation Frantic," explaining what the United States wanted and needed if the operation was to be successful. The Russians listened intently, "agreed in principle," and the meeting ended on an optimistic note. Once again, however, the Americans learned that the Soviet Union, instead of acting as an ally, seemed more intent on disrupting plans for attacking Germany from eastern bases.

The six air bases that Harriman had stated were a requirement for "Operation Frantic" were soon reduced by the Soviet officials to three—Poltava, Mirgorod, and Piryatin. Instead of the desired 2,100 Americans needed to operate the bases and repair the American aircraft, the figure was cut by the Soviet Union to 1,200 —and for a time it appeared that even this limited number would not be permitted to cross the Russian border. Prior to "Operation Frantic," foreigners entering the Soviet Union had been investigated thoroughly before they were given entrance visas. And once in the Soviet Union, these foreigners were kept under strict surveillance. When Stalin realized that "Operation Frantic" would bring hundreds of American ground personnel and aircrew men into the Soviet Union; he knew that detailed investigations and surveillance would not be possible in every case. The fact that these men would be allies didn't alter Stalin's suspicions that capitalistic America would use this as a means to plant agents in the Soviet Union.

It took until late March 1944 for General Deane to work out a procedure whereby all Americans scheduled to be permanently stationed in Russia for "Operation Frantic" would enter the Soviet Union on group visas. In practice, even this procedure often broke down, and hundreds of Americans vitally needed to get the bases ready were unnecessarily delayed. Ironically, Russian pilots and personnel were entering and leaving the United States at the same time with a minimum of red tape and practically no surveillance.

One necessity for the success of the operation of American heavy bombers from Russian bases was American control of its own communications. It had to be possible to send up-to-date weather reports to Britain or Italy, to relay operational and administrative messages to task force commanders of the heavy bomber units, and to have interbase communications within the Soviet Union. Combat operation requirements simply did not permit the time lag that was involved in using Russian communications personnel and having the messages interpreted. Language differences often caused errors in interpretations and one such error could cost the lives of many American airmen. After long negotiations, the problem was settled by permitting Soviet representatives to be present at all American communications offices and to have access to all messages sent or received.

This is the way it went, right down to the smallest detail. The Soviet officials disagreed, refused to reply, or bluntly said "no" to nearly every proposal made by the Americans. Perhaps it was the Americans' unflagging optimism, perhaps it was an assumption that they were merely dealing with red tape similar to that of their own government and military, but the United States negotiators pressed on blithely with the confidence that "Operation Frantic" would succeed and that the Soviet Union would work for its success. However, the difficulty of the negotiations should have served as a warning of what was to come, once the USAAF bombers began flying the shuttle missions. If they had listened to the warnings, the American leaders might have avoided the tragedy that was to occur at Poltava on June 21, 1944. But they didn't. And the disaster that was to be known as "the other Pearl Harbor" did occur. Perhaps, too, if Poltava had been avoided, the mistrust and uncooperativeness of the postwar era might have been avoided. After Poltava, there was a coldness that set in between the United States and the Soviet Union that has never thawed.

THE POLTAVA AFFAIR

1

"Prepare the Plans"

THE MEMORANDUM THAT PASSED through the offices of the United States Army Air Forces headquarters the morning of September 5, 1943, was only three paragraphs long. It was a simple, direct message that did not appear important enough to change the history of the world. The message was from Major General Barney M. Giles, Chief of Air Staff, to Brigadier General Laurence S. Kuter, who at the time was Assistant Chief of Air Staff for Plan and Combat Operations. It was titled "Employment of Heavy Bombers from Airports in Russia."

9/5/43

TO: General Kuter
FROM: General Giles

Request that you prepare plans giving the discussions, findings, and recommendations on the employment of our heavy bomber force from Russian airports. Your plans should initially include only shuttle service, that is, take-off from England possibly in very bad weather, bomb military objectives in Germany and land under favorable weather conditions on airports in Russia; re-service and bomb German targets enroute back to England or possibly enroute to Italy. I believe that we can secure permission to operate a shuttle service, whereas it might be more difficult to secure permission to operate on a more permanent basis from Russian airports.

Some of the advantages that I can think of at present are a closer tie between our armed forces and the Russian armed forces, as well as helping the political situation. We can also gain considerably from an operational standpoint since more missions could be accomplished during winter months than we have planned at the present time. Some of the disadvantages which might be encountered would be the repair and maintenance of aircraft at Russian air bases and bomb adapters, etc., that would be required in using our own bombs. Should this present too much of a problem, we could ship in our own bombs and ammunition to operate from airdromes in Russia. Request that something be prepared and presented to me on this subject by 9:00 A.M. Tuesday morning.

B.M.G.

Kuter, who had received his wings in June 1930, was a recognized expert on air power. He had been ordered to Washington for duty on the War Department General Staff in July 1939, when General George C. Marshall, Chief of Staff, U.S. Army, recognized the importance of military aviation and decided to assign junior air officers to his staff. Kuter, together with Lauris Norstad and C. P. Cabell, formed an Advisory Council under General H. H. Arnold, Commanding General of the Army Air Forces, to make recommendations to him and plan the basic employment of air power in World War II. He was well aware that this was not the first time that the USAAF had considered asking for air bases in Russia.

On September 2, 1942, the USAAF Plans Division had proposed an "American Component of a Joint Anglo-American Air Force for Operating in Transcaucasia." At the time the U.S.S.R. was faced with tragedy at Stalingrad, and American military leaders made the offer of help despite the fact that the nation was still very short of planes, men, and supplies. The Joint Anglo-American Air Force, the offer stated, would operate under the strategic control of the Russian High Command but would remain a homogeneous allied force under the command of a British air officer with the right of appeal to United States or British governments. The components of the Joint Anglo-American Air Force would be: eight British fighter squadrons, three British medium-bomber squadrons, one U.S. B-24 group, and one United States troop carrier group.

After contemplating the offer for more than three months, the Soviet Union abruptly refused to accept it. Stalin stated that he would accept the aircraft but he did not want allied personnel on Russian territory.

British Prime Minister Winston S. Churchill wrote to President Franklin D. Roosevelt on December 3, 1942, after the rejection:

It was hoped that by sending [the] Velvet force [code name for the Joint Anglo-American Air Force] to [the] Caucasus an example would be given of Allied forces working hand in hand with the Russians for the same military objectives and under unity of strategic control on a bigger scale than anything yet attempted. Not only would there have been practical cooperation on a considerable scale, but there might have also developed a genuine spirit of comradeship in arms which would have opened up considerable possibilities in the political and military fields.

The Pacific war made the establishment of American bases in the maritime provinces of Siberia of primary importance for bombing Japan. President Roosevelt, understanding Stalin's reluctance to antagonize Japan while Russia was still engaged in a battle for survival with Germany, also understood Stalin's fear that Japan might attack the Soviet Union. Using these fears as a basis for negotiation, on December 30, 1942, Roosevelt offered Stalin 100 heavy bombers and crews and selected logistic support to defend the Soviet Union in case Japan did attack. Stalin promptly refused the offer—once again stating that he would take the planes but not the crews. On January 8, 1943, President Roosevelt tried again, restating the offer and requesting that a survey of airbases suitable for the bombers be made by American personnel. Stalin, angry and insulted, dismissed the proposal by replying: "It should be perfectly obvious that only Russians can inspect Russian military bases. . . ."

This was the last attempt to obtain bases for American bombers in Russia until August 1943, when Arnold, realizing that constant bombing of Germany was necessary if the planned cross-Channel invasion the following year was to be successful, told Giles to study the project again. The USAAF had been having a difficult time during the summer of 1943 with high-altitude daylight precision bombing, especially against strategic targets deep in Germany. During the last week of July with fine weather working to their advantage, the Eighth Air Force in Britain had sent its bombers out in force. Optimism had been high, but before the week ended approximately 100 of the 330 aircraft available for the missions had been lost or scrapped because of extensive damage, and nearly 900 airmen were missing or dead. After a two-week respite to regain its strength, the Eighth Air Force again began pushing deep into Germany to hit important targets, and the cost mounted. Missions to bomb aircraft factories and ball-bearing works at Regensburg and Schweinfurt were near-disasters. It became obvious to USAAF leaders that they could not continue the long-distance missions. If these targets deep in Germany were to be bombed, a new procedure had to be developed.

One solution to the problem appeared to be the use of bases in Soviet Russia to shorten the distance to targets in eastern Germany and to minimize the chance of counterattack. It would also permit the American heavy bombers to fly missions when the weather in Britain and Italy prevented takeoffs and landings. Consequently, the order went out from Arnold to Giles to explore again the possibility of obtaining airfields in the Soviet Union.

Early in September 1943 President Roosevelt approved a change in the United States representation in the Soviet Union. During the initial stages of the war, the American ambassador and the military attaches had conducted negotiations with their respective Russian counterparts, and the United States Supply Mission in Moscow facilitated Lend-Lease matters. For various reasons, this standard system had not been working successfully. The ambassador, William H. Standley, was not properly briefed on operational plans of the United States military forces and, since he was the only American who had ready access to Stalin, this was a distinct disadvantage. Nor was this lack of information the fault of the military attaches; they, too, had been left in the dark by Washington concerning future plans for conduct of the war. Besides, they were too busy trying to obtain information about the plans of the Soviet Union to worry about the ambassador's lack of military knowledge. The U.S. Supply Mission personnel were kept busy day and night with the perplexing Lend-Lease problems and had no time to be concerned about Standley's sessions with Stalin except insofar as these talks affected their own programs.

In the fall of 1943, when W. Averell Harriman was appointed as the new ambassador to the Soviet Union, he immediately recognized the problem of getting air bases for USAAF use and moved to do something about it. Harriman had been associated with President Roosevelt in an advisory capacity for many years, had traveled extensively in Soviet Russia, and had played an important role in setting up the Lend-Lease program. Stalin trusted Harriman as much as he trusted any other American, but Harriman was aware that Stalin could be ruthless and extremely difficult to deal with, even with men he liked.

Harriman insisted on being well informed on military and political matters before entering into any negotiations. Consequently, he proposed a complete reorganization of United States representation in the Soviet Union. Instead of the standard military attache system, Harriman suggested a U.S. Military Mission that would be under his control but would act, with him, as a single team with one purpose. General Marshall agreed with him, so the search was started immediately for someone to head this new command.

Major General John R. Deane was noted for his unflappable temperament and for his organizational abilities, both of which were characteristics vitally important for the man who would head the U.S. Military Mission to the Union of Soviet Socialist Republics. At that time, Deane was the Secretary of the Joint Chiefs of Staff in Washington. He had joined the U.S. Army in 1917 and had served at various posts both in the United States and overseas. When Harriman asked Deane if he would head the new unit, he agreed immediately.

The stated objective of the U.S. Military Mission was "to promote the closest possible coordination of the military efforts of the United States and the U.S.S.R." Deane had permission to discuss with Soviet authorities all information pertaining to United States military strategy and operations he thought appropriate; but, as the directive made clear, he was "to make no commitments which cause an increased deployment of U.S. Army supplies or troops without War Department approval." His unit would absorb any personnel remaining in the attache offices and the Supply Mission. To help him at the top level he chose Brigadier General William E. Crist to head the Army Division; Rear Admiral Clarence C. Olson, the Navy Division; and Major General Sidney P. Spalding, the Supply Division. Later, as the shuttle-mission project was to develop, Deane would add another unit to his command— the Air Division.

Before his departure for Soviet Russia, Deane met with Arnold, who explained his desire to obtain air bases in the Soviet Union, pointing out the advantages he hoped would accrue if the bases were obtained. Deane agreed that one of the first actions of the U.S. Military Mission would be to request such bases. Harriman, who had also been briefed on the project, favored the move.

Both Harriman and Deane were confident that the logic of the request and the mutual benefits would easily convince Stalin.

Deane and Harriman arrived in Moscow on October 18, 1943, aboard a C-54 transport. Before the general was settled in his apartment in the embassy on Mokhavaya Street and the ambassador in the Spasso House, the Moscow Conference began. At the initial meeting on the afternoon of October 19, Deane met some of the Russian political and military leaders he would be dealing with throughout his stay in the Soviet Union. There was an impressive array of Soviet officers and party leaders around the huge circular table in the conference room. They included A. I. Mikoyan, head of the Commissariat of Foreign Trade, and his staff; Marshal Klementy Voroshilov, Vice Commissar of Defense; Lieutenant General A. A. Gryzlov of the General Staff; V. M. Molotov, Foreign Minister; Andrei Vishinsky, the feared prosecutor in the Moscow purge trials; and Maxim Litvinov, who had preceded Molotov as Foreign Minister.

Representing the British at this exploratory conference were Sir Archibald Clark-Kerr, General Sir Hastings Ismay, Anthony Eden, and William Strang. Americans in the conference room beside Deane and Harriman were Secretary of State Cordell Hull and his staff, which included James Dunn, Green Hackworth, and Charles E. (Chip) Bohlen.

Molotov was elected chairman of the conference. Immediately after deciding on an agenda, the Soviet Foreign Minister passed a list of Russian proposals to the other delegates. This list suggested:

1. That the Governments of Great Britain and the United States take in 1943 such urgent measures as will ensure the invasion of Northern France by Anglo-American armies, and, coupled with powerful blows of Soviet troops on the main German forces on the Soviet-German Front, will radically undermine the military-strategical situation of Germany and bring about a decisive shortening of the duration of the war.

In this connection the Soviet Government deems it necessary to ascertain whether the statement made in early June, 1943, by Mr. Churchill and Mr. Roosevelt, to the effect that Anglo-American forces will undertake the invasion of Northern France in the spring of 1944 remains valid.

2. That the three Powers suggest to the Turkish Government that Turkey should immediately enter the war.

3. That the three Powers suggest to Sweden to place at the disposal of the Allies air bases for the struggle against Germany.

Deane and Ismay of the British delegation detailed as closely as they thought appropriate at that time the plans for the invasion of Europe and assured the Russians that such an invasion would take place in the spring of 1944. After considerable questioning by the Soviets, Molotov appeared satisfied and Deane immediately presented three American proposals. They were:

1. That, in order to effect shuttle bombing of industrial Germany, bases be made available in the Soviet Union on which U.S. aircraft could be refueled, emergency repaired, and rearmed.
2. That more effective mutual interchange of weather information be implemented and, in order to effect this, U.S. and U.S.S.R. signal communications be improved.
3. That improved air transport be effected between the U.S. and the U.S.S.R.

For a moment, Molotov seemed stunned by the American proposals, as though, as Deane said, "he had been struck by a bolt from the blue." The American general learned very quickly that no one but Stalin himself could make such a decision, and any Soviet official faced with answering the questions of a foreigner would either avoid answering or present a case against it until he could consult with Stalin. It took two days before Molotov even formally recognized the American proposals, two days during which he obviously discussed the matter with Stalin. At that time, he stated that the Soviet government had considered the proposals carefully and approved them "in principle." At that moment Deane learned his second lesson concerning negotiations with Soviet officials—"approved in principle" meant exactly nothing. The phrase was an evasive answer that did not commit Molotov and Stalin to any of the proposals. Secretary Hull immediately suggested that the Red Army General Staff and the U.S. Military Mission work out the details at once; but he might as well have kept quiet, because the only action that was to result from the "approved in principle" statement during the next weeks was the foreign minister's adroit sidestepping of any discussion of the subject.

In fact, prior to the end of the Moscow Conference, Molotov made it clear that he refused to allow the American proposals, or the discussions pertaining to them, to become a part of the minutes. When Secretary Hull heard about the matter he arranged for Deane to meet with Vishinsky in private to persuade the Russians to accept the American proposals. During this meeting the general received his third lesson in Soviet negotiations, and it was a shock.

Andrei Vishinsky's reputation as a ruthless prosecutor during the Communist purge trials in the 1930s was well known to Deane, and it was with some apprehension that he met with him in a Moscow office building. The general atmosphere of the meeting was established when he was greeted at the door of the building by a member of the Secret Police and escorted under guard to where Vishinsky was waiting. The Soviet official stared at him for several seconds and then, without warning, lashed out in a verbal tirade that took Deane completely by surprise. The official conference had, on the whole, been serene so Deane was not pre-pared for the vigorous attack.

In icy tones he told the startled Deane that neither the United States nor the United Kingdom were seriously opposing Hitler and that the Soviet Union was not deluded into thinking that a second front was planned. He also insisted that it was "heartless" of the western allies not to force Turkey into helping the Soviet Union, bellowing "What would be lost if Turkey was overrun by the Germans? At least some of the Germans would then be di-verted from the Russian front, wouldn't they?" His remarks and his manner were reminiscent of the same ruthlessness and cruelty he had shown the world during the Moscow purge trials years earlier.

Deane, once he had overcome his initial surprise at the tirade, listened intently, hoping to determine the real reason for the out-burst. A cool-headed negotiator who had faced many furious indi-viduals during his long career, Deane finally decided that Stalin was using Vishinsky to let the American and British delegations know his true feelings about his disappointment with regard to the Turkish problem and the delay in opening the second front. The American general took the tongue-lashing gracefully. The following day he had reason to be relieved that he had done so. Molotov, without any further urging, suddenly agreed to include the American proposals into the minutes of the conference. Once Vishinsky's message had been delivered to the western delegation,

Stalin had no objection to the inclusion of the proposals—including the shuttle-mission plan.

After the Moscow Conference ended, Deane spent many long days in his apartment on Mokhavaya Street waiting for a summons from the Red Army General Staff to begin working on the shuttle-mission operation. The summons did not come.

In Washington, Arnold and the Joint Chiefs of Staff began to grow impatient. Most of the USAAF officers were now demanding quick action, but they had never dealt with the Soviet Union and could not understand why there was any difficulty in getting an agreement on the air bases. Arnold was not known for great patience even under the best of circumstances. But none of the officers could have understood in the fall of 1943 that the Russians conducted negotiations very differently than did Americans. Deane tried to explain this to Washington. "For one answer to one question it is necessary to wait until an answer comes from Stalin," he said, "and no other questions will be accepted until the first one is answered. It is very time consuming."

Unfortunately, none of Deane's explanations lowered Arnold's blood pressure. The USAAF, in the fall of 1943, was engaged in a battle for its very survival in Europe. The Combined Bomber Offensive (CBO) that had been approved on May 18, 1943, by the Combined Chiefs of Staff was facing an autumn crisis. Originally the CBO plan established target priorities as follows:

1. Intermediate objectives:
   German fighter strength
2. Primary objectives:
   German submarine yards and bases
   The remainder of the German aircraft industry
   Ball bearings
   Oil (contingent upon attacks against Ploesti)
3. Secondary objectives
   Synthetic rubber and tires
   Military motor transport vehicles

However, by the fall of 1943 the objectives had been altered, and the target of greatest importance was the German Air Force. Before the invasion across the English Channel could be accomplished successfully, the Allied strategic air forces would have to gain air surpremacy over Europe. It was not an easy task to accomplish; by October, Arnold was beginning to wonder just how he could defeat the Luftwaffe in the time allotted prior to the date set for opening the second front. The costly missions of the summer had hurt the German Air Force somewhat, but they had also prompted the Nazis to disperse their industrial plants, moving many of them eastward or northward out of range of the American heavy bombers from Britain and Italy, so that bombing missions were extremely hazardous. Often the long distances, combined with bad weather, hampered Allied bomber crews to such a degree that missions had to be cancelled entirely.

The second week of October 1943, at approximately the same time that Deane was desperately trying to penetrate the Russian wall of noncooperation in Moscow, the daylight bombing campaign of the USAAF in the European Theater of Operations (ETO) reached a critical point. On October 8 the American bombers from the British Isles were dispatched to bomb the city of Bremen. The Third Bombardment Division of the Eighth Air Force, accompanied by the First Bombardment Division, led the mission. Of 399 B-17s sent on the mission, 30 were lost and 26 received major damage. The following day, 378 B-17s and B-24s bombed port facilities and German naval units in the Polish corridor at Gdynia; and the submarine slips at Danzig; a Focke-Wulfe assembly plant at Marienburg, over 200 miles east of Berlin; and the Arado aircraft factory at Anklam. The targets in Poland and East Prussia were much closer to air bases in the Soviet Union than they were to those actually used in England. Consequently, the loss of 28 aircraft and nearly 300 airmen aggravated Arnold's impatience for the airfields in Russia.

But the worst was yet to come. On October 10, Arnold's planes flew to Münster, an important Ruhr traffic junction, and this time the Luftwaffe was waiting in strength. From the initial point to the target and all the way out of enemy territory, the heavy bombers were under attack by FW-190s, Me-109s, Ju-88s, Me-110s and Me-210s. The Germans flew parallel to the bombers, staying out of range of the bombers' guns in groups of 30 to 40 stacked in echelon down. When they discovered a bomber formation that looked vulnerable, the enemy planes peeled off singly or in pairs to attack. The entire lead formation of the Allied 100th Bombardment Group was lost. And other groups also suffered heavily. Out of a total force of 236 aircraft that took off for Münster,

30 bombers were lost and 300 airmen were dead or missing. The tragedy eventually reached a peak on October 14, when the heavy bombers of the Eighth Air Force returned to Schweinfurt to bomb the ball-bearing plants. The air battle between the American bombers and the Luftwaffe fighters that day developed into epic proportions. Two forces were dispatched to Schweinfurt: 149 B-17s from the First Bombardment Division and 142 B-17s from the Third Bombardment Division. A third force of B-24s from the Second Bombardment Division was scheduled to go to Schweinfurt also, but weather conditions over the British Isles were so bad on October 14 that the Liberators were unable to assemble. Each of the B-17 forces was assigned one group of P-47s to escort them to the maximum range of the fighter. The turn-back point for the P-47s was Aachen, 240 miles from the British coast. As soon as the American fighters headed for home, the German fighters made their appearance. The tactics the Luftwaffe used that day had been used before—formation attacks, rockets, large-bore cannon, air-to-air bombing, concentration on one group of heavy bombers or on stragglers—but they had never been used with such coordination and expert-time. Wave after wave of enemy fighters attacked the B-17s on the way to the target, over the target, and during the return flight. Despite the heavy losses before the target was reached, the bombing was unusually effective. The 228 aircraft that bombed the target areas dropped nearly 400 tons of high explosives and 90 tons of incendiaries on or near the three ball-bearing plants. Eighty-eight of the bombs made direct hits on the factories, and approximately 150 more fell within the factory area.

The losses, however, were too high to bear. Sixty B-17s and crews, each crew consisting of ten men, failed to return to their bases. Major damage was sustained by 17 more aircraft and reparable damage was suffered by 121 other planes. The Eighth Air Force was unable to make further penetrations to any target deep in Germany from bases in England. The Schweinfurt mission losses, added to the losses of the previous six days, totaled 148 bombers and crews. More important, and tragic, was the fact that the Eighth Air Force had, for the time being, lost air supremacy over Europe.

In Washington, Arnold was desperate. On October 26, he convinced the Joint Chiefs of Staff to send a message to Deane:

Desire you explore shuttle bombing possibilities. An estimated ten bases are needed. Operations not to be regular practice but employed whenever weather and tactics favor.

Deane understood the implications of the message. Arnold knew that the Moscow Conference "approval in principle" by the Russians had not led to any action, and the message was a subtle hint for him to get some action started. The "not regular practice" phrase was intended as an additional lure for the Soviet Union, the thinking being that Stalin might not want American planes and personnel in Russia too often or for too long a time. But Deane knew that it would take more of an enticement than that to get Stalin to act. He knew, too, that Arnold was concerned over his commitment to keep control of the skies over Europe until the invasion, scheduled for the spring of 1944.

Deane attempted to break down the Russian barrier again by using a new tactic. In Moscow all foreign military officers came under the control of the Foreign Military Mission Office, commonly known as the O.V.S. The O.V.S. was headed by Major George V. N. Estigneev, and all meetings with Soviet military authorities were supposed to be arranged by him. However, since Estigneev had ignored and refused all requests by Deane to arrange any meetings to discuss the shuttle mission project, the general decided to circumvent him and go directly to the Soviet military authorities. He selected Marshal Voroshilov, the Vice Commissar of Defense, who had been friendly with him during the Moscow Conference. There were no telephone or office directories to help Deane locate Voroshilov, so the general took his interpreter, Captain Henry H. Ware, and headed for the nearest building that he knew was occupied by the Red Army General Staff.

Walking directly up to the startled Russian sentry at the door, Deane ordered Ware to tell him they had come to see Marshal Voroshilov. For a moment the sentry was too stunned to move, but finally he telephoned someone inside the building. In quick succession, Deane was directed to two other buildings, interviewed by a Russian officer he had never seen before, and finally was told by an officer from O.V.S. that Voroshilov "was not in Moscow" and that, in the future, if Deane wished to see any Soviet military officers, he should make all arrangements through Estigneev.

After this failure, Deane again went through the proper Soviet channels; within a few days a meeting was finally set up with his "friend" Voroshilov. When he arrived at Voroshilov's office, he discovered that the Russian officer was not a "friend." His manner was icy, his comments sarcastic, and his rudeness deliberate as he bellowed tirades against the United States. When he finished berating Deane about United States conduct of the war and bragging about the manner in which the Soviet Union was saving the world from Hitler, Deane asked about the shuttle-bombing project. The marshal bluntly told him that he would have to conform to the established routine in the Soviet Union and conduct his business with the appropriate Red Army General Staff officer—and to make certain he requested all meetings through Estigneev!

After this rebuff, Deane suggested to Washington, through Harriman, that the matter of the shuttle bases be brought up by President Roosevelt when he conferred with Stalin and Churchill at the Tehran Conference scheduled for late November 1943. He and Harriman both felt that if the project was ever to get under way, the President would have to put pressure on the Russians. Deane, Harriman, and Chip Bohlen left Moscow on November 18 for Cairo to attend a preliminary meeting between Roosevelt and Churchill prior to the three-power conference in Iran. Over Stalingrad, one engine of their transport plane lost oil pressure and they were forced to land. During their overnight stay in Stalingrad, the Americans were given a tour of the shell-damaged metropolis and a dramatic eyewitness recounting of the Battle of Stalingrad. Deane still did not agree with Voroshilov's angry statement that "the Soviet Union was saving the world from Hitler" by itself, but by the time the aircraft was headed toward Cairo again, he did understand the Russian pride in the part they had played in turning back the German tide.

The Tehran Conference was the first meeting between the three heads of state—President Franklin D. Roosevelt of the United States, Prime Minister Winston S. Churchill of Great Britain, and Marshal Joseph Stalin of the Soviet Union. They discussed the overall status of the war, but they emphasized specifically a commitment by the western allies to open a second front in the spring of 1944 to divert German divisions from the Russian front; a commitment by Stalin that once Germany was defeated Soviet

Russia would join in the battle to defeat Japan; the desire of Churchill for further operations in Italy and the Balkans; postwar Germany and Poland; the entrance of Turkey into the war; and the part China would play in the war in the East. Arnold and Deane both reminded the President's staff that the matter of the shuttle bases should be brought to Stalin's attention, but it wasn't until the second day of the conference that the opportunity arose. President Roosevelt gave Stalin three memoranda that day, one of which dealt with the shuttle bases:

> 1. A request for permission for U.S. bombers from Britain to use Russian air bases for refueling, rearmament and emergency repair in the proposed shuttle bombing of Germany.
> 2. A request that planning be started at once with a view to establishing bases for upward of 1,000 U.S. heavy bombers in the Siberian Maritime Provinces for an air offensive against Japan.
> 3. Requests for exchange of information and further preliminary planning for eventual operations against Japan.

Stalin promised he would study the documents and reply at a later date, stating at that time that he certainly "agreed in principle" with the proposals, but certain considerations had to be studied before he could make any commitment. Deane, learning about Stalin's "agreed in principle" statement, shook his head. He had learned quickly. Later, General George C. Marshall, U.S. Chief of Staff, called Voroshilov aside and told the Russian officer that he had complete confidence in Deane and that Deane was authorized to speak for him in Moscow. Voroshilov slapped Deane on the back and assured Marshall that they were "old friends."

Marshall was delighted, but Deane was far from convinced of the Russian's sincerity. He had good reason to be: it was to be nearly three months before the "agreed in principle" would develop into actual steps toward augmentation of the shuttle-bombing project.

2

Stalin:
"We Favor Your Plan"

THE WINTER OF 1943-44 was a difficult time for the USAAF.
The autumn crisis had left the Eighth Air Force depleted of
planes and men when they were needed more than ever. Air
superiority over Germany had been lost, and the lack of long-
range fighter escort made the possibility of regaining air supremacy in the near future improbable. The P-47s could not accompany the heavy bombers deep into enemy territory; as soon as
the fighter escort turned for home the bombers were extremely
vulnerable to the German fighters.

However, near the middle of October 1943, a few of the P-38s
of the 55th Fighter Group in England were operational. With
75-gallon twin-engine wing tanks, these twin-boomed fighters
could boast of an escort radius of 520 miles. And when 108-
gallon tanks became available, the P-38 radius of escort increased
to a maximum of 585 miles. But this was still far short of the
range of the heavy bombers, and the Eighth Air Force heavy
bombers continued to be unable to make further penetrations into
Germany during the remainder of 1943.

A new development in the war situation, the invasion of Italy
in September 1943, brought about a reorganization of the USAAF
which would eventually affect the shuttle-mission project. In
October, when Arnold suggested using captured Italian air bases
for bombing missions to German-held Europe, both Lieutenant
General Dwight D. Eisenhower, Supreme Allied Commander in
the Mediterranean, and Major General Carl Spaatz, Deputy Commanding General of the Mediterranean Allied Air Forces, agreed.
Arnold promptly submitted a plan to the Joint Chiefs of Staff to
split the Twelfth Air Force into two forces—one tactical and the
other strategic. He recommended that the strategic unit become a
new force designated the Fifteenth Air Force, to be composed of

the six heavy bomber groups presently assigned to the Twelfth Air Force with the addition of fifteen heavy bomber groups from the Eighth Air Force. By using Italian air bases, the heavy bombers could hit German targets that were too far to bomb from Britain, and they hoped that the Italian bases would substitute temporarily for the Russian bases that could not be obtained.

On November 1, 1943, the new Fifteenth Air Force was activated, and Major General James H. (Jimmy) Doolittle became its first commanding general. Spaatz, in addition to his other duties, was to head all USAAF units in the theater. The build-up of the Fifteenth Air Force progressed very slowly, mainly because of lack of equipment, supplies, and manpower, and because of a very successful Luftwaffe bombing attack that had destroyed badly needed supplies. By January 1944, the Fifteenth Air Force was still not strong enough to have any effect on the CBO against Germany.

On January 1, in another reorganization action by the American and British military leaders, Spaatz became commanding general of the newly-formed U.S. Strategic Air Forces in Europe (USSTAF). This led to other changes that were to have a far-reaching effect on the proposed shuttle missions to the Soviet Union. Doolittle was transferred from the Fifteenth Air Force to the Eighth Air Force in England; Major General N. F. Twining took over command of the Fifteenth Air Force; and Lieutenant General Ira C. Eaker, one of the most valued leaders of the USAAF, became Commander-in-Chief of the Mediterranean Allied Air Forces. If there was one officer in the USAAF who could handle the air operations of shuttle missions to Soviet Russia, the broad-faced, husky Eaker was that man. It appeared at first that his transfer from Great Britain, where he had been in charge of the Eighth Air Force, to the Mediterranean area would completely eliminate him from the project—but fortunately this was not so.

While the reorganization of the USAAF was taking place, Deane and Harriman were still attempting to get the shuttle-mission talks underway in Moscow. The Russians continued to refuse to discuss the project except to say that they "agreed in principle." Harriman maintained pressure on Molotov while Deane pursued the subject with the Red Army General Staff; but except for a message late in December from Molotov to Harriman stating that ". . . in reply to the memoranda handed Stalin by Roosevelt at Tehran the shuttle bombing project was approved in principle. Discussions would begin regarding coordination with other Soviet war plans," there was no further action by the U.S.S.R.

When? Where? By January 1, 1944, these two questions had still not been answered by the Soviets.

Although he had been in Moscow not quite two months, Deane had learned several things that would be verified over and over again before he returned to the United States. "Everyone agrees," he wrote in a secret report to Washington, "on the importance of collaboration with Russia but unless it works both ways it will not be worth anything. After [Russian] banquets we sit around and scratch our heads to see what other gifts we can send and they scratch theirs to see what else they can ask for. . . ." He added later: ". . . our files are bulging with letters to the Soviets and devoid of letters from them."

The new year opened with the shuttle-mission project no further advanced than when it had first been proposed to the Russians in October 1943. Four days before the New Year, 1944, Arnold addressed the following message to the commanding generals of the Eighth and Fifteenth air forces:

> a. Aircraft factories in this country are turning out large quantities of airplanes, engines and accessories.
> b. Our training establishments are operating twenty-four hours per day, seven days per week training crews.
> c. It is a conceded fact that Overlord [cross-channel invasion] and Anvil [invasion of southern France] will not be possible unless the German Air Force is destroyed.
> d. Therefore, my personal message to you—this is a MUST— is to "Destroy the Enemy Air Force wherever you find them, in the air, on the ground and in the factories."

Although the German air force, and particularly its fighter strength, had been designated in the original CBO directive as "an intermediate objective," the growing resistance to Eighth Air Force missions in the fall of 1943 had made it clear that overpowering and destroying the Luftwaffe before the Normandy D-day was the USAAF's most immediate task. In fact, the code name "Pointblank" which had been used to refer to the combined offensive generally came to mean the attack on the Luftwaffe. In an attempt to destroy the German air force, the Eighth Air

Force flew twenty-one missions from January 4, 1944, until February 15, 1944. The number of missions flown was encouraging to Arnold, especially the ever-increasing over-the-clouds radar missions, but he realized that these were not the badly needed raids against the German aircraft factories. To bomb these factories, which were in central and eastern Germany, it was necessary to have long-range fighters or bases in Russia that would be closer to the factories. Neither were available in January 1944.

The Fifteenth Air Force, flying out of Italy, was having even more problems than the Eighth Air Force had been having. The new air force was seriously hampered by bad weather in the base area, shortages of equipment and skilled personnel, and long distances to the targets. In addition to the bomber missions the heavy bombers of the Fifteenth Air Force had to fly many missions to support the American and British ground troops engaged in the Italian campaign. This reduced the number of "Pointblank" attacks that could be made. Between January 1, 1944, and February 21, 1944, the new air force flew 35 missions, each involving between 50 and 325 heavy bombers, but only four of the missions involved targets of the strategic bombing program aimed at destroying the Luftwaffe. The remainder were attacks on targets that directly or indirectly supported the Anzio beachhead.

As the final weeks of January 1944 ran out and the early days of February 1944 passed, Arnold and his USAAF commanders were apprehensive and impatient. Time was getting short.

At 6:00 P.M. on the evening of February 2, 1944, Ambassador Harriman met with Stalin and Molotov in the Kremlin to discuss the subject of "Russian Bases for American Shuttle Bombers and Photo Reconnaissance Planes." This meeting was held at Harriman's request to discuss once again the memoranda President Roosevelt had given Stalin at the Tehran Conference in November 1943. Despite his official request for the meeting, Harriman was mildly surprised that Stalin had even consented to discuss the matter with him. However, he was to be in for a shock before the evening was over.

As the meeting began, Harriman was wary. A shrewd, cool, persuasive negotiator, he had experienced many complex and irritating meetings with officials of the Soviet Union requiring great patience—and he was prepared to be patient.

His first contact with the Soviet Union had been in the middle twenties when he took part in the negotiations for a manganese mining concession financed by a private group. In December 1926, he went to Moscow to discuss certain contract difficulties with government officials. Most of his dealings had been with Leon Trotsky, then Chairman of the Concessions Committee. He did try unsuccessfully to arrange a meeting with Stalin, who was Secretary of the Communist Party. Then in September 1941 after World War II began, Harriman traveled to Soviet Russia with Lord Beaverbrook, Minister of Supply and a member of the British War Cabinet, to negotiate supplying war materials to the Soviet Union. This time, he dealt with Stalin. The week he spent talking with Stalin was an interesting one. Moscow was beseiged at the time, and he could hear the German guns on the outskirts and felt the threat of the possible loss of the city to the Nazis. But what was perhaps more important was what he learned about Stalin.

During the first meeting, Stalin was so agreeable that Harriman thought the rumors he had heard about the Marshal must be wrong. Both Harriman and Beaverbrook were elated with the friendly atmosphere. Towering over the short Russian leader, Harriman noticed that Stalin often doodled while listening to others talk—and more often than not he drew pictures of wolves. Harriman, accustomed to watching a man's eyes when he talked to him, soon discovered that Stalin could give him as cold and as penetrating a stare as any man had ever given him. At other times, he evaded the eyes of the other men in the room completely.

The next evening they met again, and the atmosphere was frigid and unfriendly, exactly the opposite of what it had been at the initial meeting. Stalin refused to accept U.S. production limitations as an explanation for the lack of items he requested but was told he could not get at the present time. He was very argumentative about everything. The two visitors left the Kremlin puzzled and discouraged that night, wondering if a third meeting was worthwhile. On the third night, however, Stalin was even more friendly than he had been during the first meeting and they succeeded in making the necessary agreements without further problems. Stalin even invited Harriman and Beaverbrook to dinner. As Harriman learned—and as the other Americans associated with the shuttle-mission project would learn later—this was

the "one-two-three punch" method often used by Soviet negotiators, a kind of "shock" technique they found effective for their
purposes.

Although Harriman had learned more about the workings of
Stalin's mind than any other American, he still was not immune
to the sense of optimism that Stalin's good humor could generate
and at the February 1944 meeting Harriman could barely conceal
his pleasure at the interest Stalin finally showed in the shuttle-
mission project after so many long months of ignoring it completely. After Harriman stated the official American case for the
project, listing the reasons that he, Deane, and Roosevelt had
given the Russians many times in previous months, Stalin began
asking questions. He wanted to know the number of aircraft and
types the USAAF intended to use, the amount of fuel and the
octane content required, where the fuel would come from and
how, the length of runways needed by the heavy bombers, and
other detailed questions that indicated he had an amazing knowledge of air operations. Finally Stalin nodded, looked at Harriman,
and said simply, "We favor your proposal and I shall have our
air staff work out the details with General Deane."

It was difficult for Harriman to believe that, after all the re-
buffs the leader of the Soviet Union meant what he said. He immediately conveyed the startling news to Deane and then cabled
the details of the meeting to President Roosevelt. Meanwhile,
General Deane of the U.S. Military Mission in Moscow informed
the Joint Chiefs of Staff.

True to his word, Stalin arranged for more talks on the project.
Three days later, on February 5, 1944, Harriman and Deane
again traveled to the Kremlin to meet with the Russians. Molotov
conducted the meeting, and with him in the conference room
were Marshal A. A. Novikov, Commander of the Red Air Force;
Colonel General A. V. Nikitin, who was in charge of air operations; and Lieutenant General N. V. Slavin, of the Red Army
General Staff.

Molotov opened the meeting by stating that he had been in-
structed by Stalin to discuss the matter of Soviet bases for American heavy bombers. Neither Deane nor Harriman could determine
whether Molotov favored the proposal—or even favored having
the meeting. He did not smile, he did not frown. In fact, there
was no expression on his face at all as he asked Deane to outline

the proposal. Very carefully, and with as many details as possible, Deane explained the American conception of how the shuttle-bombing operation should be conducted. He asked for six air bases, 2,000 gallons of 100-octane gasoline per aircraft, 6,000 pounds of bombs per plane, and runways approximately one mile long for landing and takeoff. It was hoped, he said, that facilities would be available for 360 heavy bombers. Deane also pointed out that this type of bombing operation would require very detailed reconnaissance information. Up to this time the USAAF had not been able to obtain this type of information regarding targets deep in Germany and in southeast Europe because they were out of the range of English bases.

"For photo reconnaissance aircraft," Deane explained, "we would like to have one airfield in the north and one in the south, or a field centrally located that could serve reconnaissance planes both from the United Kingdom and from Italy at the rate of one plane per day. It might be possible to use two of the same bases that are placed at our disposal for shuttle bombing."

As he presented the request for the bases that could be used by photo reconnaissance aircraft, Deane saw Molotov shaking his head and looking across the table at Novikov. Deane thought he could understand the apprehension of the foreign minister about aircraft of another nation using Russian air bases and he did his best to assure him that there was no reason for suspicion.

"We will keep American personnel down to the minimum required for key administrators and technical specialists," he emphasized, "and rely on your country to provide personnel who do not require special training."

After he had completed his presentation of the plan, there was a long silence in the conference room. Molotov kept nodding, but said nothing. Both Deane and Harriman were aware that the proposal was so far outside the normal type of relations between Russians and foreigners that it was difficult for the Soviet representatives at the meeting to comprehend exactly what was involved—or so it appeared at the time. Later, they, as well as other Americans, believed that Stalin—and Molotov—had known exactly what they intended to do and how they intended to do it, and any hesitation, reluctance, or stubbornness exhibited during the negotiations were merely calculated moves in one of the greatest deceptions of World War II.

Finally Novikov, the Commander of the Red Air Force, picked up a map from the table and moved closer to Deane. After the Americans became better acquainted with Novikov, they discovered that he was one of the most beloved military leaders in the Soviet Union. He was an excellent administrator as well as a skilled pilot who had proved his courage many times before his appointment to head the Red Air Force in 1942. Novikov understood what Deane needed and throughout the shuttle-mission project appeared to want to cooperate completely. As he showed the map to Deane, he spoke near-perfect English.

"These bases might be available," he said.

To be within heavy-bomber range of the targets in eastern Germany the USAAF hoped to attack, the Soviet air bases had to be in territory that had previously been occupied by the Germans. This would entail some difficulties because the Nazis had razed all buildings, hangars, runways, and other facilities as they retreated. The Russians had moved into this once-occupied territory and quickly established fighter bases, but these runways were too short for American heavy bombers. After Novikov and Deane had studied the various possible locations, Novikov pointed to Kiev.

"I think that the best area would be in the Ukraine just east of Kiev," he suggested. "The ground dries out faster in that area."

Again he spoke in English, but the Americans observed that the Russian interpreter quickly translated his statement into Russian and repeated it to Molotov. They learned later that it was not safe for any Soviet military leader to have discussions with Americans in English unless the statements were immediately repeated in the Russian language to all Soviet representatives present. A private meeting with American representatives by any Soviet official, except for Stalin or NKVD agents, was strictly forbidden. No Soviet official or party leader trusted any other Soviet official or party leader.

Novikov was correct in his analysis of the air bases. Any fields in the north that were selected would probably not be ready for use by the American heavy bombers until the middle of the summer, because construction work on the runways could not be started until after the spring thaw. Most of the land near Kiev was flat and much drier than the land in the north. It was agreed that a selection of six air bases in that area would be made "as soon as it could be arranged for USAAF leaders to tour that section of Russia." . . . That was Novikov's way of putting it politely. What he really meant was as soon as Stalin permitted any foreigners to inspect air bases near Kiev.

The subject of the defense of the air bases was brought to the attention of the Russians. Both Deane and Harriman hoped that it would be possible to use American antiaircraft batteries and fighter planes to defend the air bases, because the aircraft would be extremely vulnerable to attack by the Luftwaffe. Novikov was ready with his answer.

"The Soviet authorities feel that the defense of the bases should be their responsibility and we will undertake to deal with it," he stated without hesitation, leading both Deane and Harriman to believe that this matter had been settled with Stalin prior to the meeting.

According to the limited amount of intelligence the Americans had available concerning Red Air Force fighters and antiaircraft installations, Deane would have felt much safer if the defense of the air bases was in American hands. The Russian Yak fighters were no match for the Me-109 and FW-190 or even the Ju-88. They couldn't fly high enough or fast enough to repel an attack by these German aircraft. Although he had no way of verifying this fact, Deane understood that most of the Russian air bases were defended only with .50-caliber machine guns mounted on American jeeps. If this were true, the Luftwaffe could bomb the bases without worrying about a high loss to their own bombers. It was not a satisfactory solution, and Deane knew it, but there was nothing else he could do at the time except agree. Otherwise, he might upset the delicate negotiations that had finally gotten underway after so many months delay. It was a decision he was to regret many times in later years.

The meeting with Molotov ended with a general agreement between the Russians and the Americans concerning the project and a promise by the Soviet foreign minister that further talks would soon be scheduled with other Russian military leaders. Deane was optimistic although wary about future negotiations. He couldn't forget the warning of Brigadier General Joseph A. Michela, who had been the American military attaché in Moscow prior to the organization of the U.S. Military Mission. In a report sent to Washington, Michela had offered little encouragement in regard to Russian collaboration:

> In reviewing the attitude of the Soviets toward this office during the past three years, it becomes quite clear that no fundamental changes in attitude have taken place, and at the present time I see little difference in attitude from what it was prior to June 22, 1941, during which time the U.S.S.R. had a pact with Germany.
>
> The Soviet Government intends to exercise as much influence and control as possible throughout the world and definitely in Europe. Contrary to expert opinion, this observer believes . . . the net result is that the Soviets are determined to control Europe if they can."

With this warning in mind, Deane moved carefully through the web of Russian intrigue—but not carefully enough.

Three days after Harriman notified Washington that the shuttle-mission project was finally underway, Arnold sent a three-man military mission to the Soviet Union to work out the details for the air bases. Colonel Paul Cullen, Colonel John S. Griffith, and Colonel Alfred A. Kessler were all experienced officers who had been personally selected by Arnold for the trip. Griffith was to be Spaatz's representative and was to "work with," not "under," Deane. Already, during the preliminary steps of the project, there was rivalry over control between those who would handle the actual operations of the USAAF and those who had to make the arrangements with the Russians. The USAAF personnel wanted to get on with the flying and ignore the delicate negotiations and appeasement tactics which Deane knew were necessary. Deane, who had learned the hard way about the pitfalls of dealing with the Soviet military and Communist party leaders, was destined to have a two-prong campaign on his agenda throughout the entire project. One was to handle the Russians, the other was to handle the USAAF officers who thought he was too slow and too timid with the Russians. Chief of Staff Marshall, however, knowing that the Soviet leaders would deal only with the American officials who had already been "established" overruled Spaatz and placed Griffith "under" Deane while he was in the Soviet Union. To start all over again with new "faces" was not logical. A change could upset the always delicate negotiations and cancel out the entire shuttle-mission proposal.

Paul Cullen was an expert in aerial reconnaissance. Earlier in the war he had been in charge of operational reconnaissance procedures with the USAAF in Washington and at the time of his trip to Soviet Russia he was commanding officer of the Seventh Photographic Group based at Mount Farm, Great Britain. His assignment in the Soviet Union was to set up the complicated reconnaissance procedures with the Russian leaders so that the information necessary for target folders could be obtained without the American reconnaissance planes going unrecognized and being shot out of the sky by Russian antiaircraft or fighters. The reconnaissance operations were of utmost importance to the success of the shuttle-bombing plan. Without the intelligence information required by the aircrews, there would be no point in risking the long flights across Germany. Of the entire project, Cullen's task would be one of the most difficult to accomplish, both on the ground and in the air. He was forewarned of this during his stay in the Soviet Union with Griffith and Kessler.

Colonel Alfred A. Kessler was selected for the Russian base operation because of his earlier trip to the Soviet Union in 1943. At that time he had accompanied Donald M. Nelson, Chairman of the War Production Board, on a three-week tour of Soviet Russia, and had been impressed by the Soviet Union's efforts to hold off the Nazis. Arnold knew this, and he considered that it would be good to have an officer sympathetic to the Russian military in Moscow to help convince the Soviet leaders to collaborate with the United States. "Uncle Ugly," as the tall, stoop-shouldered Kessler became known among the Russian officers he worked with, did everything possible to assure the success of the project.

On the way to the Soviet Union Kessler came down with pneumonia and had to remain in Cairo for medical treatment. He did not arrive in Moscow until March 6, 1944. Cullen and Griffith, however, reached the Soviet capital on February 24 and immediately met with Deane and Harriman to be brought up to date on the negotiations.

Never was the difference between the viewpoints of those dealing with the actual operational problems and those with the responsibility for dealing with high Soviet officials more evident. Before leaving the United States, the three-man advance party had been briefed by Spaatz, who, as commanding general of

USSTAF, would be in charge of the air missions and the ground operations necessary to support the aircraft. He had listed the main purposes of the project for Cullen, Kessler, and Griffith, emphasizing that the primary aim of the shuttle-bombing proposal was to bomb "Pointblank" targets so that the USAAF would have air superiority in the skies over Europe by D-day.

But Deane and Harriman, during their briefing to the three men, presented the shuttle-bombing project as having a different overall purpose. They listed the aims as:

1. Primary purpose is to establish a precedent for American forces operating from Soviet territory with the aim of obtaining air bases later from which to bomb Japan.
2. Closer cooperation with the Soviet Union and the U.S. would improve relations and morale of the fighting men of both countries.
3. Tactical and strategical advantages for the USAAF.

This difference in overall aim of the project caused considerable dispute between the American diplomatic-political faction and the military faction. The USAAF officers in charge of the missions did not understand or appreciate the difficulties facing Deane and Harriman as they negotiated with the Russians. And not all of the USAAF leaders were aware of President Roosevelt's true aim in activating the shuttle-mission project, an aim that Stalin understood and cleverly blocked. While Spaatz fought for air bases to bomb "Pointblank" targets, Arnold sought them as a preliminary to obtaining additional bases in the Siberian Maritime Provinces in order to strike at Japan. On a still higher level of planning were Deane and Harriman who, on instructions from President Roosevelt, sought entry into the Soviet Union of American military personnel as the first step in a much broader program of international gamesmanship . . . the future of postwar Europe and who would control it! This goal was dramatically exhibited during the final shuttle-bombing mission to Poland.

In February 1944, however, Cullen, Griffith, and Kessler were unaware of the "secret" presidential goal of the project and were confused and irritated by the Deane-Harriman briefing that altered, in their minds, the primary aim of the shuttle bombing. This confusion carried over into many of the meetings that were held later with Soviet military leaders, resulting in indecision on many of the issues when the American stand should have been firm and uncompromising.

Four days after the arrival of the three-man American team, they had their initial meeting with Colonel General A. V. Nikitin of the Red Air Force who had been placed in charge of all the arrangements for the project. Since Nikitin was also very busy with the day-to-day planning of the Red Air Force's operations against the Germans, the Americans had difficulty arranging an appointment with him. However, most of the American officers grew to like this tall, thin, stooped Russian officer who was invariably courteous even at the end of his usual fifteen-hour day. Never one to berate those he was negotiating with, Nikitin managed to remain firm and to follow Stalin's instructions to the last detail. During this first meeting, he handed Griffith a list of possible Russian air bases that American heavy bombers could use. The United States and Soviet military officers also discussed the length of the runways that would be required, whether hard-surface runways were a necessity (or even if they were possible because of the weather) or whether steel matting would be suitable, the signals that would be used to identify incoming American bombers, and many other details that would be involved in the operation. It was agreed that the three Americans would inspect the possible air base sites in the near future. As the meeting came to a close, however, Nikitin shocked the Americans with one final request. Through an interpreter, he stated: "We would like to have one of your Norden bombsights."

The highly secret Norden bombsight was the prized possession of the USAAF. It had been developed by C. L. Norden, a civilian consultant, and was very accurate from high altitudes. No one, not even Great Britain, America's closest ally, had been provided with the Norden bombsight. When twenty B-17s were given to the RAF in the spring of 1941, all the equipment normally installed on the aircraft was included except the Norden bombsight. The Sperry bombsight had been substituted! Now the Russians, who thus far had refused to cooperate with the United States to any noticeable extent, wanted one. Griffith acknowledged the request by Nikitin, promised to forward it to Washington, but had to make an effort not to smile in front of the Soviet officer. To his way of thinking, such a request was ridiculous.

Knowing it was a waste of time, Griffith forwarded the Russian request through Deane to Washington as he had promised Nikitin he would. To his amazement, on March 2, 1944, Arnold sent the following message to Spaatz, and a copy to Deane in Moscow:

> Reference Deane message, you are authorized to ship to Moscow for presentation to Soviets one Norden bombsight.

Griffith had barely recovered from that surprise when, on March 15, 1944, another message was delivered to the U.S. Military Mission in Moscow:

> Reference Deane message, you are authorized to ship to Moscow for presentation to Soviets one C-1 automatic pilot with stabilizer for operation with Norden bombsight previously given to Soviets.

Stalin's rape of technical secrets of the USAAF was well underway.

Two days after this message arrived, Kessler and Cullen met with Lieutenant General Grendal, Chief of Intelligence and Reconnaissance of the Red Air Force, to discuss joint intelligence problems. Grendal had little data—or at least, he had little data he would release to the Americans—about Luftwaffe disposition. He stated that the Germans were known to have a complete radar net over the eastern front, but he insisted that he did not know the location of the stations. Enemy antiaircraft batteries were located along the front to a depth of approximately 85 miles. Kessler gave him a list of "Pointblank" strategic targets that the American heavy bombers wanted to strike on the initial mission, and Grendal agreed to submit the list to Soviet authorities.

Tragically for the Americans, Grendal insisted on postponing any discussion involving Russian antiaircraft batteries for defense of the air bases to be used by the American heavy bombers, the fighters available for the same purpose, and the possibilities of American installation of radio direction-finder stations for guiding their bombers. Except for the radio direction-finder stations, these subjects were not to be discussed by the Soviet leaders again until after the tragedy at Poltava. And then it was to be too late.

Early in March, Deane, now confident that the Soviet Union would approve the project, sent a message revealing his thoughts to Washington:

> I have had repeated assurances that the Soviet Government has approved the shuttle bombing project and will do what is

necessary to make it a success. This does not mean they surrender complete determination to us as to what is necessary. In getting in with this operation we are breaking a traditional resistance to foreigners that is as old as Russia. I can only assure you that we here can understand how you would like to see the project develop and will do our best to bring it about. I shall not attempt to discuss our difficulties by cable. I will say that I am confident of success if we play our cards right and keep patiently plugging. Having given their approval to the venture, I am sure the Soviets will make certain that a flop cannot be attributed to them.

Spaatz knew that if the shuttle-bombing project was to help the USAAF regain air superiority in the skies over Europe before D-day—tentatively scheduled for late May or early June 1944—the necessary supplies had to reach the Soviet Union by April at the latest. He decided to gamble that the Russians would soon assign the air bases for the heavy bombers and started to ship the supplies, knowing that it was going to be extremely difficult to obtain the necessary cargo space for the large amount of materials and equipment. At the outset of the shuttle-mission project a study had been made of the possible supply routes available, and Spaatz now reviewed the options open to him. The report, dated December 1943, detailed the advantages and drawbacks of all possible supply routes:

I. Persian Gulf—This route is now being used to its maximum capacity of 216,000 long tons per month for Russian Lend-Lease supplies. Of this capacity, 110,000 tons are by rail, the remainder by road. Supplies now moving by this route include items of the same type as required for shuttle bombing operations. As there is a general shortage of trucks for U.S. requirements, it would not be feasible to increase the capacity of this route. Note: The rail capacity can be increased by 160,000 long tons per month using present U.S. equipment and personnel if the U.S.S.R. can clear this amount from Tehran by rail and truck.

II. Murmansk—The Northern Route through Murmansk can be used without heavy losses only in bad weather. At present its use is not projected beyond March, 1944, for U.S./U.S.S.R. Lend-Lease. If this route is used for shuttle bombing supplies a loss rate due to enemy action of fifty percent would have to be assumed thus doubling all requirements. This route would also require heavy naval convoy commitments and these would probably not be available unless this route is kept open after March, 1944, for Lend-Lease purposes.

III. Vladivostok—The Pacific route to Vis is now used to near-capacity for U.S.S.R. Lend-Lease. All cargo is carried on U.S.S.R. bottoms (sixty-two percent formerly of U.S. registry) and for normal operating conditions is subject to Japanese inspection. It is not believed that the U.S.S.R. would jeopardize this route by carrying U.S. supplies.

General Conclusion—The Persian Gulf Route is the only practical one, U.S. aid being furnished U.S.S.R. to help the Soviet Union with clearance problems at Tehran.

Reading this report in March 1944, Spaatz decided that there was only one option open to him. A Lend-Lease convoy was scheduled to leave England for Murmansk early in March and Spaatz was informed that his five ships could join it if he could get the vessels to Britain in time. Deciding that this was his best chance to get the shuttle-bombing supplies to the Soviet Union in time to accomplish *his* primary aim, he agreed. The ships carrying the supplies were:

SHIP	TONS	CARGO
George T. Angell	2260	gasoline
	353	vehicles
	2571	landing mat
	348	miscellaneous
Total	5532	
George M. Cohan	3719	landing mat
	2225	gasoline
	416	vehicles
	164	miscellaneous
Total	6524	
Edward P. Alexander	62	oil
	654	gasoline
	237	parts
	691	bombs and ammunition
	2250	landing mat
	171	vehicles
	1	medical
	100	quartermaster stores
Total	4166	

SHIP	TONS	CARGO
John Davenport	29	oil
	432	gasoline
	35	signals
	221	parts
	255	vehicles
	1991	landing mat
	687	bombs and ammunition
	3	medical
	292	quartermaster stores
Total	3945	
William McKinley	1703	gasoline and oil
	273	parts
	1862	landing mat
	706	bombs and ammunition
	146	vehicles
	24	engineering
	1	medical
	135	quartermaster stores
Total	4850	

The ships were due to dock at Murmansk on April 4, four days after it was considered safe to send supplies by this route because of German submarines. Spaatz, knowing that the prediction was that he would lose as much as fifty percent of his supplies, took the gamble.

While the ships were still at sea, Deane sent a message to Washington saying that the air bases had been selected and that the Russians approved of the selection! Spaatz's gamble would pay off, if the supplies reached the Soviet Union safely.

3

"Is Russia on Our Side?"

O N MARCH 22, 1944, Deane sent confirmation to Washington
that the air bases for the American heavy bombers had been
selected. Instead of the six bases requested, however, Nikitin, obviously under orders from the Kremlin, had permitted Kessler,
Griffith, and Cullen to select only three. They were Poltava, Mirgorod, and Piryatin, all in the Kiev area of the Ukraine. The
Americans knew that none of the three airfields were really suitable for B-17s, but they were the only ones that could be adapted
for the heavy bombers within a reasonable time. Several others
were as suitable as Poltava, Mirgorod, and Piryatin but three bases
were all that the Russians permitted them to choose, so they selected these three because they were the nearest to the eastern
front.

Piryatin, designated #560 by the USSTAF, was the furthest
west and nearest the eastern front in March 1944. It was only
270 miles from the nearest German airfield. It was planned that
this base would be used by American fighter aircraft that would
accompany the B-17s, as well as some of the bombers.

Mirgorod was approximately fifty miles east of Piryatin and six
miles from the town of Mirgorod, which had once had a population
of 30,000 before the Germans occupied the area. The open na-
ture of the terrain around this base provided little or no shelter
from the Siberian winds or the scorching summer sun. It had been
reoccupied by the Russians within the past eight months after a
two-year occupation by the Nazis. All of the buildings of any size
that had a potential for war use had been destroyed by the retreating German armies, which meant that the USSTAF had to practically rebuild the air base before it could be used by the American heavy bombers.

The third base selected by Kessler, Griffith, and Cullen was

Poltava. It was earmarked to be the headquarters base for the permanent American personnel stationed in the Soviet Union for the duration of the shuttle-mission project. Poltava had once been the pride of the Ukraine, the center of a thriving agricultural area, with a population of 130,000. Now its population was one-third of what it had been prior to the war and every public building in the city had been razed by the Germans. Since the Ukraine had often been a prize of war, the Nazis were sympathetic with the citizens and few homes had been destroyed. After the Russians reoccupied the city they had removed most of the litter, rebuilt a few parks, and kept the damaged remnants of the city as clean as possible. The airfield itself was two miles west of Poltava and had two concrete runways. One runway was 3300 feet long, the other 1900 feet long, and both were much too short for the American heavy bombers . . . even if the bomb craters had been repaired.

The Americans knew that they had to start from scratch at the bases before they would be suitable for the shuttle-mission operations. Facilities for housing, mess halls, medical care, aircraft servicing and repair, communications, navigation, and a host of other details had to be worked out with the Russians. Each air base had to have runways at least one mile long to handle the B-17s that would be coming in to land and since there was no time to construct hard-top runways it was decided to use steel matting. It was a job that required a great deal of cooperation from the Russians in providing manpower, getting the supplies from the ships at Murmansk to the air bases, and permitting the skilled American personnel needed into the Soviet Union immediately.

The Soviet Union, rather than cooperating, put every conceivable obstacle in the way of the USAAF. It was not that Stalin wanted the shuttle-mission project canceled; he had found in it an ideal method for brazenly blackmailing the United States into getting what he wanted, when he wanted it.

No sooner had the bases been approved than the Russians began balking at every request made by Deane or Harriman in behalf of the USAAF or the USSTAF, which would actually be flying the missions. It was vital that the American advance party personnel be allowed to enter the Soviet Union and go directly to the air bases to begin the necessary preparations for the shuttle missions. After haggling over the number of such personnel needed

—the United States asked for a minimum of 2,100—there was nothing Deane could do but agree with Stalin's ultimatum that 1,200 Americans was the absolute maximum he would permit into the Soviet Union. Once this matter was settled, even though it was unsatisfactory to the USSTAF, Spaatz began sending the skilled ground crewmen, administrators, communications experts, and others to Tehran, from where they would fly to Moscow and on to the air bases. Since Stalin had approved the 1,200 maximum, no further trouble was anticipated.

An initial echelon of sixteen officers and six enlisted men were given orders to proceed to the Soviet Union by way of Tehran, but when they arrived in Iran they discovered that the Soviet Embassy refused to issue the proper visas without contacting Moscow. This took time, valuable time if the project was to get underway prior to D-day as planned. Deane immediately protested, as did Harriman, but to no avail. The advance echelon remained in Tehran waiting . . . waiting . . . waiting. Warnings from Spaatz to Deane forwarded by Deane to the Red Army General Staff and by Harriman to Molotov and Stalin brought only silence. Spaatz threatened to cancel the entire project but Stalin, with all the cards in his hand, knew it was a bluff. Stalin sat tight until he decided what he wanted next to "sweeten the pot." He decided that what the Soviet Union needed was permission to base a Red Air Force unit in Italy!

This request was made by the Mediterranean Theater of Operations representative Alexander Bogomolov to the Chief of the Allied Control Commission, Lieutenant General Mason MacFarlane. MacFarlane was immediately suspicious of the request because of the timing. The Russians had asked for the air base facilities at the same time they had suddenly recognized the Badoglio government in Italy. (By supporting the Badoglio government the Soviets felt they could get a foothold in postwar Italy and the Balkans.) This led General Henry Maitland Wilson, Supreme Allied Commander, Mediterranean, to have misgivings, but because of the wishes of the Americans connected with the shuttle-mission project, he agreed to submit the request to the Combined Chiefs of Staff.

Once Stalin was assured that he could have an air base from which the Red Air Force could operate in Italy he agreed to discuss the visa problem again. It was obvious even to the Kremlin that their previous procedure of thoroughly investigating every foreigner before he entered the Soviet Union was not possible in the case of the Americans waiting to be admitted to man the three Russian air bases. Nor could each of the American airmen be kept under strict surveillance once they were in the Soviet Union. Deane's argument was that the United States and the Soviet Union were allies against a common enemy—Germany—so why were the Russians so suspicious? But as he said privately later: "I would much prefer to risk my chance of survival on a landing in an African jungle than on a landing in Russia without the proper documents."

Finally, near the end of March, he and Harriman had negotiated an agreement with the Russians whereby all Americans who were to be permanently stationed at the Soviet bases would enter the country on group visas. The details were worked out carefully by Deane since he was well aware that Stalin's approval of an agreement did not necessarily include the approval of the supporting action that made the agreement workable. It was decided that the American personnel would travel to Tehran, where they would be double-checked by Major General Donald H. Connolly, commanding general of the Persian Gulf Command. Once he had a list of their names, he would present the list to the Soviet Embassy in Tehran and the list was to be stamped "Approved" by the Soviet ambassador. This would constitute a group visa. A duplicate of the list was to be sent to Deane who, in turn, would give it to the Foreign Office in Moscow. Once the men arrived in the Soviet Union, each was given an identification card.

"Without the identification card in Russia, an American airman is treated as though he is a capitalistic secret agent," Kessler complained to Nikitin later.

The Russian general shrugged and replied: "It is our custom."

The group visa plan was fine on paper, but in practice it didn't work well. Usually, after Connolly presented the list of American personnel in Tehran ready to enter the Soviet Union to the Soviet ambassador he would refuse to stamp it "Approved," saying, "he had to check with Moscow." Since Moscow had no record of the men waiting to enter the Soviet Union, the Foreign Office would have to wait until Connolly's duplicate list was cabled to Deane in Moscow. Deane would then pass it on to the Foreign Office, which would check the list and notify the Soviet ambassador in

Tehran. The Soviet ambassador would then stamp the list "Approved" and the Americans were permitted to enter the Soviet Union. If, during this delay, it was necessary to change any of the names on the list, the entire procedure had to be repeated. The project was delayed many weeks by the visa problem.

Not everyone assigned to the project had the patience, tact, and diplomacy to work with the Russians. It was much too one-sided, with the United States "backing down" at every meeting in an effort to keep the project alive. Few persons in the USAAF were surprised when the shuttle-mission project was given the code name "Frantic." It fitted the operation perfectly. Griffith, who had been sent to Russia to represent Spaatz personally, was not adept at dealing with the unpredictable Russians, and after several unsuccessful negotiations conducted by him, Deane asked Spaatz to relieve Griffith.

Deane made the request because he believed Griffith "lacked the temperament and personality suited to the difficult task of working closely with the Russians." He feared that Griffith's manner "would irritate the Russians to the extent that when we want to come in here on a large scale, they would be inclined to say 'We've tried it once and it is too difficult for us to operate together so you give us bombers and we will. . . .' "

Reluctantly Spaatz recalled Griffith, and Kessler, "Uncle Ugly" to the Russians, took command of the American personnel assigned to Russia for "Operation Frantic" and assumed responsibility for the operation of the three Russian air bases. At that time the entire contingent of Americans assigned to the project became known as the Provisional Eastern Command, USSTAF.

Kessler faced seemingly insurmountable odds—lack of Russian cooperation, late-arriving supplies, air bases that needed major renovations before operations could begin, bad weather, and a host of other problems. Surprisingly, "Uncle Ugly" tackled the obstacles with an optimistic attitude that pleased even the Russians. Slowly he began to win the confidence of the lower-level echelon of Red Air Force officers with whom he had to work. The Russians had selected Major General A. R. Perminov to command the Soviet forces stationed at the bases selected by the Americans and Kessler and Perminov took an immediate liking to each other. Perminov took an intense interest in the operation and did everything he could under the restrictions placed on him by Moscow to aid in getting the bases ready for the American bombers involved in the shuttle missions.

Perminov furnished two labor battalions to lay the steel matting used for the landing strips at the three air bases and agreed to send 800 maintenance specialists such as mechanics, fabric workers, and communications repairmen to aid the American personnel when the bases began to operate. In all, the Russians set up an organization totaling approximately 1,400 men to help at the three bases, 200 more than the Americans were permitted to send to the Soviet Union! The five merchant ships that had joined the convoy headed for Murmansk docked early in April with the supplies needed so badly by Kessler. By April 23 the ships had been unloaded and 10,000 tons of the supplies had been reloaded into 538 freight cars for transshipment to Mirgorod, Piryatin, and Poltava. Four hundred and fifty of the Russian freight cars had reached the bases by the middle of May, less than one-fifth of the 2,100 freight cars required to carry all the supplies that had been on the ships. By a carefully planned priority system, however, Kessler received enough supplies to get the bases in operational order by June 1, 1944.

The Russian labor battalions consisted of exceptionally good workers, none of whom resented the Americans or tried to take advantage of them. These laborers, supervised by American engineers, constructed steel mat runways at Mirgorod, Piryatin, and Poltava.

Two weeks after Kessler and his staff moved into the five-story building at Poltava, the one building that the retreating Germans had not razed, Russian and American security men discovered twelve German bombs totaling 5,500 kilograms under the building. These bombs were connected with an elaborate radio-controlled exploding mechanism in a large waterproof box buried 250 yards south of the headquarters. The mechanism was a complex device consisting of a radio receiver with 31 dry-cell batteries. The radio receiver was connected to a rectangular antenna 80 yards long and 20 yards wide that had been laid on the surface of the ground under straw and weeds. It was obvious to the security men of both countries that the Germans intended to set the explosives off at an opportune time by transmitting a radio signal from an aircraft.

All Americans and Russians were evacuated from the building

for two days while the German bombs were disconnected from the activating device. As Kessler said later: "Unknowingly the Germans could have wiped out the shuttle-mission operation with one signal from a Ju-88."

Kessler and his men faced other problems. One was the difficulty the Americans had becoming accustomed to living day after day with the Russians, working with them, eating with them, and socializing with them. At the beginning both Kessler's men and Perminov's men outdid each other making concessions so that relations were peaceful, but as the weeks passed small irritations grew in magnitude until both sides were ready to kill each other and probably would have tried if certain rules had not been established. Finally, Kessler posted the following notice to his men at Poltava in an effort to avoid further controversy:

> Haircuts—two barbers will be furnished every Wednesday.
> Bath Day—from 1300 to 1800 hours on Wednesday or any other [day] twenty men are available for baths.
> Sheets and Pillowcases—will be changed by the Russians every Wednesday.
> Laundry—will be collected every Thursday and returned the following Wednesday.
> Vodka—to be ordered in bulk for cash.
> Repairs—will do upon request.
> Rats and Mice—Russians will supply a cat.

American publications were in great demand by the Russian personnel on the three bases and at first the American personnel distributed their magazines freely after they had read them. This too was brought to an abrupt halt after a few weeks when Perminov, the Russian commander, gave strict orders to Kessler that the Americans should not give the magazines to either Soviet military or civilian personnel.

"Of course, Perminov himself would often come to my room and read the American magazines for hours," Kessler said.

As more and more of the allowable 1,200 Americans came to the three bases, more and more unpleasant incidents occurred. At Mirgorod, where a club had been built for use by the Russians and Americans, a USSTAF officer misinterpreted a remark by a Soviet airman. The Russian was calling him "friend" but, unfortunately for all concerned, the word for "friend" in his language sounded like "my droop" in English and after a few drinks fists began to fly. After the ensuing riot was halted, the club was closed. At the mess hall at Poltava, several American airmen taught one of the pretty girls who served food a few words of English.

As a bad joke, they taught her an obscene phrase and told her that it meant "How are you?" When she greeted a visiting American general with the obscene statement, he was promptly insulted and reported her to Perminov. An investigation revealed what had happened and that evening several husky Russian soldiers, friends of the girl, proceeded to get their revenge on the Americans. The fight was a draw but relations at the base were tense for weeks and never did return to the happy, easygoing early days of the project.

As "Operation Frantic" developed, it became apparent to Washington that a better unit organization was needed. The Provisional Eastern Command, USSTAF, was replaced by the Eastern Command, USSTAF, and a table of organization was set up for the new organization:

BREAKDOWN (Permanent)

	OFFICERS	ENLISTED	TOTAL
Command Headquarters, Poltava	78	217	295
Poltava Base	33	285	318
Mirgorod Base	36	313	349
Piryatin Base	29	230	259
	176	1045	1221

Lieutenant Colonel Curtis P. Boas was named commanding officer at Poltava, which was designated Station #559; Colonel David B. Lancaster, Jr., at Piryatin, Station #560; and Lieutenant Colonel James R. Irish at Mirgorod, Station #561. Kessler had been doing an excellent job as overall commander of the Americans preparing the bases in Russia for the American heavy bombers but Deane felt that he needed a higher-ranking American on the staff of the U.S. Military Mission in Moscow to deal with the Red Air Force officers. The Russians were extremely rank-conscious and no Soviet officer would conduct business with an American officer unless the American was of comparable rank or higher. General Arnold, in Washington, began searching for a USAAF officer who could meet the vital personal requirements needed for the position, and his attention centered on a little-known major general named Walsh who was in South America at the time on a special assignment.

Major General Robert L. Walsh was an officer who had a way of making friends with people very quickly. Energetic and intelligent, he was a favorite of Arnold.

General Arnold discovered that Walsh was on an aircraft en route to the United States for a rest when he decided that the major general was the man he wanted to go to the Soviet Union. The plane's pilot was contacted as soon as he crossed the United States shoreline.

"Is General Walsh aboard?" was the query radioed from the tower at Arnold's request.

Assured that the major general was on board, Arnold sent his personal driver to the National Airport at Washington to take the startled Walsh directly to USAAF headquarters. Greeting the major general with a smile he said, "Bob, you're going to Russia in the morning!"

The shocked Walsh asked for a few days' delay of the assignment so that he could return to Brazil on the next flight to pick up his personal belongings and clothes and also wind up a few matters pertaining to the ferry route. Harriman, who was headed back to Moscow after a Washington visit, agreed to wait for him. Both men then flew to Moscow in Harriman's converted B-24. In Moscow Walsh assumed a double command. He became head of the Air Division of the U.S. Military Mission in Moscow and also commander of the new Eastern Command, USSTAF. Kessler became his deputy commander, Cullen was named deputy commander for operations, Colonel Laurence B. Hickam deputy commander for administration, Colonel Lewis L. Mundell acting chief of staff and also chief of the weather service, and Lieutenant Colonel William M. Jackson was assigned to the Eastern Command as its surgeon. Under Walsh the Eastern Command became a very efficient organization despite the obstructions placed in his path by the Russians.

As the construction at the bases neared completion and the ground crews became organized and more settled at Poltava, Mirgorod, and Piryatin, the Americans' attention turned toward the operation of the first shuttle mission. Intelligence information was badly needed but, as usual, the Russians offered none despite the fact that United States military leaders knew they had bulging files concerning eastern Europe. In rare instances Lieutenant General Grendal, Chief of Intelligence and Reconnaissance of the Red Air Force, permitted limited intelligence "tidbits" to be turned over to Eastern Command's G-2 personnel. On April 21, 1944, a map showing a few Russian antiaircraft areas was given to Kessler. During the month of May a map of Soviet airdromes was handed to Deane in Moscow. Later that same month Poltava-based American officers began receiving the daily Soviet intelligence bulletin. In specialized fields such as navigation, Eastern Command navigation experts met with Red Air Force experts, but despite the fact that the American personnel answered nearly all the specific questions asked by the Russians about USAAF navigational techniques, the Soviets did not reciprocate. About all the Eastern Command experts learned was that Russian navigators preferred to use "magnetic" rather than "true" headings, reversed the "plus" and "minus" signs in designating magnetic variations, and interchanged the American terms of "heading" and "course."

This lack of cooperation in intelligence matters severely hampered the flight operation plans for the shuttle missions. It also emphasized the need for permission from the Kremlin for American reconnaissance planes to fly photographic missions as soon as possible. Target folders were needed for the flight crews, specific targets had to be selected for the initial shuttle mission, up-to-date information was needed on the location of Luftwaffe units on the eastern front. Except for a special display of Red Air Force aerial photographic equipment in Moscow on April 11, 1944, for the benefit of Cullen and his staff, no collaboration was extended by the Soviet Union in regard to target photos or other reconnaissance information they obviously had available. And the camera equipment displayed was inferior to American equipment already in use.

Arnold, in Washington, decided that a mission of high-ranking USSTAF officers to Russia was required to impress Stalin with the importance the United States attached to "Operation Frantic" and to help solve the many problems that were threatening the start of the project. The mission was headed by Major General Fred Anderson, Spaatz's deputy, and included Brigadier General E. P. Curtis, Colonel Elliott Roosevelt, and Colonel F. J. Sutterlin of the USSTAF, Colonel S. J. Gormly of the Mediterranean Allied Air Forces (MAAF), and Colonel J. A. Thomas of the Fifteenth Air Force. Harriman had insisted that Roosevelt be included on the mission because he was the President's son and might be able to convince Stalin of the need for immediate reconnaissance missions by American aircraft throughout the sector of eastern Europe that would be covered by the American heavy bombers on the shuttle missions.

Other subjects were on the agenda, too. Originally, the plan for the shuttle missions had suggested that U.S. fighter aircraft would provide escort for the heavy bombers as far as their fuel supply would permit and then Red Air Force fighters would fly cover and project the B-17s from the Luftwaffe. The many delays in the project, however, had changed this fighter escort concept. The P-51 long-range fighter had been developed to the point where these planes had the range to go all the way with the American heavy bombers. The USSTAF high command much preferred this new idea, but it was problematical whether the Russians would permit the American fighters to fly into the Soviet Union. Anderson was to discuss this new proposal in Moscow during his trip. Also, during the long delay in getting "Operation Frantic" underway the situation on the eastern front had changed. The Red Army was moving west fast, forcing the Germans to retreat all along the front, and this placed Poltava, Mirgorod, and Piryatin farther from the front lines than the USSTAF had desired. A main advantage of having the Russian air bases was to reduce the distances the American heavy bombers had to fly to bomb German targets in eastern Europe. Consequently, the question of air bases farther west that the USSTAF could use was to be introduced into the negotiations. In addition, information on targets that the Soviet Union wanted bombed was needed and a bomb line boundary between Budapest and Constanza had to be drawn to prevent Allied aircraft from accidentally bombing Soviet troops.

The mission arrived in Moscow on May 10, 1944, and began discussions with high hopes. The American officers met with Nikitin and Slavin, with Deane acting as intermediary. While they encountered the usual obstinacy and unpredictability of the Russians, the negotiations moved forward fairly smoothly. Roosevelt managed to obtain a temporary agreement on photographic flights by American planes and on May 15 Nikitin notified Deane, who notified the mission, that permission had been granted for 50 to 70 American fighter aircraft to enter the Soviet Union with the heavy bombers. The trip by Anderson and his companion officers was considered a success at the time and Spaatz made an optimistic report to Arnold on May 21, 1944.

SUBJECT: USSTAF Mission to Russia

TO: General H. H. Arnold, Commanding General, Army Air Forces, Washington, D.C.

Dear Hap:

This letter and the report submitted by Fred Anderson on his return from Russia are being brought to you by Colonel Jack Griffith. It will give you some additional and up-to-date information on the situation as we see it now. I firmly believe that we have accomplished a substantial step forward in the successful negotiations of the "Frantic" project; and if this project is followed up vigorously, and I intend to do so, the possible dividends which will accrue to the United States in its prosecution of the Japanese war are substantial. The use of our own fighters, to which the Russians have agreed, will aid in the success of our operations and will lead toward the establishment of a complete integrated unit on the Eastern Front. While we all realize that the present limitation as to the number of fighters permissible is going to create a handicap, we feel that reasonable success in initial operations will cause the Russians to open up even more and work actively with us.

I feel that we can afford to divert a group of fighters and three (3) groups of bombers to this project if necessary, and be well repaid in future dividends. I hope that commitments in support of our Ground Arms will not interfere with the immediate carrying out of operations to and from Russia. The tremendous benefits which are potentially available from the Russians, both on their own Western Front and on our Pacific Front, are well worth the temporary setting aside of this much of our force. It may not be necessary for much combat time to be lost by reason of our "Frantic" operations, but I feel very strongly that we should be prepared to accept such a reduction.

I believe we can create more of a strategic manner of thinking on the part of the Russians through shuttle operations on which they have taken part, than we could through many months of diplomatic negotiations. I am convinced that the Russians have done little thinking on any strategic air plan, and that they have operated up to this time on a purely tactical basis as far as their Air Force is concerned. Through our use of their fighters as well as our own and through the results of our PRU operations, I expect to see the Russians gradually adopt strategic operations along the same lines.

Our PRU operations from Russia covering the Eastern areas may reveal some lucrative targets currently unknown to us. I think it is highly probable that the Germans have installed considerable industrial facilities in that area. We should know about this in a very short time.

> *Carl Spaatz*
> Lieutenant General, USA,
> Commanding

In addition to giving Arnold an up-to-date report on "Operation Frantic," this letter also revealed the fact that Spaatz had widened his objectives for the project. He was now emphasizing that success in using the Russian air bases would convince Stalin that he should provide the USAAF other bases from which heavy bombers, probably the new B-29s, could attack Japan. Initially, Spaatz had concentrated on the task of attaining air superiority over the Continent prior to D-day and on the bombing of "Pointblank" targets in eastern Germany.

His comment that "I believe we can create more of a strategic manner of thinking on the part of the Russians through shuttle operations . . ." would probably have made the scowling Stalin smile had he known about it. It became obvious after the beginning of "Operation Frantic" that one of the reasons the traditionally isolationist Russians agreed to American air bases in their own territory, even after the tide had turned and the war was going in their favor, was that they were interested in the American technique of strategic bombing. Stalin, as events proved later, was already planning such strategic bombing by the Red Air Force as a long-range development. The Red Air Force policy of assigning, and to some degree rotating, personnel to work at the Eastern Command bases soon made it evident that the Russians were seeking to develop heavy bomber skills. Russians of all ranks learned their technical skills from American ground crews. Moreover, through Lend-Lease they kept making attempts to obtain B-17s, B-24s, B-29s and other heavy bombers of the Allies. Even as the shuttle mission project was developing, the Russian technicians put together for their own use individual American aircraft from salvaged materials made available. when

U.S. heavy bombers crash-landed or made emergency landings in Soviet territory!

Even an experienced USAAF officer such as Spaatz, whose opinion was valued highly right up to the White House, had tragically underestimated the subtlety and subterfuge of which Stalin was capable.

Despite the success of the Anderson trip to Moscow, all the major problems were not settled. The communications problem in particular horrified the Russians. Arnold, Spaatz, and other USAAF and USSTAF commanders had decided that there could not be any shuttle missions unless the radio communications vital to such missions were controlled by Americans. There were several important reasons for this nonnegotiable decision. Administrative and operational messages had to be sent, weather reports were required by the air commanders, radio direction-finding equipment had to be operated so that the American heavy bombers could find the air bases in the Ukraine, and there had to be communications between Poltava, Mirgorod, and Piryatin. The lives of the entire flight of American aircraft en route to or departing from the Russian air bases might depend upon a single radio message and the USAAF leaders were determined that no chances would be taken on this important part of the project. It was American-controlled communications or no shuttle missions.

The Foreign Office under Molotov was just as determined that no foreigners control any radio facilities in the Soviet Union, and for several weeks the matter was not discussed further. Red Air Force officers, however, understood the American demand that their own personnel operate the radio equipment, knowing that there was no time for translations in the air when a vital message was radioed to the flight leaders or formation commanders. Nor could procedural differences be taught the American airmen in time so that they would understand them when they reached Soviet territory. Nikitin and Novikov finally worked out an agreement that satisfied both Washington and Moscow. The Americans could operate their own equipment if Soviet representatives were present at all the communications stations. This was an excellent agreement because the Soviet representatives sent to the communications stations were Red Air Force experts who understood the problems involved as well as the Americans and did not interfere in any way.

Once this agreement was reached the Airways and Air Communications Service (AACS) of the USAAF was assigned the duty of handling all communications for "Operation Frantic," including point-to-point and range facilities. The Twenty-fourth Region of the AACS selected an initial cadre of sixteen enlisted men, including eight radio operators and eight cryptos, and two officers. In addition, ten enlisted men and an officer from the Signal Airways Service were chosen, all from the cream of the AAC's skilled technicians. This cadre was directed by a headquarters party consisting of Lieutenant Colonel William Day, commanding officer of the Twenty-fourth Region and three other officers. Supplies needed for the project were trucked from all over Britain to Prestwick and Saint Mawgan, jumping-off places for "Operation Frantic" cargo planes. The Air Transport Command (ATC) earmarked 20 transport planes to carry the 70,000 pounds of equipment, and Day chose one man to accompany each plane.

One week after departing from the United States the headquarters party, the initial cadre of communications personnel, and the 70,000 pounds of equipment were at Tehran ready to move into Russia. Then, as throughout the entire project, the Russians said "Nyet!" For three and one-half weeks the Soviet Embassy at Tehran and the Foreign Office in Moscow refused clearance into Russia. Deane's request for visas for the communications personnel, relayed to Molotov by Harriman, was ignored. The Soviet ambassador to Iran stated that he could not issue the visa unless Molotov gave him permission. For several weeks the AACS party marked time in their 4,000-foot high tent camp near Tehran. Finally, Russian aircrews were assigned to each of the ATC cargo planes destined to fly to the three American air bases in the Soviet Union—but the visas still had not been granted. Most of the headquarters party was forced to return to London on urgent business. Not until the end of April 1944 did word come from Moscow that the communications party would be permitted to proceed north, not to Poltava direct, but to Moscow first, where Day would have to deal through diplomatic channels with the appropriate Russian officials.

Day and his men, despite being discouraged about the lack of Soviet cooperation, accepted the offer and were in Moscow two days later ready to continue their efforts to proceed to Poltava.

Surprisingly, in Moscow the colonel found the Russians "cordial and obliging" and within three days he was on his way to Poltava. At Poltava the party was met by Major Rodininoff, in charge of liaison, who was formal but cooperative. Day, however, discovered what most Americans learned during their stay in the Soviet Union for "Operation Frantic." Rodininoff and his staff had a great "thirst for knowledge." Before the shuttle mission project ended, the Russian communications experts knew every technique the American communications personnel used, were experienced in the use, upkeep, and repair of all American radio equipment, and understood every detail of USAAF ground-to-air-to-ground transmissions. In the years after World War II, the Soviet experts would put this information to extensive use against the country from which they had learned it.

During the last week of April 1944 AACS installed its circuits on one floor of the Russian operations building at Poltava. Just as the radio facilities were ready to go on the air, however, the American and Soviet security investigators discovered the explosives the Germans had left in the building with the intention of blowing it up at a later date. The AACS had to evacuate the building until the explosives were removed but by early May 1944 the radio stations were ready for use in "Operation Frantic." They were ready, Day said, despite the fact that the Russians at Poltava who were supposed to help the Americans were "tongue-tied by Moscow."

Another important factor in the success or failure of "Operation Frantic" as well as bombing operations by USAAF aircraft against Japanese targets was weather. The Japanese attack at Pearl Harbor, when the enemy aircraft reached Hawaii after following bad weather that concealed the planes, was ample evidence of the value of weather as a weapon of war. Weather stations in the U.S.S.R., and there were many since the Soviet Union represented one-sixth of the earth's land mass, sent reports to Moscow, but Stalin refused to allow these reports to be passed on to American personnel. This weather information would have been invaluable to the USAAF. Weather conditions in western Russia, if they had been known, would have aided the American heavy bomber campaign against Germany, while information from Siberia and the Far Eastern maritime provinces would have removed the blackout that existed, as far as weather was concerned, in Japanese-controlled areas. On his trip to the Soviet Union in 1941 when he consulted with Stalin about Lend-Lease, Harriman had requested a weather exchange between the United States and the Soviet Union but Stalin had refused despite the fact that he was asking for millions of dollars worth of supplies from the United States. A year later, when the Alaskan-Siberian air route was established to deliver American aircraft to Soviet Russia, weather information from Soviet weather stations was requested but only an exchange between Irkutsk weather station, near Lake Baikal, and the United States weather station at Fairbanks, Alaska, was negotiated successfully. The Russians agreed to this exchange to safeguard the Lend-Lease aircraft on their way to the Soviet Union.

When Deane arrived in Moscow to head the U.S. Military Mission he immediately tried to instigate a complete weather exchange between the stations of the two countries—and was ignored. President Roosevelt, at the Tehran Conference, also brought the subject to Stalin's notice but it wasn't until late March 1944 that Andrei Vishinsky notified Harriman that the Soviet Union was ready to broaden the exchange of weather information "on a basis of reciprocity." Deane assigned Rear Admiral Clarence E. Olsen to work out the details of the new agreement with Lieutenant General Eugene K. Fedorov, Chief of the Russian Weather Service. Fedorov was more a scientist than a military officer and was an advocate of international weather exchange, so this made Olsen's job much easier. Under the ever-watchful eye of the Foreign Office, Olsen and Fedorov agreed on a pact that provided an exchange of weather information from 100 weather stations of each country. The United States was to provide weather coverage of the United States, the Atlantic Ocean, and as much of western Europe as possible, while the Russians were to provide coverage of the entire Soviet Union. Also, long-range forecasts were included in the agreement. This weather exchange agreement was honored by the Russians throughout "Operation Frantic" and even after the shuttle mission project ended. It was one of the most successful collaboration efforts between the two countries during World War II.

The shuttle-bombing project had progressed slowly but steadily between February 2, 1944, when Stalin had finally given his approval to the idea, and the middle of May 1944. It had been a constant struggle by Deane and Harriman in Moscow, Kessler and Walsh at Eastern Command headquarters at the Poltava airfield, and Connolly at Persian Gulf Command headquarters in Tehran, but by the middle of May the facilities for handling the American bombers and fighters and their crews at Poltava, Mirgorod, and Piryatin were sixty-five percent completed, with the work yet to be done considered by Kessler not important enough to delay the shuttle missions any longer. The weather reports from Soviet Russia were being received at Eighth Air Force headquarters in Britain and at Fifteenth Air Force headquarters in Italy in accordance with the Olsen-Fedorov agreement. The AACS radio stations and direction-finding equipment were in operation. The Anderson mission, with Elliott Roosevelt doing the negotiations, had arranged a temporary agreement on photo reconnaissance flights by American planes over Russian territory and these planes were being prepared for the initial reconnaissance missions by the middle of May. All that remained was to select the target for the first shuttle mission, and this appeared to be a simple matter.

4

The Target Controversy

As PREPARATIONS FOR "Operation Frantic" continued in the Soviet Union, the Eighth Air Force in Great Britain and the Fifteenth Air Force in Italy were still trying to achieve the necessary air supremacy over Europe that was needed for "Overlord," the code name for the cross-Channel invasion plan. Bad weather, lack of long-range fighter escorts, and depleted aircrews had seriously impaired the efficiency of the two units, however, and it was not until the middle of February 1944 that the heavy bombers once again began to operate in strength against targets deep in Germany.

On February 19 the weather in the areas of the German aircraft factories began to open up and the plan that had been put on paper by the Combined Operational Planning Committee four months earlier became feasible. This plan, code-named "Argument," placed airframe and final assembly factories producing single- and twin-engine fighter aircraft at the top of the target list. The Combined Operational Planning Committee members felt that if these factories were bombed out of operation, the results would show up much quicker in combat than if the aircraft engine plants were attacked. In addition, the antifriction-bearing industry was considered highly important to the Luftwaffe because without the bearings, regardless of how small they might be, no aircraft was operational. This industry was concentrated in a small number of factories which, if eliminated, would mean a critical loss of bearings to the German Air force.

The primary responsibility for the series of heavy bomber missions that began on February 20 and ended on February 25 belonged to the USSTAF, the same organization planning the Russian shuttle missions. Spaatz's operations deputy, Major General Frederick L. Anderson, was placed in charge of these concentrated raids that later became known as "Big Week." His orders: "Take more than ordinary risks in order to complete the destruction of German fighter production, including the risk of exceptional losses that might occur from missions staged under conditions of adverse base weather." It was an all-out effort to regain the required air supremacy over the Continent.

During "Big Week" more than 3,300 bombers from the Eighth Air Force and 500 from the Fifteenth Air Force dropped approximately 10,000 tons of bombs on "Pointblank" targets. The losses were heavy but not as overwhelming as had been anticipated by many USAAF officers. The Eighth Air Force lost 137 bombers during the six-day attack while the Fifteenth Air Force lost 89, with nearly 2,600 crewmen either killed in action, missing, or seriously wounded. As a result of "Big Week" the German aircraft industry was ordered to disperse its plants. Also as a result of the damage caused by the heavy bombers the overall responsibility for aircraft production was shifted from Goering's Air Ministry to Albert Speer's Ministry of Armaments and Munitions. In estimating the effects of "Big Week," however, USSTAF and USAAF leaders failed to take into account the phenomenal recuperability of the German aircraft industry. The successive heavy bomber raids forced the Germans into feverish action that resulted in reducing the effects of the bombers to only a temporary reduction in overall aircraft production. The dispersal of the German plants also put many more of the factories out of reach of both English and Italian air bases and made "Operation Frantic" more necessary than ever to American military leaders. The situation became even more critical with "Overlord" set for early June.

Initially, plans had been made for the Eighth Air Force to fly the first shuttle-mission to Soviet Russia. It was the largest of the USSTAF air forces, their crews had the most experience, and many of the choice enemy targets were on the route from the British Isles, where the Eighth was based, to the Soviet Union. However, early in May, Spaatz and Arnold decided that the Eighth Air Force would be needed for "Overlord," and consequently that they didn't want 150 of its heavy bombers in Russia during the critical cross-Channel invasion. Thus the Fifteenth Air Force was selected for the mission. On May 3, 1944, Spaatz notified Major General N. F. Twining:

SUBJECT: Shuttle Bombing Operations to Russia

TO: Commanding General, 15th Air Force, APO 520, U.S. Army. (Thru Commanding General, MAAF)

1. You have been provided with a letter from the U.S. Strategic Air Forces in Europe, subject "Shuttle Bombing Operations Utilizing Bases in Russia," date 28 April 1944. This letter outlines the planned installations and logistic support for these operations.

2. Although Paragraph 6 of this letter indicates that the initial operation will be made from U.K., I believe that the OVERLORD situation may make it essential that the first operation be conducted by a combat wing of the 15th Air Force.

3. In accordance with our conversation on this subject, I wish you would make plans to move a combat wing of approximately 150 heavy bombers and one group of fighters to the Russian bases early in June. The actual timing of this operation will depend upon the state of completion of the air bases in Russia and your own local commitments.

4. Upon arrival at the Russian bases, desire that the combat wing be prepared to make several attacks against the German aircraft industry in the Posen area. It is assumed that the 15th Air Force has complete target folders covering these targets. If not, send to this headquarters a request that they be provided to you.

5. I will obtain from the Russian government their desires as to the targets to be hit en route into Russia.

6. The necessity for the full utilization of the Russian facilities provided is well known to you, as well as the necessity for fullest cooperation with the Russians during FRANTIC operations to assist them by attacking targets of their selection. To achieve this end, at least one additional strategic target should be selected by the Russians in addition to their selection of the target for the first shuttle operation.

7. This headquarters will keep you fully informed as to the status of our arrangements in Russia, to include command setup in the Poltava area, our headquarters setup in Moscow, and all further developments in our negotiations and preparations.

Carl Spaatz
Lieutenant General, USA,
Commanding

Fifteen days after Spaatz sent this message to Fifteenth Air Force headquarters in Italy, he received a message from Deane in Moscow to the effect that he had informed Nikitin that the USAAF proposed to fly three or four missions from Russian bases prior to the beginning of return shuttle trips. No objections were raised so Deane suggested to Spaatz that he plan on going ahead without seeking formal Russian approval.

It appeared that most of the necessary details for the initial "Operation Frantic" mission had been settled. Only the seemingly simple matter of selecting targets that would aid both the American and Russian war objectives remained.

During the last six days of May a final conference on "Operation Frantic" was held by most of the principals involved in the complex project at Park House in Wimbledon, a few miles outside London. Walsh, Harriman, Spaatz, Eaker, and several other officers from their staffs were present. It was definitely decided that the initial shuttle mission to Russia should be flown prior to "Overlord" so that the Germans would realize that they faced attacks by American heavy bombers from the east as well as from the west. It was hoped that Goering would then shift a sizeable number of his fighter planes from the western front to the eastern front. This would, of course, help guarantee the success of the cross-Channel invasion. Another decision, regretted later, was that any target that the Soviet Union requested the American heavy bombers attack while the B-17s were operating from Soviet air bases would have priority over other targets.

The decision that was to cause the most controversy during the initial shuttle mission to the Soviet Union was the revision of the USSTAF target list to focus on German aircraft production at Riga, Latvia, and Mielec. The Heinkel plants in this area were important targets, high on the priority list at this date, and extremely difficult, if not impossible, to attack from Italy if the heavy bombers had to return to their home bases after dropping their bombs. Spaatz also decided to request prior authority to photograph these targets so that adequate target folder data would be available for the aircrews. These decisions were considered routine as was the formal request Spaatz later made to Moscow, which was considered a matter of courtesy. He and the others concerned with the success of the operation soon discovered that these points were anything but "routine."

While the conference was going on in England, Deane was meeting with Nikitin in Moscow. Their discussion centered on the important matter of defense of the Russian air bases while the American heavy bombers were in the Soviet Union. The Russians had insisted during earlier negotiations that they would provide all the defense necessary for the three bases, but Kessler had been complaining to Deane that there was no indication that this agreement was being complied with at Mirgorod, Piryatin, or Poltava. As Deane told Nikitin: "It was my understanding originally that the arrangements for both fighter and antiaircraft defenses were to be coordinated through General Perminov but he has now stated that the coordination must be expected in Moscow. Apparently it needs some clarification."

Nikitin gave no clear answer but implied that there was nothing to worry about. Two days later several Russian fighters appeared at Piryatin and the following day American Lend-Lease trucks fitted with special mounts holding 50-caliber machine guns moved onto all three bases. Kessler was still not satisfied, but there was nothing he could do about the matter.

While Spaatz confidently awaited Russian approval for the heavy bombers of the Fifteenth Air Force to strike the targets in the Riga, Latvia, and Mielec area, he decided to send the first American reconnaissance aircraft to Soviet Russia. Cullen, the Eastern Command's deputy for operations and considered one of the best reconnaissance pilots in the USAAF, was chosen to fly the mission. Cullen had flown many dangerous photo reconnaissance missions during World War II but as he told Spaatz prior to his takeoff for Poltava: "Usually all I have to worry about are enemy guns. Now I have to worry about the Russian guns, too."

During the long negotiations in Moscow the Russians had agreed that American pilots could make reconnaissance flights over targets in eastern Germany and continue eastward to land in the U.S.S.R., but had insisted on a twenty-four-hour notice. The Soviets insisted that this advance notice was necessary because of the difficulty of alerting the Russian fighter and antiaircraft units that "friendly" aircraft would be crossing the eastern front. Without the alert, all Russian defenses, on the ground and in the air, attacked any aircraft heading eastward. This was not a satisfactory procedure for the USAAF since twenty-four-hour notice seriously interfered with the efficiency of the reconnaissance operations. Many times a reconnaissance plane in other areas of the combat zone would take off with only a few minutes notice to photograph a target about which more information was needed. Spaatz had tried for weeks to get the Soviets to change their minds but had not been successful. Consequently, when Cullen took off on the first shuttle reconnaissance mission on May 24, 1944, he had good reason to be worried.

Cullen and a wingman, both flying F-5 reconnaissance aircraft (converted P-38 fighters, with guns removed and all excess weight discarded), flew across German territory without incident, taking the pictures required for the target folders to be used later by the heavy bomber crews. They had little difficulty staying away from the Luftwaffe fighters but once the two American pilots reached Russian-occupied territory all radio contact with them was lost. It was not known whether Cullen and his wingman had reached a Soviet air base safely or not. On May 26 the following message was received by Spaatz:

Cullen and Carney arrived safely at Poltava on time and without incident.

The following day, however, Cullen made a reconnaissance flight in his F-5 from Poltava and as he was returning from his mission he passed near Mirgorod. Without warning the antiaircraft battery on the air base opened fire on him and only quick evasive action saved his life. It was an omen of what would face both the heavy bomber crews and other reconnaissance pilots operating within the borders of the Soviet Union. At first, such incidents were considered accidental. Later events indicated that many of the attacks made on American aircraft had been intentional.

To further strain the situation, four American photo-reconnaissance planes on a shuttle run from Italy to the Soviet Union tried to land at Poltava on May 30 and because of a mixup in the advance notice procedure, the Russian gunners tried to shoot down all four planes. The F-5s were easily distinguishable from the ground by their twin booms and twin engines but this did not deter the Russians gunners, who continued to fire at them until the furious Kessler demanded that Perminov order the shooting stopped. Fortunately, no one was injured but Soviet authorities, stating that the F-5s had landed on Russian soil without permission, forced the cancellation of other reconnaissance flights already scheduled by the USSTAF. On June 1, 1944, Kessler radioed the news to Eaker in Italy:

> Clarifying our confusion regarding photo recon cite your 34. No photo recon flights have been permitted by the Soviets. No shuttle flights to or from Italy are cleared although requested. Mission accomplished en route from Italy only partial successful because of cloud. These photos are being printed in sufficient quantity for return operations. You will be immediately notified when Soviets grant requested clearance for either shuttle or local photo recon missions.

Time was getting very short for the first "Operation Frantic" mission if it was to be flown prior to "Overlord." Since it was still undetermined whether "Big Week" by the Eighth and Fifteenth air forces had been successful in its aim to limit German aircraft production to a level where Allied air supremacy over the Continent was assured during the invasion, it was important for the shuttle missions to begin as soon as possible. The opportunity to force Goering to withdraw some of his fighters from western Europe could not be missed. But with only a minimum of photo coverage of the targets available, all reconnaissance flights cancelled by the Soviets, no formal approval of the proposed targets, and the weather conditions forecast as poor for the following week at both ends of the proposed shuttle, Spaatz was getting more and more discouraged. There was nothing he could do except wait for the results of the last-minute negotiations taking place in Moscow.

Shortly after Spaatz learned the bad news about future reconnaissance flights, Deane was summoned to a meeting with Slavin, of the Red Army General Staff, who told the commander of the U.S. Military Mission to Moscow that the Red Army General Staff had disapproved all the targets Spaatz had selected for the initial shuttle mission. The reason given was that the targets were "within the Russian sphere of operations." Slavin insisted that the American heavy bombers attack targets in the Bucharest-Brasov-Debrecin-Budapest area. To Deane this was ridiculous since all the targets in this area could just as easily be attacked from Italian bases. "If these are the targets," he told Slavin, "there was no need to continue on to Russia." The Russian quickly became angry when Deane protested his selection of targets and demanded to know why the Americans had indicated they wanted to assist the Russian advance in the Balkans but now, when the time came to help, they refused? Despite all of Deane's arguments, Slavin refused to compromise on the target selection. Deane could do nothing but transmit the information to Britain, Italy, and the United States.

After explaining Slavin's statements concerning the targets Spaatz wanted to attack in the Riga, Latvia, and Mielec area, Deane suggested agreement on the Russian target selection.

> . . . once started [the operations] will meet with great enthusiasm and we will be allowed a great deal more freedom of action, not only in the selection of targets, but on all other questions. The opening of the second front will, of course, have a beneficial effect. If this is done, I think that on subsequent missions we shall be perfectly safe in selecting our own targets and announcing them without asking for specific approval.

Wanting to launch the first shuttle mission prior to the cross-Channel invasion, now scheduled for June 5th, or 6th, depending upon the weather, Spaatz reluctantly bowed to the Soviets and selected the inconsequential targets they had suggested. He sent word to Eaker at MAAF headquarters in Italy to proceed with his preparations for the initial mission, using Fifteenth Air Force crews, and to schedule the operation on the first day the weather was favorable. He also requested that Eaker personally lead the formation to Soviet Russia. He couldn't have chosen a better man.

Lieutenant General Ira C. Eaker was a tough-minded flier with courage to spare and the intelligence to plan the operations that required this courage. Fifty years of age, he had probably had as much experience as any man in the USAAF. After the United States entered the war he was promoted to brigadier general and in January 1942 was given the assignment to organize and command the Eighth Bomber Command, which later was redesignated the Eighth Air Force. Not only did he organize and command this unit but he personally led attacks on enemy targets in Germany and France, for which he was awarded the Legion of

Merit, the Silver Star, and the Distinguished Service Medal. On September 13, 1943, Eaker was promoted to three-star rank. This was the same month and same year that "Operation Frantic" was first proposed.

When Eaker received the assignment to personally lead the first shuttle mission to the Soviet Union he was delighted but cautious. He was certain that the Fifteenth Air Force crews could handle the mission successfully, and that the American heavy bomber units assigned to the operation could and would impress the Russians with their skill and courage. He was, however, one of the USAAF leaders who remained unconvinced that the Soviet military and political leaders were sincere in their promises of collaboration. The preliminary negotiations conducted by Deane and Harriman had only served to strengthen this belief, and as he prepared for the initial "Operation Frantic" mission, Eaker was still skeptical about the reception he and his crews would receive in the Soviet Union. Concerning the targets the Russians had selected for the first American task force and their demand that only these targets be attacked, he said: "The Soviets do not want us to attack the targets in the Riga, Latvia, and Mielec area because they do not wish us to be able to say that our bombing contributed even partially to their successes. . . ."

In later months Eaker was proved absolutely correct.

Nor did he like the decision made at Park House late in May and verified by a message from Spaatz to him on May 26, 1944:

> At meeting in London, May 25, 1944, herewith points decided upon for your information. *Russians may be given freely information on American technical equipment now in operational use. . . .*"

Eaker also requested, and received approval from Spaatz, that if the Soviets refused to approve targets he selected to attack while at the Soviet air bases he could immediately bring his Fifteenth Air Force crews back to Italy, bombing any target he wanted on the way. Eaker didn't want his planes and crews stuck in Europe while Moscow haggled over targets. Despite his irritation with and suspicion of the Russians and his feelings that they were certainly not cooperating as an ally should cooperate, he assured Arnold that he intended to do his utmost to make the operation a complete success.

In this respect, one of the first briefing notes Eaker gave to the Fifteenth Air Force crews selected for the shuttle mission was a warning:

> . . . not to enter into political or social discussions based on comparisons with our own institutions. The Russians do not recognize personal opinions in the armed forces. Statements made by individuals are considered official opinions of the government.

However, another briefing note Eaker's intelligence officers received clearly indicated that he did not intend to tell the Russians everything:

> In briefing for Frantic Joe [code name for first mission] instruct all personnel on operation that they *must not* speak disparagingly of the B-24. Questions will be asked about it. Instruct all personnel to speak highly of it. The reason for this, not to be divulged at briefing, is that a number of these B-24s are earmarked on a Lend-Lease basis.

The selection of the aircrews and fighter pilots to fly the initial Russian shuttle mission was made very carefully since the prestige of the United States as well as the USAAF, USSTAF and the Fifteenth Air Force was involved. Although the Fifteenth Air Force had only been activated November 1, 1943, the winter bombing campaign had given it much-needed experience. Prior to and during the Anzio landings and the weeks after the Anzio operation, the Fifteenth Air Force had been busy. However, most of these missions were in direct support of ground troops, not strategic bombing operations for which the heavy bombers were designed and which would be required on the Russian shuttle mission. Eaker, however, was certain the Fifteenth Air Force could handle the assignment successfully.

He selected his task force carefully. One of the first units he picked for the shuttle-mission to Russia was the Second Bombardment Group, which had proved itself during "Big Week." It was commanded at the time by Colonel Herbert Rice. Another combat unit chosen for the mission was the Ninety-seventh Bombardment Group, commanded by Colonel Frank Allen. The Ninety-seventh had been organized in January 1942, and initially flew antisubmarine patrols with B-17s. Moving to Great Britain, the group entered combat on August 17, 1942, on the first mission flown by the USAAF's heavy bombers from the British Isles. Five squadrons of the Ninety-ninth Bombardment Group were selected by Eaker to go on the initial shuttle mission with the Ninety-seventh and the Second Bombardment groups. This unit, which was commanded by Colonel Ford J. Lauer, had received a Distinguished Unit Citation for its performance on July 5, 1943, when the group helped neutralize fighter opposition prior to the invasion of Sicily by penetrating enemy defenses to bomb planes, hangars, fuel supplies, and ammunition dumps at the Gerbini airfield. The Ninety-ninth had received a second Distinguished Unit Citation for withstanding severe fighter assaults while bombing a German aircraft factory at Wiener Neustadt on April 23, 1944. This outstanding mission, flown during the time that "Operation Frantic" plans were being negotiated, caught Eaker's attention and was probably the reason this group was chosen.

The "baby" of the Fifteenth Air Force units selected for the first "Operation Frantic" mission was the 483d Bombardment Group, commanded by Colonel Paul L. Barton. The 483d began combat operations in April 1944, at a time when the plans for "Operation Frantic" were well underway. However, Eaker felt that this new unit had proved its worth while bombing targets such as factories, oil refineries, marshalling yards, and airfields in Italy, France, Germany, Poland, Czechoslovakia, Austria, Hungary, Rumania, Yugoslavia, and Greece. The Soviet Union would soon be added to this impressive list.

For fighter protection Eaker took no gamble when he chose the famous "Checkertail Clan," the 325th Fighter Group. Headed by colorful Colonel Chester L. Sluder, the 325th had been in combat since April 17, 1943, operating out of North Africa and Italy. The "Checkertail Clan," so named because of the black-and-yellow checkered design on the tails of their fighters, had been extremely busy. The unit received a Distinguished Unit Citation for action over Sardinia on July 30, 1943, when the group, using diversionary tactics, forced a superior number of enemy planes into the air and destroyed more than half of them. Moving to Italy and changing from the P-40 fighter to the newer P-47, the 325th began escorting the heavy bombers of the new Fifteenth Air Force on long-range missions. The group also flew cover for reconnaissance aircraft and made many low-level strafing runs on enemy trains, vehicles, and airfields. On January 30, 1944, the group flew more than 300 miles at very low level to surprise the enemy fighters defending German airfields near Villaorba and caused so much havoc among the Luftwaffe planes that the Fifteenth Air Force bombers could bomb vital targets without encountering serious opposition. For this mission the unit was awarded its second Distinguished Unit Citation. As Eaker said when selecting the 325th to escort the American heavy bombers to Soviet Russia on the first shuttle mission: "I'll feel much safer with the 'Checkertails' flying cover above my plane."

The crews selected for the shuttle mission to Russia were sworn to secrecy. They were not permitted even to tell other crews of their group that were not listed to fly the mission that they were flying to Soviet Russia. Sluder, commander of the 325th, first learned where he was going when he was called to Headquarters, Fifteenth Fighter Command, by Brigadier General Dean C. Strother, its commander. Strother told Sluder that the 325th had been selected to escort B-17s on a shuttle-bombing mission to the Soviet Union and warned Sluder that the operation was classified "Top Secret." Back at the fighter base at Lesina, Sluder had to find a way to plan the mission for his group and make the necessary preparations without compromising security. He took Lieutenant Colonel "Buzz" Toner, deputy group commander, Major Ken Setterdahl, the group intelligence officer, Major Sherman Hoar, group materiel officer, and Lieutenant Sam Brown, group operations officer, into his confidence and the preliminary planning was begun immediately.

Adding to Sluder's burden during the weeks just prior to the shuttle mission was the group's transition from P-47 fighters to P-51s. Even during this transition, however, the group had to maintain its full quota of combat missions. Two days after Sluder's visit to see Strothers, he was summoned to Fifteenth Air Force headquarters in Bari, Italy, where Eaker gave him a detailed briefing of the upcoming "Operation Frantic" mission that was now commonly known as "Frantic Joe."

"It is to be a maximum effort," Eaker explained, "requiring every P-51 and every pilot available. The bombers must be protected at all costs."

Sluder and his pilots were to pick up the bombers over the Adriatic Sea and escort them as long as possible. When their fuel became low, the 325th fliers were to head for Piryatin. Eaker warned the colonel that if his fighters left the bombers too soon the Luftwaffe would probably attack in force and reduce the American task force to an ineffectual formation that could not complete its assigned mission. If they left too late, the P-51s would not have enough fuel to reach the Soviet air base. There was no room for error.

On May 30, 1944, the 325th was granted a "stand-down" from missions and Hoar concentrated on getting the P-51s into top shape for the mission. He also had to gather the necessary spare parts for the "Mustang" fighters to ship to Russia aboard some of the B-17s and select the ground crewmen who would also go to the Soviet Union on the bombers to repair battle damage or mechanical problems. Setterdahl spent the last few days prior to the mission collecting the necessary information on the enemy's "Order of Battle" along the proposed bombing route, identification material on Soviet fighters, and a myriad of other details that were the responsibility of the intelligence officer. Brown, group operations officer, was busy planning the route, rendezvous point with the bombers, duration of escort, magnetic headings, and elapsed time. Deputy commander Toner coordinated the efforts of the others.

On the evening of June 1, 1944, after Eaker had given orders that "Frantic Joe" would be scheduled for early on the morning of June 2, Sluder briefed his squadron commanders: Major "Herky" Green, at the time the leading ace of the Mediterranean Theater, 317th Squadron; Captain Roy B. Hogg, who had four victories to his credit, 318th Squadron; and Captain Raymond E. Hartley, Jr., the aggressive leader of the 319th Squadron. That same evening the ground crews were taken to bomber fields for their trip to the Soviet Union. By this time rumors were rampant but since security was still tight at Lesina, the ground crews were not certain of their destination until they reached the fields and discovered that they were going to fly across German-held territory to the Soviet Union. The information came as a distinct shock to the men, most of whom had never been on a combat flight prior to this time. As yet, however, the pilots of the 325th, except for the group commander, his staff, and the squadron commanders, still did not know they were going to fly to Soviet Russia and would not know until 0300 hours the next morning.

Hogg, commander of the 318th Squadron, went to bed early the night of June 1, 1944, feeling that he was as ready for the shuttle mission to Russia as he would ever be. His escape kit was prepared, including the out-of-uniform picture he had been ordered to obtain. The happy-go-lucky Hogg had worn a nurse's blouse, a beard, and had his hair as unkempt as possible in the photograph. "That picture is bad enough to scare both the Germans and the Russians," he told the flight surgeon who was his roommate at Lesina. Hogg also took one more precautionary step in his preparation for the mission. Since his squadron had the highest VD rate in the Fifteenth Air Force at the time, he had the ammunition removed from the right-wing guns and the boxes filled with prophylactic kits and contraceptives. He wanted his men as ready for the Russian women as for the Luftwaffe fighters.

At the bomber fields similar preparations were in progress for "Frantic Joe," now definitely scheduled for the morning of June 2, 1944. Eaker had sent a final message to the bombardment groups involved in the operation, once again emphasizing the importance of the shuttle mission to the Soviet Union.

> The ultimate objective of 'Frantic Joe' is to impress the Russians with the power and capabilities of the Strategic Air Forces. To do this effectively this relatively small Task Force must be in good fighting trim. Since maintenance and supply in Russia will, at best, be relatively inferior, the Task Force must not be wilfully subjected to strong opposition with consequent possibility of heavy battle damage en route to Russia. This factor has considerable bearing on the selected route. . . .

Eaker was worried about the security surrounding, or supposedly surrounding, "Operation Frantic." He was aware that the original code name for the first mission, "Baseball," had been learned by the Germans, requiring a change in plans by Eaker's headquarters. He had also been informed that the Japanese diplomats in Moscow had become increasingly curious about the growing number of Americans attending the Bolshoi Theater and sitting in the United States Embassy's reserved boxes. The general knew that his Fifteenth Air Force task force would be comparatively small and if the Luftwaffe learned the route of the heavy bombers prior to the mission, German fighters could subject the formations to concentrated attacks. At this late date, however, he could only hope that the breaches of security concerning the shuttle missions to the Soviet Union had not been serious.

The crew chiefs of the B-17s, both those flying to the U.S.S.R. with the bombers and those permanently stationed at the three Russian air bases, were given a list of detailed instructions that included:

1. When aircraft arrives each one will be led to its parking place where it will be parked by the crew chief to whom it will be assigned. Conventional hand signals will be used. (In parking the aircraft, stay where the pilot can see you and make positive motions with your hands so that there can be no doubt as to what you want the pilot to do.)

2. Give mimeographed "Instructions for Combat Crews" to the pilot as soon as possible.

3. Instruct the crew that they must remain together until they have been billeted.

4. See that the entire crew gets on the truck which will meet the plane, with the exception of one member who will remain as guard. There will be two crews to each truck.

Due to the enthusiastic reaction of most American pilots and crews when they are on a new airfield or in a new country, Eaker wanted to avoid, at all costs, any damaging incidents that might occur immediately after the "Frantic Joe" crews arrived in the Soviet Union and were "feeling" their way with the Russian personnel they would come in contact with at the air bases. Consequently, "Instructions to Combat Crews," a mimeographed sheet, was issued to the Fifteenth Air Force personnel scheduled to fly the mission. In addition, another copy was given to the fliers when they landed just to make certain that everyone had a copy. While little mention was made of Russian personnel in the mimeographed instructions, the steps outlined for the crews to follow after landing definitely minimized the chances for the occurrence of a damaging incident.

Instructions to Combat Crews

These instructions must be followed implicitly. American personnel at this station is extremely limited. Full cooperation is requested in order that you may be made as comfortable as facilities permit; also that operations may be carried out with the utmost efficiency.

I. Airplane Commander:
   a. Keep your crew with you until you have all been assigned billets.

b. Before leaving your aircraft the following forms must be completed.
   (1) Intelligence Interrogation Form (by A/C commander). This form is to be turned in at the interrogation tent.
   (2) Maintenance Form (by aerial engineer).
   (3) Loading List (These forms to be given to the ground crew chief who met your A/C).
c. Retain all escape kits and purses.
d. Leave all flying equipment in ship, except what is to be worn while here.
e. Leave photo equipment intact.
f. In addition to filling out the enclosed forms, group and squadron lead crews will be given complete interrogation. In case the lead A/C is missing, the deputy leader and crew will be given complete interrogation.
g. Leave one of your crew members as A/C guard.

II. Bombardiers and Navigators:
a. All intelligence material, target folders, etc. will be removed by you and turned in at the interrogation center.
b. Navigators will carry their logs with them. Navigators who do not have complete information on A/C in distress should gather all available additional data from other crew members before arrival at the interrogation tent.
c. Bomb sights will be left in A/C.
d. Navigator of lead ships will report at Hot News Table immediately upon arrival at interrogation center.

III. Aerial Engineers:
a. Fill out Maintenance Form and Loading List before leaving A/C.

IV. Gunners:
a. Remove guns and stow them in your A/C.
b. Report number of rounds fired to Aerial Engineer before leaving A/C.

V. General Information:
a. A truck will take you from your A/C to the interrogation tent.
b. Another truck will take you from the interrogation tent to the Billeting Officer.

The other forms, such as the Interrogation Form, Maintenance Form, and Loading List were similar to those used in Italy by the Fifteenth Air Force on nonshuttle missions, with several exceptions. The Interrogation Form, for example, had four additional questions that pertained strictly to the Russian air bases: (1) Which radio beacons were used for homing? (2) Which radio beacons were used for fixes? (3) Results of use of beacons—satisfactory or unsatisfactory and if unsatisfactory give reasons. (4) Malfunctions of radio equipment. Eaker was worried that his pilots might have trouble finding the grass-and-pierced steel matting runways of the Russian air bases and he definitely wanted to know how well the radio facilities at the fields—scant as they might be—were working. He had good reason to be worried, as events on the first mission proved.

No Loading List in Italy or England was as important as the one the aerial engineer of each crew was responsible for during the shuttle missions. The names on these loading lists were checked closely by the Russian officers at the air bases as soon as the bombers landed, and if the names did not correspond with those on the groups' visa in Moscow, there was trouble.

While the Fifteenth Air Force personnel in Italy made their final plans for the mission scheduled for the morning of June 2, 1944, the permanent American contingent at the Soviet air bases also prepared for the incoming flight crews. Ted Morris and "Bony" Russell had completed their work at Poltava early on June 1 and decided to take a short walk. As they topped a small rise Russell, a fatherly-type maintenance technician who was older than most of the American ground crew personnel at Poltava, stopped in surprise and nudged Morris.

Ahead of them was a small lake and as the two Americans stared they saw Russians soldiers, male and female, swimming in the lake nude. Russell turned and urged Morris to do the same but Morris just grinned and kept watching until the older man finally pulled him back down the slope out of sight of the lake. Morris laughed all the way back to his tent at Russell's embarrassment and, for the moment, the tenseness created by the next day's planned operation was forgotten.

As darkness fell on the evening of June 1, 1944, the airmen and officers of the Fifteenth Air Force tried to get some rest in Italy, but sleep was hard to come by that night. The rumors had taken their toll in nerves and now the fliers were patiently waiting for the briefing hour when the curtain would be taken away from the map and they would see their mission for the day.

5

"Frantic Joe"

AT 03:00 HOURS on the morning of June 2, 1944, the pilots and their crews assembled in the briefing rooms in Italy. The 325th Fighter Group at Lesina, the Second Bombardment Group and the Ninety-sixth Bombardment Group at Amendola, the Ninety-ninth Bombardment Group at Tortorella Airfield and the 483d Bombardment Group at Sterparone Airfield all gathered at approximately the same time to listen to their group commanders and group S-2 officers detail the mission for the day. Sluder, commander of the 325th, watched the faces of his pilots as the drape was pulled away from the briefing map and they saw the black course line extending all the way across Europe. Their jaws dropped in unison! The route was approximately 1,200 miles in length, which was really no problem for a P-51, but the 325th pilots had been flying P-47s so long that they were not yet "thinking" P-51. They still didn't have enough experience in the Mustang to appreciate its much greater range. The briefing at Lesina proceeded routinely, however, except for such information as the flare pistol color code to be used in the event the group was intercepted by Russian fighters and the frequency of the homing station which was supposed to be in operation at Piryatin, where the 325th was scheduled to land in the Soviet Union. Strother, commander of the Fifteenth Fighter Command, made some encouraging remarks to the apprehensive fliers and, just before he sat down, cautioned them about their deportment while in the Soviet Union.

Roy Hogg, commander of the 318th Squadron of the 325th Fighter Group, smiled to himself as he listened to the general.

"You will not engage the enemy," Strother stated, "unless they attack the bombers."

With four German planes to his credit at the time, Hogg

needed only one more victory to become an "ace." He didn't intend to hunt the Luftwaffe, but if they came near. . . .

At the bomber stations the officers and airmen of the crews scheduled for "Frantic Joe" stared at the long course line just as the fighter pilots at the 325th had done and there was the same momentary silence in the briefing room. Eaker, scheduled to ride in a bomber of the Ninety-seventh Bombardment Group piloted by Captain Leslie Gates, understood the shock the men felt as they suddenly discovered there was no return course line to Italy on the map. The course line just kept going and going and going until it ended in the Soviet Union! Even while the group S-2 officer was talking, he could see the eyes of the men in the briefing room keep returning to the map time and time again.

At the Second Bombardment Group First Lieutenant James S. Stewart, the group navigator, was checking his maps and photos in the target folder to make certain he had all the required material. The tall, slender ex-postal clerk from Atlanta, Georgia, didn't want to get over the Soviet Union and then discover that one or more of his maps were missing. Not after the S-2 officer's warning that the Russians didn't welcome "strangers" and that there were certain inherent dangers in a lost Flying Fortress landing at a Russian airfield other than the one where it was scheduled to land.

Robert Sitterly, a bombardier with the 340th Squadron of the Ninety-seventh Bombardment Group, spent his last few minutes before takeoff studying the target folder photos of the railway center at Debrecen, Hungary, that the Fifteenth Air Force was going to attack on the way to the Soviet Union. He had heard Eaker emphasize that the Russians would want strike photos of the mission to study, that the Soviet Union was doubtful about the prowess of the Fifteenth Air Force and about strategic bombing as practiced by the USAAF. If the photos indicated that the railway center at Debrecen was destroyed or badly damaged, Moscow would be impressed. If the bombs missed, Stalin would get a good laugh at the expense of the United States. Sitterly had no intention of missing the target.

The bombers of the Fifteenth Air Force, led by Eaker in "Yankee Doodle II," took off at 06:55 hours on the morning of June 2, 1944, and headed across the Adriatic Sea. Each B-17 carried ten 500-pound bombs and several disposable wing tanks for the fighters accompanying the bomber formations. Eaker lighted one of his customary big black cigars as the "Yankee Doodle II" climbed to flight altitude, recalling that two years earlier he had led the first daylight raid over Europe by American heavy bombers in another Flying Fortress that had been named "Yankee Doodle." To his right he saw the plane in which the Ninety-seventh's commander Frank Allen was riding, while to his left was the B-17 piloted by Second Lieutenant Alfred Bond. The lieutenant's aircraft was so close that the general could read the serial number on the tail easily: 42-30319. It was a number Eaker would never forget.

The four bombardment groups had an uneventful trip over the Adriatic Sea and across Yugoslavia. The fighter planes of the 325th, led by Sluder, also took off shortly before 07:00 hours and the 70 Mustangs, once they had formed-up, streaked toward the rendezvous with the bombers. The weather was good along the route, with scattered cumulus clouds and unlimited visibility so Sluder had no difficulty locating the B-17s and maneuvering his fighters into the top cover position he wanted. The colonel was a top fighter pilot who knew exactly what was expected of him and his pilots on this first shuttle mission. His selection as leader of the fighters flying escort for the heavy bombers on "Frantic Joe" was a popular choice with the other fliers. They knew they could trust Sluder . . . and with both the Luftwaffe and the Red Air Force as possible obstacles to completing the mission successfully, they needed someone they could trust.

The Fifteenth Air Force bombers were at altitudes ranging from 21,000 to 25,000 feet as they neared the target area in Hungary. The Ninety-ninth Bombardment Group turned at the initial point and made their bombing run first over the railway yards at Debrecen, followed by the Ninety-seventh Bombardment Group. The 500-pound bombs of the Ninety-ninth raised so much smoke and dust that the Ninety-seventh had to abort its initial bomb run over the target and make a second pass. Usually, this was a fatal move for a bomb group since both the enemy fighters and ground defenses, knowing the course and altitude of the formation making its second try at the target was zeroed in on the formation, but the Ninety-seventh was fortunate. By the time the B-17s were over the rail center the second time visibility was unlimited for the bombardiers, and the antiaircraft fire was still sporadic and inaccurate. There were no enemy fighters in the area. Then someone yelled "Look! That Fort's on fire!"

One of the B-17s attached to the same squadron as Eaker's "Yankee Doodle II" had pulled out of the formation and was flying parallel to the other bombers about 500 feet to the north. Flames were visible on the right wing but it was impossible to determine whether it was one of the engines or a fuel tank. Eaker, looking closer, saw that it was the Flying Fortress piloted by Alfred Bond. For nearly two minutes the aircraft flew straight and level under full control, ample time for the crew to bail out, but no parachutes appeared in the sky. It was obvious that the crew thought they could control the fire and put it out before the plane exploded. It was a gamble often taken in combat. This time the gamble paid off in tragedy. One moment there was a B-17 in the sky, the next there was nothing but a black cloud of smoke and four flaming fuel tanks falling earthward.

As the bombers continued east the tail gunners in the B-17s reported that the target appeared badly damaged. Later reports and photographs obtained by the reconnaissance planes verified these reports. All tracks in the main marshalling yards were cut and a large quantity of rolling stock was damaged or destroyed. The bombs blasted or burned the central railway station, the chief building of the engineering facility located near the rail center, and destroyed all controls for the rail yards. Officially, the USSTAF reported that of the 130 Fifteenth Air Force bombers dispatched on the morning of June 2, 1944, from bases in Italy, all 130 attacked the target, dropping 1,030 five-hundred-pound bombs with "good" results.

As the Fifteenth Air Force task force approached the German-Russian front the cloud cover began dropping lower and lower. Eaker, aware that the three Russian air bases did not have the proper radio facilities to enable the heavy bombers to make instrument let-downs and afraid that the entire formation might wander off course and either be attacked by Red Air Force fighters or Russian ground defenses that had been previously alerted to expect the B-17s to fly a certain in-bound corridor, the general gave the order to stay below the overcast. Within a few minutes the remaining 129 Flying Fortresses were down to an altitude of 500 feet above the flat Ukrainian countryside, startling the awed inhabitants as the planes roared overhead. By the time the weary crews neared the Russian city of Vinnitsa it was raining hard. With fuel at a minimum and knowing that the airfields would be difficult to locate because of their size, their location in strange territory as far as the American navigators were concerned, and the camouflage used at the air bases to prevent detection by the Luftwaffe, Eaker was worried.

Sluder, leading the fighters, was worried, too. As long as the cloud cover had remained "broken" he was able to navigate visually, but shortly after spotting the Dnieper River, the overcast formed a solid curtain that concealed the ground entirely. Since he had orders to maintain radio silence so as not to endanger the entire task force by permitting the Luftwaffe to home in on his radio transmissions, Sluder had only one choice. He had to get under the overcast. Leading the 325th fighters through the clouds, he soon discovered that the visibility was fairly good underneath. Fortunately, the colonel and his pilots were far enough ahead of the bombers so that they missed the heavy rain that later engulfed the Flying Fortresses. He took up a compass heading for what he hoped was a direct course for Piryatin. The part of the Ukraine he was flying over offered very few checkpoints for the worried colonel, however. It was flat and featureless and everything looked the same. The last definite location he recognized was the Dnieper River and as he tried to navigate using the three overlapping maps, each one using a different scale and color scheme, there being no other maps available in Italy, Sluder felt less than confident.

D. J. MacDonald, who was to add a footnote to history before he saw home again, followed Sluder as did the other pilots of the "Checkertails," knowing full well that while the group wasn't lost "no one was certain exactly where we are." He noticed a railroad track pass under his P-51 but according to his map there wasn't supposed to be a railroad track at that spot—or else he wasn't where he thought he was! The entire group, flying loose formation, continued straight ahead for twenty minutes and then, to add to MacDonald's apprehension, the colonel led the entire group, 64 brand new Mustangs, in a wide 180-degree turn and flew directly back to the railroad tracks!

Sluder had come to the decision that he had flown far enough east to reach Piryatin and evidently had missed it. With several pilots radioing—despite radio silence restrictions—that they were getting very low on fuel and were unable to pick up the Piryatin direction finding station that was supposed to be transmitting a homing beacon, he had elected to return over his in-bound course with the idea of finding the Dnieper River again, following it to Kiev, and getting the group on the ground before the Mustangs ran out of gas. When he reached the railroad track on his return course, however, he saw a P-39 on the ground a short distance to the north. A closer look also revealed an American two-and-one-half-ton truck and two well-camouflaged runways. Without hesitation, Sluder led the group to the Russian airfield, not knowing for certain whether it was Piryatin or not, but wanting to get the P-51s down safely. He landed, taxied into the parking area, and discovered that he was just where he was supposed to be—Piryatin!

The Periodic Intelligence Report published by Group S-2 for this period stated simply:

> Mission Report 2 June 1944. 24 P-51s of the 317 Fighter Squadron, 24 P-51s of the 318 Fighter Squadron, and 22 P-51s of the 319 Fighter Squadron took off at 0700 hours to provide cover for B-17s attacking Debrecen marshalling yards, Hungary, 6 P-51s returned early. 64 P-51s met bombers at target at 0930 hours, 25,000 to 28,000 feet, and escorted to Russian bases until 1145 hours. 64 P-51s down at Russian bases at 1220 hours. No encounters.

It sounded easy but it wasn't. MacDonald's fuel warning light had been glowing on his instrument panel for fifteen or twenty minutes before Sluder led the group over Piryatin. As soon as he spotted the field, MacDonald peeled off and landed right behind the colonel, and as he turned off the runway his Mustang stopped —completely out of gas. Hogg, who had more fuel left than most of the pilots, signalled his wingmen to land ahead of him since he knew that their "throttle-jockeying" to stay in formation during the long trip had used more gas. As soon as the wingmen were on the ground, Hogg banked his Mustang sharply and giving the Russians their first view of an American fighter pilot's "wing-scraping" approach to a runway, eased his P-51 down in a perfect landing. Proud of his exhibition, Hogg began taxiing toward the parking area when he suddenly heard shots. Looking out of his cockpit he saw several Russian soldiers with guns in their hands firing in his general direction. For a moment he was tempted to open the throttle on his Mustang and get back into the air, but while he was trying to decide on his next move he saw a rabbit—"so big it looked like a small bear"—running across the air base and realized that the Russians were shooting at it, not him.

Meanwhile, the bombers were en route to their intended landing areas at Mirgorod and Poltava, farther east. Eaker, leading 64 of the Flying Fortresses, landed at Poltava at 1424 hours, the first American heavy bomber of the "Frantic Joe" task force to touch down on Soviet soil.

It was raining and the steel matting runway, when wet, was slippery. In addition, about six inches of grass had grown up through the steel matting and the wet grass was also very slick so that when Gates, pilot of "Yankee Doodle II," tried to stop the aircraft the B-17 began to slide. In an all-out effort to get the Flying Fortress stopped at the end of the steel matting run-way, the pilot maintained his pressure on the brakes and blew out both tires on the landing gear. The Russians, however, cheered the landing. They had no bombers as large as the B-17 and thought that Gates had made a normal landing. No one told them otherwise.

Sixty-five other B-17s landed at Mirgorod in a drizzle without incident, although they had difficulty locating the well-camouflaged field. Finally, several Russian Aircobras took off from the air base, and the American fliers discovered that they were practically over the field they had been hunting so desperately. While Mirgorod, Piryatin, and Poltava were each equipped with 75-watt homing beacons, on this initial shuttle mission the beacons either did not transmit at all, as at Piryatin, or transmitted only inter-mittently, as at the other two bases, and were of little help to the American crewmen incoming from Italy. Yet, except for the B-17 that caught fire over the target in Hungary, all the Flying Fortresses and P-51s landed safely in the Soviet Union on the afternoon of June 2, 1944.

In Moscow and at Poltava matters were not progressing as successfully—as usual. Once the target controversy was settled, despite the fact that it was to the detriment of the USAAF, Deane thought that, as far as the initial mission was concerned, everything was agreeable with the Russian leaders. His fond hope

was, of course, that Eaker would lead such a successful mission to
Soviet Russia on his first attempt at shuttle flights that the
Soviet officials, military and political, would be so elated that
most of the obstacles previously presented by them would fade
away in their appreciation. Deane soon learned, however, as he
was to learn many more times during his stay in the Soviet
Union, that the Russian leaders had no intention of cooperating
on either important or minor matters. The "battle of the correspondents" was typical.

Deane, Spaatz, Eaker, Arnold, Harriman, and all other American military and diplomatic officials who had worked so hard to
make "Operation Frantic" a reality were anxious that American
press and radio correspondents in Moscow be at the Russian air
bases to see the first American heavy bombers land on Soviet
soil. They knew that the Russians intended to have a welcoming
ceremony for the American fliers and that the Soviet press and
radio would certainly be present in large numbers to show the
world the Russian side of the collaboration. Deane wanted the
American correspondents to be the ones to break the story to the
world under a Moscow dateline. In fact, prior to the date of the
first scheduled shuttle mission he had briefed the correspondents
on his plans for their coverage of the landings at the Russian
air bases and had asked them to avoid any conjecture stories
based on the influx of American personnel. They had agreed. He
had also asked Nikitin to obtain permission from the Foreign
Office for the correspondents, numbering approximately 30, to
fly to the Russian air bases the day before the American heavy
bombers were scheduled to arrive. Deane considered this a routine
request and assumed that permission would be granted promptly.
It was not. No word was received from the Foreign Office until
ten o'clock on the morning of June 1, 1944, and this word was
frustrating.

"Only five correspondents may go to the air bases," the approval report stated.

Deane was indignant, as were the correspondents. He immediately protested the restrictions the Foreign Office had made to
the Russian Chief Censor, but after more than an hour on the
telephone he had only managed to get the number of American
correspondents that would be permitted to go to the air bases
raised to ten. As a last resort the American Newspaper Guild

staged the first labor strike in Soviet Russian history, saying that if all the correspondents could not go none would go. The confused Soviet officials, fearing the obvious consequences on world opinion if no American press coverage was made of such a unique operation that was supposed to show the close cooperation existing between the Soviet Union and the United States, relented and at noon all the correspondents were loaded aboard a Soviet C-47 and flown to Poltava.

At Poltava both the American and the Russian officials had planned a warm welcome for Eaker and his fliers. Harriman, his daughter Kathy, and Deane came down from Moscow. Walsh, who had recently arrived to take charge of the Eastern Command, was present, as was Kessler and his staff, Curtis P. Boas, commanding officer at Poltava, and other ranking United States officers stationed in the Soviet Union with the Eastern Command, the U.S. Military Mission in Moscow, and the U.S. Embassy staff. The dark, overcast day and intermittent rain only added to their concern about "Frantic Joe." They knew—or at least thought—that the future of the entire shuttle mission operation hinged on the success or failure of this mission. In fact, it was generally thought at the time that future collaboration between the United States and the Soviet Union, particularly in regard to future operations against Japan, would be easy to obtain if "Frantic Joe" was a success and the Russians were impressed by the American task force. This assumption, believed by most top military and political leaders of the United States in June 1944, was a costly error.

The Russians, too, had made preparations to welcome the Americans. Slavin, Deane's contact with the Red Army General Staff, had flown down from Moscow. Unfortunately, Nikitin, the Russian officer who had worked so closely with Deane to set up the shuttle missions, was unable to attend the ceremony because of other duties. While Nikitin had not always been agreeable, he had been more harmonious in his relations with the U.S. Military Mission in Moscow than the other Soviet officers. He sent Grendal, the tight-lipped head of Red Air Force Intelligence and Reconnaissance, to represent him. Both Slavin and Grendal had several of their staff officers with them at Poltava. Reporters from *Izvestia*, *Red Star*, and *Pravda*, as well as Soviet newsreel photographers, were also waiting. Overseeing the entire Russian contingent was the wiry, slightly-graying Perminov, the Soviet officer stationed at Poltava to work with the Eastern Command officers.

It was a tense wait for the Americans. By noon the Eastern Command had still not heard whether Eaker and his task force had taken off from Italy or not. Deane knew that this could be due to the unreliable communications system that the Americans in the Soviet Union had to depend on, or it could also mean that the mission had been "scrubbed" because of the bad weather. Looking around the air base at the Russians who had gathered— the military officers in their full-dress uniforms, the Russian Aircobra pilots lounging by their fighters, the well-scrubbed women waiting to serve food to the incoming airmen, and the Soviet media personnel—Deane hoped the B-17s were on the way. It was going to be a disappointing and frustrating day for the Americans stationed in the Soviet Union if the Flying Fortresses did not make an appearance. He could picture in his mind the sneering, disdainful looks Grendal and Slavin would give him if he had to announce that "Frantic Joe" had been cancelled.

At 12:30 Eastern Command headquarters at Poltava received a flash that Eaker and his bombers had left Italy shortly before 0700 hours that morning. Kessler quickly relayed the message to Deane who, in turn, proudly announced the fact to the Russian officers. Neither Perminov nor Grendal changed facial expressions at the news. It was evident to Deane that they intended to remain publicly unimpressed by the operation, neither wanting the Soviet media to recognize the fact that the American bombers meant much to the Red Army or to Red Air Force's overall plans. However, Deane noticed that as he and the remainder of the American contingent got into their jeeps and command cars and drove to the airdrome from the Eastern Command headquarters area of the air base, the Russians quickly followed.

"There they come!" an American reporter said quietly, pointing to the west where several small black dots were visible just above the horizon. "One . . . two . . . three. . . ."

Deane turned to inform Slavin, but the Soviet general was nowhere in sight. He suddenly remembered that he had not seen Slavin all morning, and had been talking only with Perminov and Grendal. He started to walk over to Perminov to ask the Russian where Slavin was, but at that moment the frozen expression on Perminov's face changed completely as the B-17s came nearer the air base and he could see them better. The firm mouth broke into a wide smile and he shook his head in disbelief at the size of the Flying Fortress formation. The roar of the engines of the 64 bombers made him hold his ears and made talk impossible, but Deane saw him nudge Grendal and point excitedly toward the American planes. The Red Air Force Intelligence and Reconnaissance chief was smiling, too, and it was obvious he was impressed by the B-17s flying overhead at 1,000 feet. The sky was filled with the bombers and even the Americans, who had often seen much larger bomber formations in Italy and Britain, watched in fascination as the silver-colored Flying Fortresses flashed against the black, rain-filled sky. Eaker led the entire task force section scheduled to land at Poltava directly over the field in perfect formation, then began a huge circle to the left. The aircraft began "peeling off" at planned intervals, leaving the formation and making a short downwind leg during which the pilot dropped the wheels and flaps and adjusted his power setting for landing. After Eaker's plane skidded to a stop and taxied clear of the runway, the other bombers came in and landed one by one without incident. At times there were three B-17s on the steel matting at once. The landing procedure was so perfect that the Russian Aircobra pilots, who had previously exhibited a "you'll-have-to-show-me" attitude, were clapping their hands excitedly. Deane had never felt more proud of the USAAF.

Both the American and the Russian contingent—still minus Slavin—hurried to the "Yankee Doodle II." Eaker was the highest-ranking American officer of the USAAF yet to visit the Soviet Union and his reception at Poltava by the Russians was gracious. Perminov greeted him as he stepped from the B-17, giving a prepared speech of welcome that seemed much more sincere now that he had been so awed by the appearance of the American formation a few minutes earlier. A huge bouquet of roses was given to Kathy Harriman and while the newsreel cameras focused on the scene, Deane spoke a few words emphasizing the fact that Hitler now had to fear bombing from both the east and the west since the arrival of the American bombers in the Soviet Union. The Soviet media was careful to eliminate all of his remarks from their releases. Stalin did not want the world to think that the United States was of any help whatsoever to the Soviet Union in winning the war. Eaker had come prepared for the welcoming ceremony, too. In a surprise move that made Perminov very happy, Eaker presented the Russian officer with the Legion of Merit and a citation expressing the gratitude of the United States for the part he had played in preparing the air bases for use by the American heavy bombers.

There was only one incident that marred the welcoming ceremony. As each pilot alighted from his aircraft he was handed a bouquet of flowers by a Russian girl in a Red Army uniform. Since the only greenhouse in Poltava had been destroyed by the Germans, the flowers had been picked from the nearby meadows and there was only one bouquet. As each of the embarrassed American pilots started to walk away with the bouquet, an NKVD man would jerk it from his hands and give it back to the Russian girl, who would then give it to the next American pilot to get out of his aircraft. This had been going on for several minutes when there suddenly was a loud shout from the direction of the flight line. Deane, startled, turned to see what had caused the commotion and was amazed to see Slavin striding angrily toward Perminov. Perminov was still fingering the Legion of Merit Eaker had presented him when Slavin arrived and began berating him in a loud voice. Deane thought the Red Army General Staff officer would have apoplexy, so intense was his attack on the hapless Perminov. Feeling sorry for Perminov, he moved to the side of the pair. Upon inquiry he learned that no one, including Perminov, had remembered to awaken Slavin for the ceremony and he had only been aroused from his nap by the roar of the B-17s as they passed over Poltava prior to landing. He had hurried to the landing area, only to discover that the Americans guarding the runway section of the base with orders to keep all unauthorized personnel from getting close to the Flying Fortresses refused to permit him to join the other Russian officers welcoming the Americans. The red trimmings of his Red Army General Staff uniform had not impressed the American sentries in the least so he had been forced to watch the ceremony standing among the peasant farmers of the Ukraine. To a class-conscious officer such as Slavin this was an unpardonable sin and he took his anger out on the unfortunate Perminov. Deane, holding back a smile, tried to pacify Slavin and shoulder part of the blame but it was a wasted effort. Slavin's face was still flushed with anger long after the ceremony ended.

Eaker was driven to Eastern Command headquarters where quarters had been prepared for him. Meanwhile, the pilots and their crews were hastily interviewed by both the American and the Soviet media representatives. The American correspondents knew what to expect from the brash, energetic, "I-don't-give-a-damn" American fliers but the Russian newsmen were taken by surprise at some of the answers the pilots gave to their questions.

Through an interpreter, one Russian correspondent asked a first lieutenant, "What do you think of Russia?"

"It is rugged and sure as hell all messed up by the Germans."

"Are you glad to be in the Soviet Union?"

"Yeah, I like to stretch my legs in a new country whenever I can."

The Russian wasn't particularly pleased with that answer since he thought the American pilot should be much more grateful to have the opportunity to visit the "great" Soviet Union. When he told the first lieutenant this, the pink-cheeked pilot looked around at the austere surroundings of Poltava and said, "Yeah? What the hell is so great about it?"

He was hurried away by an American S-2 officer before he had an opportunity to elaborate on his impression of the Soviet Union any further. Another pilot was asked if the formation had encountered any Luftwaffe fighters during the mission and when he replied that it had not, the Soviet correspondent smiled and began writing in his notebook.

"No Luftwaffe fighters encountered by the American aircraft because the German fighters were engaged by the Red Air Force."

The American flier quickly interrupted. "Hey, I didn't see any Red Air Force fighters, either. Those Germans were afraid of our gunners. That's why they didn't bother us."

He, too, was rushed out of the press tent before he could continue.

At Mirgorod and Piryatin the same sort of incidents were occurring but on the whole, the initial contact with the Russians, including the press correspondents, went well. All news releases were carefully reviewed by both the Americans, who didn't want to incur any further anger from the Russians in regard to the shuttle operations, and the Russians, who wanted to make certain that the Soviet Union's part in the shuttle operation was emphasized to the world. Two days after the "Frantic Joe" mission the Soviet newspaper *Red Star* published the Russian version of the operation. It was written by Lieutenant Colonel L. Vysokoostroysky, a *Red Star* special correspondent who was at Poltava for the landing:

> The final preparations for the welcoming of the American aircraft are in progress on the airfield. The landing strips are carefully marked and the landing "T" is in place. Ground crewmen stand ready with flags. Cars, gasoline trucks, and other vehicles are parked on the edge of the field.
>
> The sky is quiet. From time to time the loudspeaker in the signal room reports on the progress of the American planes. Meanwhile the weather deteriorates. A fine rain starts falling. Then suddenly from behind the clouds comes a heavy increasing roar and with every minute it grows louder. Then through the mist appear the first eight huge ships. These are American Flying Fortresses arriving at one of the air bases on Soviet territory.
>
> In a moment the gusty wind tears asunder the blanket of mist and then all see overhead a multitude of heavy American bombers. The Flying Fortresses fly in perfect formation as if on parade. They circle widely over the airfield for two or three minutes. Then the flagship peels off to the left, turns and lands. . . .
>
> The bombers continued to land while a large group of Soviet and American officers gathered by the flagship. They congratulated the fliers on the success of their flight. An American general who flew in with the task force told how the mission was accomplished. He led the first group of Flying Fortresses and the bombing of important targets on enemy territory was carried out under his leadership. The general presented Soviet Major General of the Air Force, Perminov, with an American military decoration for his excellent work in preparation of the base for the reception of the American planes. This decoration was presented in the name of the President of the United States, Mr. Roosevelt.
>
> An hour after the last plane landed the field was silent. The fliers had gone to camp, only the guards paced up and down at the edges of the vast field, guarding the planes.
>
> Late in the afternoon we visited the camp where the American fliers were staying. These men had just completed a long and arduous flight at a considerable height using oxygen, and had carried out a combat mission and had been through considerable

excitement. One might imagine that they were tired and should rest but we found the camp full of strenuous and cheerful activity. Young men lightly clad were playing football and various other games. Among the strenuous football players we noticed a young officer with the rank of captain who proved to be the chaplain of that aviation unit. We chatted with him.

The American fliers made a most favorable impression on all Soviet officers. These husky youngsters are efficient in any job they undertake. If they are servicing the plane, they do it quickly and efficiently. If they are working in camp they do everything carefully and conscientiously. They help each other a great deal. When an American officer is riding in a car and sees someone walking he considers it his duty to stop and offer him a ride. The fact that now they can attack enemy territory in its entire depth makes both American and Soviet fliers especially happy.

The Americans value highly the mere fact that they can land on Soviet territory after long flights and raids on principal enemy targets. They testify that previously, owing to the great distances, they could not deal heavy blows to certain areas of enemy territory. One captain said that once they were flying to bomb a railway junction in eastern Germany. Everything had been calculated correctly but a strong wind prevented their reaching the target. They ran the risk of running short of gas for their return trip and, 10 kilometers short of their goal, turned around and dropped their bombs on a secondary target.

This won't happen anymore. The Americans now can reach any point in enemy territory without turning back but heading for bases in the Soviet Union. This possibility of coordinating blows against the enemy has been achieved as a result of the successful advance of the Red Army westward, so that the region of its activities is now within the range of the air forces of the United States and Great Britain.

Despite the obvious propaganda incorporated in the news release printed in the *Red Star*, American leaders were generally satisfied with it. There was no question that the Fifteenth Air Force aircraft had made a fine impression on the Russians, who had no strategic bomber force of their own, and the Americans involved with the shuttle mission operation were well satisfied with "Frantic Joe."

When it came to "slanted" news, the American press did as well as—or perhaps better than—the Soviets. For days prior to the initial shuttle mission the American heavy bomber crews had been cautioned against making any remarks that might be considered critical of the Soviet Union or its people and while some of the pilots and other flight personnel were not too careful during the debriefing, none of their remarks saw print. A news item that appeared in many American newspapers a few days after "Frantic Joe" was typical of the "good news today" attitude that predominated in the releases in general:

> The Fifteenth Air Force is the toast in this corner of the Soviet Union. American and British correspondents journeyed here to observe what kind of a welcome this great flock of Flying Fortresses got from the Russian people seeing for the first time such things as American heavy bombers in their skies and GIs in their streets.

The news release gave several examples of short interviews with American airmen—and all the comments were flattering to the Russians:

> "It is wonderful," said an airplane commander from upper New York state. "I even got kissed by one captain with a long black beard."

A lieutenant from Georgia, a pilot from New York, and an officer from Massachusetts all agreed that they were happy to be in the Soviet Union:

> "This is beautiful country and fine people. I've done a lot of traveling and seen lots of people and lots of countries since this war began," the Georgia native said, "but when it comes to foreigners, give me the Russians."
> "Look what I got," the Massachusetts officer said. "A Russian gave me his cigaret lighter."
> "No better than mine," countered the pilot from New York. "The Red Army Red Star button. I'm wearing it on my cap."

The American correspondents visited Poltava and called it a "typical village with a long main street and pretty houses strung out for a long distance. The girls and women stood out in gay-colored dresses and the old men and young boys had bright shirts." Before many more weeks passed, the "typical village" image changed and the correspondents were calling it as they saw it: "A battered, war-torn village where everyone wore drab clothes," although these comments did not get into print because of censorship. One statement in the news release summed up the situation with an accuracy that was proved again and again during "Operation Frantic." The typical American and the typical Russian got along very well. Almost to a man the American soldiers liked the plain Russian citizen and in most instances the plain Soviet citizen welcomed the plain American. The distrust and unfriendliness that existed among the high echelons of both countries simply did not exist among the GIs and the Russians. The nine-day stay of the Fifteenth Air Force task force in the Soviet Union verified this fact.

6

Soviet Sojourn

THE "INVASION" OF THE SOVIET UNION by nearly 1,300 American flight personnel during "Frantic Joe" presented the United States with its first opportunity for a large group of Americans to mingle with and to observe the common Russian citizen and soldier. Members of the American heavy bomber flight crews and pilots of the P-51s took advantage of the stay in the Soviet Union to explore the areas near their bases and to get acquainted with the Russians. It was a pleasant but occasionally shocking experience for the Americans.

At Poltava the American airmen received their first close look at a Soviet city that had previously been occupied by the Germans for seventeen months during the earlier stages of the war. Poltava had been practically destroyed during the retreat of the Nazi forces. The Germans had systematically blown up every building and had then poured oil on the rubble and set it afire. In an unexpected act of kindness, however, the retreating Nazis had left untouched the individual small homes of the citizens of Poltava, two churches, and a hospital they had used to treat their wounded. The people of the city, speaking through interpreters, explained that during the first weeks of the Nazi occupation the Germans had been friendly and that many of the Russians had welcomed the Germans, believing that the Ukraine might fare better under the Germans than it had under the Soviet Union. And when the Germans were forced to retreat, large numbers of Ukrainians went with them. As a whole, however, the Ukrainians remained loyal to the Soviet Union and considered their fellow citizens who had gone west with the Germans during the retreat as traitors. "We'll get them if we have to chase them clear to the Rhine," one old man told an American pilot as he waved his clenched fist.

A photograph of the Russian who had served as a very co-operative mayor of Poltava under the Nazi occupation indicated that the old man was serious. The photograph showed the quisling with an Alpine axe sticking in his head!

The American airmen's friendliness soon won over many of the Russians. Within twenty-four hours they were teaching the boys of the area how to play softball and had organized a couple of teams for a game. A lieutenant who had flown numerous combat missions and was an expert in the art of enjoying his spare time between missions undertook a tough assignment. He taught a Russian officer how to play gin rummy. Other GIs discovered the strength of both the females and the vodka of the area. The "headache" qualities of the drink were anticipated but not the muscular power of the women. Two Americans were struggling down the walk to the mess with a couple of big pots of soup, sweating and muttering that "if God had wanted them to carry such heavy objects he would have made them horses." At that moment two giggling Russian girls came up and took the pots of soup from the Americans. They handled the pots as though they were toys.

Two musicals were performed by the Russians, one by a chorus of local girls dressed in native costumes, the second by a Cossack chorus selected from the Russian troops in the area. Some of the Americans were invited to private homes and, despite the fact that food was very scarce, their hosts insisted that the visitors eat with them. Some GIs tried to reciprocate by obtaining food from Eastern Command supplies and giving it to the Russians, but they soon discovered that the citizens of Poltava were too proud to accept it. Accustomed to the begging of the Italians near their Foggia bases, the Fifteenth Air Force airmen were amazed at the Russian attitude.

At Piryatin, Sluder and his fighter pilots met with a similar reception from the citizens. They soon discovered that the permanent complement of Eastern Command personnel at the base had already made their influence felt among the Russians. The fighter pilots used a mess hall manned by Russians. One attractive girl, a pretty blonde who caught everyone's eye as soon as she appeared to serve the Americans, would place the food on the table and invariably say solemnly, "What's buzzin', cuzzin'?" That was the extent of the English language she had picked up from the Americans. Unfortunately, some of the Russian girls were taught phrases that were not as polite. Prior to the coming of the fighter pilots, an American mechanic had informed her that the phrase: "Say, do you want to f---?" was a standard American greeting. Not understanding English, she believed him and delighted many GI visitors with the greeting until an American officer who was fluent in Russian explained the true meaning of the phrase. The girl was mortified and for a couple of days refused to show her face to the American visitors. Finally she was ordered to man the chow line again where she dispensed silverware at mealtime. On the second day Sluder and his fliers were in the Soviet Union, one of the pilots found himself short a piece of silver and headed back to the chow line. "I want a fork," he told the blonde. Before the shocked fighter pilot could duck, the girl hit him on the side of the face and sent him reeling. The poor guy could never understand why she hit him!

Roy Hogg, the squadron commander who had removed the ammunition from the right wing-guns of his P-51 and filled the ammunition boxes with contraceptives and prophylactic kits, discovered that he was one of the most popular Americans at Piryatin when the Russians learned of his secret. Several soldiers and civilians of the area told him that if a girl became pregnant after associating with a Russian soldier there was a likelihood that both of them would be shot. The Red Army did not have time nor the inclination to handle such matters. Therefore, he became the "king" of the base when the Russians, especially the Red Army and Red Air Force officers, discovered that he could supply them with contraceptives.

The Soviets assigned a man to each of the P-51s to assist the American crew chiefs who had been flown to Russia aboard the B-17s. At Mirgorod and Poltava, Eastern Command officials had agreed that the Soviets could assign an assistant crew chief and two helpers to work with each Flying Fortress crew chief. It soon became evident that the Russians assigned to the American aircraft wanted to know everything, down to the smallest detail, about the planes. Roy Hogg learned from a Russian officer that each of the Russians assigned to an American plane would be examined on the knowledge they acquired after the departure of the task force and those who failed to achieve a passing examination score would be reassigned to the front lines. Stalin wanted every detail of the American advanced technology catalogued by his officers and men and the Russians missed no opportunity to accomplish this goal while the American task force—and later task forces—were in the Soviet Union. Ted Morris, a crew chief stationed at Poltava, for example, added up the number of Russians he had taught to taxi his aircraft and discovered the number totaled twelve. It was little wonder that by the time "Operation Frantic" ended, the Soviet Union was well on its way to establishing a strategic bomber force for postwar use.

The Russian officers were extremely strict with their men assigned to the American aircraft. Hogg was at his P-51 one day checking it over when one of the Russians accidentally fired a flare gun inside the cockpit of the fighter. There was little damage other than a fogged canopy where the fireball of the flare impacted but a Soviet supervisor appeared on the scene within minutes with a pistol in his hand. Although it may not have been his intention, it appeared to Hogg that the supervisor planned to execute the inept mechanic for his error. The American pilot interceded in the Russian's behalf and instead of shooting him, the Soviet supervisor ordered him off the field. Hogg never saw the mechanic again.

One afternoon Sluder met with the Russian fighter squadron commander and some of the Red Air Force pilots for a session of revealing "hangar talk." Two Russian interpreters were present and their English was flawless. A major from the American base complement was also at the session and he was fluent in the Russian language so there was no difficulty in comparing ideas. The Russian squadron commander was a well-decorated ace but he looked as if he didn't have the strength to fly a fighter. Skinny, blonde-haired, soft-spoken, he was in direct contrast to the stereotype Russian pilot Sluder expected to see. Another Red Air Force pilot was a young Russian who had destroyed forty-one German tanks. He was on leave and had come to Poltava but had been unable to locate a single relative. They had either been killed or had moved out of the city during the German occupation.

One of the first questions the Russian fighter squadron commander asked Sluder was a surprise.

"How much are you paid for each confirmed victory?"

When Sluder, through the interpeter, explained that American pilots received monthly military pay and that was all, the Red

Air Force officer seemed dubious. It was obvious he did not believe the colonel. The Russian pilots, Sluder learned, were paid
a bonus for each aircraft shot down as long as the "kill" was
verified by Red Army personnel finding the wreckage on the
ground. One drawback to this arrangement was that the Russian
pilots had no desire to engage in air-to-air combat behind the
German lines since the Red Army could not verify the "kills."

The Russian aircraft that the pilots of the 325th saw were not
impressive when compared with the American planes. Barrie
Davis talked to one Russian pilot who flew a tiny biplane loaded
with hand grenades and similar ordnance. The Russian would fly
the small aircraft at its maximum altitude over the front at night,
shut off the engine, and glide noiselessly over the German lines
while his observer tossed the grenades out of the rear cockpit.
If the biplane was not shot down, the pilot would glide back over
the Russian lines, restart his engine, and fly to his home base!
The most interesting aircraft the Americans saw was a large
Soviet bomber that had an open cockpit for the pilot. It, too,
was a biplane and was in regular use by the Red Air Force.
Compared to the sleek Flying Fortress, the Russian bomber
seemed ludicrous. This was why Stalin was so interested in obtaining American technological and operational information from
the United States through the guise of "Operation Frantic."

The Red Air Force fighter pilots were enthusiastic about the
P-39s they had obtained from the United States through Lend-
Lease and the defense of Piryatin had been assigned to a P-39
squadron. Despite the fact that the aircraft were of American
origin, the Russian pilots would not permit the Americans to get
near them. Hogg watched a Russian major walk to Hogg's P-51
one day with a stick, measure the cannon on the Mustang and
then walk back and compare its length with the cannon on his
P-39. When Hogg, who knew that the barrel of the cannon on the
Mustang was longer, walked toward the Russian to chide him,
the major motioned him away from the P-39. It didn't take the
Americans long to discover that their policy of telling and showing the Russians everything about their own aircraft was definitely
not reciprocated.

It was this reluctance of the Russians to discuss the defense
of the air bases at Mirgorod, Piryatin, and Poltava and their
refusal to allow the Americans to examine their aircraft or ground

defenses that eventually led to disaster. To the American personnel on the bases it appeared that the Red Air Force fighter pilots
were ready and willing to defend the bases against any Luftwaffe
attack. The American fighter pilots could not get over their
surprise, for instance, about the procedure the Russian fighter
pilots used to get their aircraft into the air in a minimum of
time once the alert signal was given. The Yak or P-39 pilots
would start out at full throttle from their parking area once the
call came. It made no difference to them that they might be taking
off downwind instead of into the wind, across runways instead of
on runways, or that other Red Air Force fighter planes might be
taking off directly toward them or at right angles. It seemed to
be every pilot for himself, and miraculously there were no acci-
dents resulting from this unorthodox procedure while the Americans were in the Soviet Union. However, Kessler and Walsh were
worried about the capability of the Russian pilots and their aircraft for night combat and for high-altitude defense. Perminov,
when questioned, would merely reiterate that the Red Air Force
planes and the Red Army guns could effectively repel any
Luftwaffe raid that might be attempted on the Russian air bases.

As for the ground defenses, little was known by the Americans.
Kessler knew that some American trucks equipped with .50-caliber
machine guns patrolled the fields intermittently. Around the
perimeter of the air bases the Russians had dug very deep fox-
holes and gun emplacements, many of which were manned by
women gunners. The changing of the guard was a spectacular
event for the Americans until they became accustomed to it. The
guard officers not only passed the special orders of the day to
one another as the change was made but also made a thorough
test of all weapons. The air bases would reverberate with gunfire
for several minutes. Despite all the noise, however, most of the
Americans were concerned about the Russian ground defenses.
They had not seen any large guns in the area, nor did they believe
that the Russian gunners at the air bases were well trained. All
efforts to discuss the matter further, either at Eastern Command
headquarters at Poltava or at the Kremlin in Moscow, were rebuffed. The United States contingent had no choice but to rely on
the Soviet promises to defend the bases against enemy attack.

Eaker, who led the Fifteenth Air Force task force to the
Soviet Union on the "Frantic Joe" mission, was treated exception-

ally well by the Soviet military and political leaders. After the welcoming ceremony at Poltava and a chance to wash and shave, Harriman invited the general to fly to Moscow with him so that he could attend a dinner at the Kremlin. Stalin had invited Harriman and the ambassador wanted Eaker to join him so that he could tell the Russian leader about the mission the American bombers had flown that day from Italy to the Soviet Union. Harriman did not want to miss any opportunity to impress the Russian leaders with the importance of the shuttle-mission project and to improve the relations between the two countries. He knew that Eaker, with his quiet efficiency and gracious manners, would be an asset to the American contingent at the dinner in the Kremlin. Despite being awakened at 0230 hours the previous morning in Italy for the briefing prior to the "Frantic Joe" mission, Eaker was delighted to accept the invitation.

The table service at the Kremlin dinner was elaborate, with huge silver bowls filled with fresh fruit, tall thin cut-glass goblets for the red and white wines, beautiful vodka glasses, silverware encrusted with gold, and the finest china, also encrusted with gold. Bottles of wine and vodka lined both sides of the long table. Interspersed among the bottles were silver platters filled with caviar, pickled ham, candy, and many other delicacies. It was difficult for the Americans present to remember that they were in a city that a short time earlier had been threatened with complete destruction by the Nazis.

Stalin was particularly gracious to Eaker and asked many questions about the mission he had flown from Italy that day. The Russian leader seemed to take great interest in the operation, rather surprisingly, since it was a small part of the overall war effort Stalin had on his mind but, as the Americans learned later, Stalin was thinking of the future. Finally, after a last toast to the weary Eaker, he inquired of Harriman whether the general would be willing to talk with his Red Air Force officers. Harriman asked Eaker if he would do so and the veteran officer agreed, thinking that Stalin intended to schedule the meeting the following day.

"When do you want General Eaker to meet with the Red Air Force officers?" Harriman inquired politely.

"Right now!" Stalin said.

It was already after midnight and Eaker had a headache caused not only by his weariness but because of oxygen deficiency over the target when his oxygen mask had inadvertently come loose. Since he had committed himself to the meeting, however, he did not protest the late hour and followed a Russian guide to another room where Marshal A. A. Novikov, the commander of the Red Air Force, was waiting. Eaker took an instant liking to the smiling, handsome Russian officer and after a few minutes it was evident that Novikov had warmed to Eaker. The Russian spoke English, had a sense of humor, and was very friendly. He told Eaker that Stalin wanted him to ask about American strategic bombing tactics so he would start off the meeting by asking the questions for which he needed answers. Later, he said, he would be glad to answer Eaker's questions.

Eaker, as tough-minded as he was gracious, looked at the Russian a moment and asked, "How do I know that you will answer my questions after you have received all the information you want from me?"

Novikov laughed uproariously and slapped his knee. "All right, you first!"

Eaker, through his questioning of the Red Air Force commander, learned that his pilots only supported the Russian ground troops and made no effort to attack strategic targets such as railroad centers, German airfields, or industrial plants. When Germany had attacked Russia in 1941, Russia did not have the resources to do both long-range strategic bombing and tactical bombing so Stalin decided to concentrate on driving the Nazis out of the Soviet Union with every resource he had. Consequently, Soviet Russia had no strategic bombing force. Eaker learned later just how sharply the Russians divided ground support missions from strategic air missions. During this initial visit with Novikov, he asked the Red Air Force commander if Major General John K. Cannon, who was Commanding General of the Twelfth Air Force and of the Mediterranean Allied Tactical Air Force, could visit the Soviet Union and study Red Air Force tactics. Novikov said that it was not for him to make such a decision but if Stalin allowed Cannon to come he would make certain that the general saw everything he wanted to see. The necessary permission did not come until a very short time prior to the planned Allied invasion of southern France, which made it necessary for Cannon to rush to the Soviet Union and back since he was responsible

for the air cover for the operation. Cannon saw enough in this
visit to learn that there was a definite line drawn by the Red
Air Force pilots between ground support sorties and strategic
bombing. On one flight over the front lines in a Russian plane,
the Red Air Force pilot showed him a German tank under a tree
that was his target for the mission. Despite the fact that a
German train loaded with supplies was moving slowly along the
tracks nearby, the Russian flier was not permitted to attack it.

The meeting with Novikov was very satisfactory; the Russian
answered all of Eaker's questions promptly and the American
general reciprocated. When Eaker returned to Spasso House at
0400 hours in the morning, Harriman asked him his opinion of
the Red Air Force chief and Eaker answered truthfully that he
was very impressed with him, that he had not avoided any
questions, had given him the information Eaker desired, and that
he was exceptionally cooperative. Eaker related to Harriman an
example of the Russian general's thoughtfulness. Novikov, prior
to introducing Eaker to his staff, had warned the American officer
that each staff member would want Eaker to have a drink of
vodka with him.

"Since you are tired, I suggest you eat an apple first. The
apple will absorb much of the vodka and it will have less effect
on you. It is an old Russian trick," Novikov explained. Eaker
followed his suggestion and discovered that it was very effective.

Harriman and Eaker decided that, in view of Novikov's cooperative attitude, Harriman would invite him to the embassy
the next night for dinner and Eaker could award him the Legion
of Merit as a gesture of friendship. They did not, however, take
into consideration the suspicion prevalent in the Soviet Union
about all Americans. When Deane, as an intermediary, called
Novikov to ask if he could come to the dinner the Russian
general quickly agreed—if he could bring Nikitin along. Novikov,
despite being chief of the Red Air Force, was not permitted by
the Kremlin to associate with the Americans alone, not even in
the U.S. Embassy! Eaker presented *both* Novikov and Nikitin
with medals.

During the entire "Operation Frantic" project, Novikov co-
operated as well as he could with the Americans under Kremlin
restrictions and was exceptionally friendly and understanding of
the USSTAF problems in regard to operating out of Soviet air

bases. Evidently, Stalin considered him too friendly with Americans because, within six months after the end of the shuttle mission project, Novikov was in a Siberian prison. He was not restored to good graces until Nikita Khrushchev came to power years later. This was one more example of Stalin's determination to prevent any of his officers or party leaders from becoming friendly with Americans during World War II. While both Roosevelt and Churchill hoped to use wartime intimacies to develop a relationship with the Soviet Union in the postwar world, Stalin had no intention of permitting this to happen.

During his conference with Novikov, several problems that both Spaatz and Arnold had asked Eaker to investigate were discussed and resulted in various agreements, some "in principle." One agreement that was particularly satisfying to Eaker was the approval of the Russians for the Fifteenth Air Force task force to bomb Mielec on June 4 and return to the Soviet air bases. This was the target Eaker had originally wanted to bomb during "Frantic Joe" but had been turned down by the Kremlin. It was also agreed, at Eaker's suggestion, that the American heavy bombers bomb the Galatz airfield in Rumania on June 6 and continue on to their home bases in Italy. The trouble Eaker had anticipated having with the Russians over target selection once his task force reached the Soviet Union did not materialize, much to his relief. While bad weather forced a change in these original plans, Eaker was satisfied with the cooperation of the Russians on the target selection. Another important matter discussed was the matter of permission for American photographic reconnaissance flights. Eaker left the conference under the impression that it had been settled, but the Russians later reneged on their agreement. Eaker explained in detail why the twenty-four-hour notice to the Russians before each scheduled flight was not satisfactory to the United States. Novikov, familiar with flight operation problems, understood the situation and it was finally decided that five corridors would be set up across the Russian front lines leading to the air bases used by the American aircraft that could be traversed at specific hours and at specific altitude without prior notification to the Russians. Eaker quickly agreed to the proposal and left the Kremlin satisfied that this difficult problem had been solved. Within hours, however, he learned that Stalin had not approved the agreement he and Novikov had worked out concerning the five corridors. Stalin feared that the Germans would learn about the corridors and use them with captured Flying Fortresses to bomb Russian targets. As a consolation to Eaker, the Soviets cut the prior notification time requirement from twenty-four hours to ten hours. Eaker had no alternative but to agree to give this method a fair trial but stated that if it proved unsatisfactory permanently established corridors would have to be discussed again.

In a message dated June 13, 1944, from Spaatz to Eaker, Kessler, and Doolittle, the USSTAF commander clarified the approach he wanted taken in regard to the reconnaissance flights:

> Soviet air staff notified me . . . that it is essential that ten-hour advance notice of our photo mission be given them in Moscow and in all cases they will be cleared. Setting up regular corridors objected to by the Russians primarily since they would soon become known to Germans and secondarily that the Soviet AA defense vigilance in these corridors would relax. Our desired operations can be made known to them by Perminov within one-half hour after Perminov is informed and clearance, insofar as AA and fighter defense is concerned, can be established in eight hours for any corridor. Eaker agreed while in Moscow to give this method a fair trial and if unsatisfactory permanently established corridors may later be obtained. It is felt that under these arrangements photo recon planes leaving Italy and England are required only to notify Kessler as far ahead of time as possible with ten hours as a minimum. They should then execute their mission unless at any time before plane takes off word is received to the contrary.

Unfortunately, the ten-hour prior notification procedure for the U.S. photo reconnaissance aircraft did not work out satisfactorily nor were the permanently established corridors ever obtained from the Russians. It later became evident to the Americans in "Operation Frantic" that Stalin did not want a large number of photo reconnaissance flights over Soviet territory and that he did not want the United States to have a photographic file of the Soviet Union for future reference.

When Eaker returned to Poltava from Moscow, Perminov, the Russian general who commanded the Soviet forces at the air bases, invited him to dinner. Kessler, who worked closely with the Russian general at Eastern Command headquarters, had grown to admire and respect Perminov despite the fact that many of the Russian's decisions angered him. Perminov was in the same position as all other Russian officers and party leaders—under Stalin they could make no decisions on their own. Every decision, no matter how minor, had to be approved or disapproved in Moscow and this lack of freedom definitely limited the cooperation Perminov could extend toward the Americans. He had, however, done an excellent job of providing the Russian personnel needed to prepare the air bases for use by the American heavy bombers and the personnel required to operate the bases after the shuttle missions started. Perminov also made certain that the Russians assigned to the air bases did their work efficiently, sometimes too efficiently. When the Russians, mostly women, were placing the pierced steel matting in place to provide runways for the B-17s, an American engineer on the job suggested to Perminov that perhaps twelve hours a day was too long for the laborers to toil.

"Why not," the American engineer asked, "work two shifts of eight hours each?"

Perminov grabbed the idea with great enthusiasm and from then on built the airfield with two shifts. All the women reported at 0400 hours for the first shift, worked eight hours, and then labored for a second eight-hour shift without any rest. It was not what the American had in mind, but it got the job done.

The dinner Perminov arranged after Eaker's return from Moscow was held in a small room of the austere, battered officer's club on the air base. Only Eaker, Perminov, and a pretty female aide of the Russian general's staff attended the affair. While the table service, food and drink could not compare with those provided by Stalin at the Kremlin, it was obvious that Perminov had done the best he could under the circumstances to make the dinner successful. Vodka, wine, some fresh fruit, and several courses of meat, evidently scrounged from nearby farmers, were on the table. Once the United States and the Soviet Union and various individuals, organizations, aircraft, and anything else that Perminov could think of had been toasted, each with a separate glass of vodka as was the Russian custom, Eaker decided that it was time to get down to business. He had 129 Flying Fortresses sitting on the Russian air bases plus the supporting fighter task force of P-51s at Piryatin, and he wanted to put them to use. He was well aware that the bombers and fighters had been diverted by the Fifteenth Air Force for the Russian shuttle mission since they could have been used for other missions, especially with the cross-Channel invasion upcoming and the need for the Italian-based bombers to draw the German fighters away from the western front. When Eaker told Perminov that he wanted to fly a mission in the morning with his bombers but needed a cleared corridor through the front lines designated and approved, Perminov shook his head.

"Tonight let's forget the war. We will eat, drink, and be happy."

Despite every effort Eaker made during the early part of the evening to get the conversation back on the subject of a mission for his task force, Perminov refused to discuss the matter. The Russian general politely but firmly ignored Eaker's queries, filled the American general's glass, the woman aide's glass, and his own glass with vodka and suggested another toast. Finally, Eaker decided that there was no possibility of arranging a mission for the next day. He excused himself, went to another room and notified his group commanders by telephone that there would be no mission the following morning because he could not get Russian approval of a designated corridor. It was a disappointing development since he had been led to believe by Novikov in Moscow that neither target selection nor corridor selection would be a problem. Discouraged and frustrated, Eaker returned to the dining table.

After several more toasts, the Russian girl stood up and bid Eaker good night. After a few words in Russian with Perminov, she left the room. Eaker, resigned to an evening of eating, drinking, and light conversation, braced himself for the next Perminov toast. Instead, the Russian general turned to him and shrugged his shoulders.

"Now we can discuss matters of war," he said. "She has gone to make her report to Moscow."

For the first time during the evening, Eaker realized that Perminov's pretty aide was not of the Russian general's choosing. She was a member of the NKVD assigned to spy on both Perminov and the Americans at Poltava. While she was in the room, the Russian general would not discuss any military matters. Within a few minutes after she left the room, Eaker had the designated corridor through the front lines for his bombers and fighters arranged with Perminov and the information relayed to the Russian air and ground defenses.

It was one more revealing example that Stalin not only did not trust the Americans in the Soviet Union but did not trust his own officers who were dealing with the Americans.

Bad weather delayed Eaker's plans for his task force to bomb Mielec on June 4, 1944, and return to the air bases. As he waited for the weather to clear, he became more and more alarmed over the vulnerability of his aircraft as they sat on the Russian fields. Russian intelligence reports indicated increased German aerial activity in the area and the personnel at Poltava spent two hours in the slit trenches on the fourth when 47 Luftwaffe aircraft were plotted east of Kiev. One German reconnaissance aircraft was seen high above Piryatin but there was no follow-up attack by the Luftwaffe, as Eaker expected. To add to his concern, communications between Poltava, Mirgorod, and Piryatin were very poor. There was no telephone that could be depended upon, only a rudimentary teletype operated by the Russians. The Americans could plug into this circuit at will but it proved unreliable and Eaker had to depend upon courier aircraft.

The weather on June 5 was no better so there was nothing Eaker could do but keep his task force on the ground. Exactly what the general had feared might happen was happening—a large number of heavy bombers and escorting fighters were tied up in the Soviet Union when they could have been used effectively in Italy. He was considering taking his task force straight back to Italy on the first clear day when he was handed a message that had arrived earlier in the day in Moscow. The message was addressed to Eaker and Deane and was very short:

> Stay in Russia. Fly missions from Russia. Don't come home to the west.
>
> Spaatz

The meaning of the message was clear to Eaker. The long-awaited D-day had arrived. The cross-Channel invasion was imminent and Spaatz wanted the Fifteenth Air Force shuttle-mission task force on the eastern front to draw away as many Luftwaffe fighters as possible from the west!

As delighted as Eaker was to learn that the invasion of Europe was at last going to become a reality, it did not lessen his concern for the safety of his aircraft sitting on the Russian air bases. Neither did the Russian report he received later that day showing the estimated disposition of enemy aircraft. The report indicated that there were 30 Ju-87s and 20 Me-109s at Romau; the same plus 20 additional FW-190s at Bacau; 100 Ju-87s at Husi; 10 Me-109s at Jassy; 20 Me-109s at Kishinev; the same number at Komrat and Leipzig; 30 Ju-87s at Tecuci; and 66 He-111s plus an undetermined number of Ju-88s at Foscani. One concentrated attack by these scattered aircraft on the Russian air bases and Eaker knew his task force could be wiped out. He desperately wanted to get them into the air.

Back in England, however, Spaatz was looking ahead and making plans for the future use of the Russian air bases. He relied entirely on the Soviet promises to defend the American aircraft while the planes were in the Soviet Union. On June 5, the same day he ordered Eaker to remain in the Soviet Union with his shuttle-mission task force, he sent another message to Deane in Moscow outlining the plans of the USSTAF as far as using Soviet air bases was concerned. He indicated that he intended to send a task force of heavy bombers to the Soviet Union every month at double the rate designated in the original plans. This would, of course, require twice as many escorting fighter aircraft to accompany the American heavy bombers. As though this was not ambitious enough, Spaatz insisted that he wanted to base an American air unit near the eastern front permanently, preferably a unit consisting of three heavy bombardment groups and one fighter group, with the intention of later increasing this unit to an air division of from six to nine heavy bombardment groups. He preferred basing this new air unit at four new Soviet air bases nearer the front lines.

Deane, well aware of the difficulties he and Harriman had encountered in getting the Soviets to permit the American heavy bombers to use Poltava, Mirgorod, and Piryatin, shuddered when he read the message from Spaatz. Despite the success of Eaker's mission from Italy to the Soviet Union, he knew that the Kremlin had no intention of agreeing to such ambitious expansion plans for "Operation Frantic" without long months of negotiations— if, indeed, Stalin would ever agree. He immediately replied to Spaatz that the chances of getting more than one new airfield at this time were practically nil. He agreed, however, that he would try to find a suitable way to approach the Soviets on the proposal. While he thought Spaatz's proposals overoptimistic, Deane was convinced that this was the time to press the Russians for more and better collaboration because of the initial success of "Frantic Joe."

Harriman, while not as optimistic as Spaatz, also agreed that the time was right for making additional proposals to the Soviets. In a message to Roosevelt after "Frantic Joe" he expressed his sentiments about the project clearly;

> In addition to the tactical value of the operation, all the Soviet officials place great importance on the morale effect of this, our first combined operation, both in bringing the people of our two countries closer together in the development of lasting friendship as well as in undermining enemy morale through ending the Hitler-Goebbels propaganda that the Allies could be divided.

Arnold, in Washington, was also confident that most of the troubles that faced the Americans prior to "Frantic Joe" could now be resolved. He urged Harriman to quickly "clean up such problems" as delays in clearing flights into Soviet Russia, clearing photo recon flights, obtaining group visas, and the ceiling restrictions put on American personnel permitted to enter the Soviet Union. There was no doubt in his mind that these obstacles could now be resolved.

In this atmosphere of optimism, clouded only by Eaker's concern over the defense of his grounded aircraft, the weather began clearing over Mirgorod, Piryatin, and Poltava on the night of June 5, 1944.

"We'll fly in the morning," Eaker promised his group commanders.

Several hundred miles to the west the greatest invasion armada the world had ever known had already started across the English Channel toward Normandy.

7

Axis Sally: "We'll Be Waiting"

O N THE EVENING OF June 5, 1944, Axis Sally broadcast that the Luftwaffe was aware of the American heavy bombers on Soviet airdromes and that the German fighters would destroy them when they tried to come out of Russia. While the American airmen were accustomed to the Axis propaganda broadcasts to Italy and the British Isles, Axis Sally's warning sounded more ominous now that they were in a strange land and knew that they would have to fly over enemy-held territory before they could get back to their home bases. Once the airmen awakened early on the morning of June 6, however, and began their preflight preparations for the mission to Galatz, Rumania, they quickly forgot their nervousness.

The Periodic Intelligence Report for the day stated:

> Mission Report 6 June 1944. Sixteen P-51s of the 317 Fighter Squadron, sixteen P-51s of the 318 Fighter Squadron, and fifteen P-51s of the 319 Fighter Squadron took off from Russian bases at 0730 hours to provide route cover for B-17s attacking Galatz, Rumania. Five P-51s returned early. Forty-two P-51s escorted bombers between 0935 and 1145 hours at 23,000 to 27,000 feet. Sixteen enemy aircraft were encountered in the target area. P-51s attacked and destroyed six of these. Two P-51s (Lieutenant John D. Mumford and Lieutenant Donald J. MacDonald) failed to return from this mission. Forty P-51s down at Russian bases at 1210 hours. Victories were credited to the following:
>
> 1 FW-190 . . . . Lt. Col. Chester L. Sluder
> 2 FW-190 . . . . Capt. Roy B. Hogg
> 1 Ju-88 . . . . Lt. Cullen J. Hoffman
> 1 Me-109 . . . . Lt. Robert Barkey
> 1 Me-109 . . . . Lt. Wayne Lowry

The report, while factual, did not tell the entire story as witnessed by the P-51 pilots or the airmen in the 104 B-17s that bombed the airfield at Galatz. The German fighters that attacked the American formation over the target area were determined and pressed home their attacks in a skilled manner. Barrie Davis of the 317th Fighter Squadron discovered this during the air battle over Rumania. A Luftwaffe pilot taught him a combat tactic he would never forget. He had a Me-109 directly in his gun sights and was ready for the kill when the German pilot suddenly chopped his power, dropped his wheels and flaps, and nearly stopped in mid-air. The maneuver so shocked Davis that before he recovered he found his P-51 directly in the sights of the German plane he had overshot. Fortunately, the German did not hit Davis or his Mustang and the American survived to shoot down several Luftwaffe planes which tried this trick later in the war. After the violent air battle over the target, Davis joined his flight leader Ray Lowry and the two pilots, flying tight formation for protection, headed back for Piryatin. As they flew side-by-side, covering each other, Lowry saw a third plane approach from the rear. He decided that it was Bob Bass, another 317th Fighter Squadron member and the third member of Lowry's flight, so he permitted the aircraft to close behind Davis. His error was revealed when the plane, a German Me-109, opened fire on Davis' Mustang. The first round from the Luftwaffe pilot's cannon hit the canopy of the P-51, exploded, and knocked Davis unconscious. Fortunately, the Mustang continued to fly with Davis unconscious while Lowry whipped over and shot down the Me-109. Davis finally regained his senses several minutes later and, half-frozen and confused, tried to find the Russian airfield at Piryatin. His shoes, wet with early morning dew, were frozen to his feet. The canopy of the Mustang was completely shot away, his propeller had been damaged and, out of balance, was trying to shake the fighter plane apart. There were holes in the right wing, tail, and fuel tank. After he eventually spotted some other P-51s of the 325th Fighter Group and followed them to Piryatin and landed, the flight surgeon spent several hours plucking tiny bits of plexiglass and fragments of metal from the top of his head and from his thighs. The mission earned him a Purple Heart and a great deal of embarrassment because he had to explain to his fellow fighter pilots how he had permitted a Me-109 to get so close.

Sluder clobbered a FW-190 while Hogg became an ace, shooting down his fifth and sixth German planes. He also nearly got himself killed driving six more Luftwaffe planes away from Sluder during the air battle. He dove his Mustang so long and so fast to escape the guns of the German aircraft that the pitot tube was torn off, leaving him with no airspeed indicator. Fortunately, he caught up with another P-51 and followed him into the Russian airfield, matching his airspeed with the lead P-51, and touched down without any trouble.

MacDonald was not so fortunate. He did not make it back to Piryatin on June 6, 1944, but he did survive the war as a prisoner. He had fought many air battles during the North African campaign and during a hospital stay at Mostaganem in Algeria a nurse gave him a St. Christopher medal that he sewed onto his flight helmet above and just between his eyes. During the next year of combat flying, MacDonald was never touched by German gunfire and he considered the medal his "lucky piece." On the mission to Galatz on June 6 he was jumped by a number of FW-190s about ten minutes away from the target and after a scramble to get into position to intercept the German planes, he dove on two of the enemy planes, believing that his wingman was following him. After chasing the FW-190s from 24,000 feet to 10,000 feet, he selected the enemy aircraft on his left, leaving the other enemy plane for his wingman—he thought. His wingman, however, had not followed him down. MacDonald caught the FW-190 he was chasing midway in a half-roll, gave the German fighter several bursts from his guns, and watched the plane explode and burn. He then pulled away from the burning aircraft and began climbing back up to altitude where the other P-51s were grouped. It was at that moment he realized that his wingman was not with him.

Before he could rejoin the other P-51s, the fireworks began. His Mustang felt as though it had exploded underneath him as the second FW-190, the one he thought his wingman was taking care of, attacked. The German badly damaged MacDonald's instrument panel before the surprised American pilot could begin to take evasive action in an attempt to escape. MacDonald rolled his Mustang several times, did a two-turn spin, leveled out, and opened his throttle to full power. The engine lasted about one minute, coughed once, and quit. He told the rest of the story in a letter from prison camp to his sister Patricia Mary:

> After my engine quit, I looked behind me and the plane was burning. Since I was down to fifty feet altitude I knew I didn't have enough height to bail out. This left me with only one alternative—crash land! My speed, naturally, was too high for a crash landing but I knew I had to get on the ground immediately because of the fire. I dropped the flaps and headed down. When I crashed I was traveling at an airspeed of 250 miles an hour. When the plane hit the ground my shock straps on my shoulders broke and centrifugal force threw me forward causing me to strike my head on the gun sight, which is sharp and made of strong glass. My head struck the glass exactly where the St. Christopher's medal was sewn on my helmet. The next thing I realized was that I was a hundred feet back in the air with cold air blowing in my face. I had received a terrific blow on the head and blood was streaming down my face from the gash. Why or how I ever woke up can't be explained and I consider this a miracle.
>
> I had received a concussion so of course I was very dazed and didn't know what was going on for a while. But after a few hours in prison camp I discovered that the medal on the helmet was missing. I believe it saved my life.
>
> It was my own fault that I was shot down. If I hadn't been so happy and excited about shooting down the FW-190 and had concentrated more on my job, everything would have been okay.

While the B-17s were on the bomb run over Galatz, radio operators heard the British Broadcasting Company announce the Allied landings in France. The bombers did moderate damage to the Luftwaffe airdrome at Galatz and lost no aircraft. As the American crews headed back to Mirgorod and Poltava they were jubilant over the news that D-day for the Normandy invasion had arrived and that Allied ground troops were actually going ashore in Europe. Back at the Russian air bases later, however, they were disappointed to discover that the Soviet officers and other personnel were not celebrating the landings. A few Russians were crowded around bulletin boards where copies of newspapers were displayed, but there were no demonstrations as the Americans had expected.

In Moscow, however, both Deane and Harriman were elated that the Allied landings had begun. Stalin had been furious over the fact that the Allies had delayed the invasion several times in favor of other military operations and even when the U.S.

Chiefs of Staff set May 31, 1944 (with two or three days' margin on either side to allow for weather and tides, as a firm date for the Allied landing, Stalin was not convinced. As the time of the invasion drew near and Deane had to notify the Red Army General Staff of several changes in the date, his stock reached a new low. The General Staff believed just as Stalin did, that the May 31 date was a part of a deception plan the western powers were using against the Soviet Union. Deane, in a gesture that he hoped would convince the Russians of the sincerity of the Allied planners, bet Slavin twelve bottle of vodka in February that the invasion would begin in May but when June 1 arrived and the landings had still not taken place, he not only lost the bet but the confidence of the Russian general.

When June 6, 1944, arrived and the invasion actually began it was a great relief for every American in the Soviet Union as well as Allied personnel everywhere. Deane felt that D-day would mark the beginning of a period of close cooperation between Great Britain, Russia, and the United States. He was so elated when he heard the news and so certain that the Russians would be grateful for the Allied operation in the west that would draw German ground troops from the eastern front, that he took a walk through the busiest section of Moscow. He thought he would be mobbed by the happy citizens because of his American officer's uniform. Instead, he was ignored. He covered the entire distance to Spasso House without being noticed by anyone. Despite the fact that the news of the landings had been broadcast by the radio stations and published in the newspapers, there was no demonstrative outburst of enthusiasm by the Russians in Moscow. It was difficult for Deane to understand.

The following day he explained to the Red Army General Staff that since both the western powers and the Soviet Union were now fighting on the same continent he was willing to broaden the scope of the U.S. daily reports of military actions to include not only what had happened but also a forecast of forthcoming actions if the Russians would do the same. The Red Army General Staff quickly agreed to the proposal. After the agreement was made, Deane would get a three- or four-page message from Eisenhower each night outlining in detail his operations for the day and quite often his plans for the future. These reports, which were received by Deane at about 10:00 P.M., would be translated into Russian, plotted on maps, and sent to the Red Army General Staff and Stalin. In return, Deane received nothing but an advance news release concerning Russian military operations, the same release sent to correspondents around the world for the public media. Once again Stalin had duped the Americans.

During a meeting Harriman had with Stalin on June 10, 1944, while Eaker's Fifteenth Air Force shuttle bombers were still in the Soviet Union, Stalin gave the impression that he was going to be easier to get along with now that "Frantic Joe" and the mission to Galatz had been successful and D-day in the west was an actuality. Harriman had requested the meeting to present several proposals to Stalin, hoping that in the atmosphere of optimism that permeated "Operation Frantic" at the moment he could gain a favorable hearing from the marshal. He reminded Stalin that several months earlier, February 2, 1944, to be exact, Stalin had said he would permit 300 American heavy bombers to operate against Japan from Soviet bases once Germany was defeated. At that time, Harriman reminded Stalin, the marshal had promised to bring the Chief of the Red Air Force in the Far East to Moscow to discuss with Deane the details of such an operation, but that this meeting had never taken place. What, Harriman asked, was Stalin's viewpoint on this matter at the present time?

Stalin shocked Harriman with his answer. He immediately stated that in the area between Vladivostok and Sovietskaya Gavan there were twelve airfields, some new, suitable for heavy bombers. The USAAF, Stalin said, could expect to use six or seven of these airfields. It was obvious that the Soviets had watched the construction methods used by the Americans at Poltava, Mirgorod, and Piryatin and had used the same methods to build the new bases. While Harriman was still congratulating himself on solving what he had anticipated would be a very delicate and difficult problem, Stalin named his "price." He asked for immediate delivery of 240 Flying Fortresses and 300 Liberator bombers. Fortunately, Harriman had made an important decision regarding further negotiations with Stalin and other Russian party or military leaders. In a letter to Harry Hopkins he explained his new concept:

Whenever I talk to Molotov on any matter that we request he

immediately uses the word 'reciprocity.' The Lend-Lease alloca-
tions made in Washington are evidently considered by the Soviets
to be contributions to the Red Army in recognition of their offensive and they evidently do not consider that they are called upon
to do anything in return that would be helpful to our forces. As
you know, it is most distasteful to me to get a trading atmosphere
into our negotiations over mutual assistance in the war, but trading
seems to be the language they understand, and we don't find them
at all impressed by any obligation on their part to reciprocate
after commitments have been made in Washington.

Using this changed approach in his negotiations, Harriman
told Stalin that the USAAF would begin delivery of the bombers
he requested "after agreement had been reached regarding our
operation from Soviet Far Eastern bases." The USAAF would also
train Soviet crews, either in the United States or in the Soviet
Union. Hearing this statement, Stalin agreed that talks should
begin immediately between Deane and the Chief of the Red Air
Force in the Far East.

The conference ended on this optimistic note—but six weeks
later the talks still had not begun.

Meanwhile, at Poltava Eaker was still nervous about keeping
his task force in the Soviet Union so long and was anxious to
get back to Italy. Finally, Spaatz gave him permission to schedule
a bombing mission as soon as the weather cleared and, after
hitting the selected target, to return to the home bases of the
Fifteenth Air Force at Foggia. The airmen were delighted to get
the news, too, since living conditions at the Soviet air bases were
not good. They could not shower, had no change of clothes except the small supply they brought with them, the tents were
crowded, and the food adequate but far from outstanding. Time
began to drag. Vodka could not replace cold beer, the Russian
dance, the Kazatsky, was interesting the first time but dull
after that, and even the large-breasted women all began to look
alike after the first week.

Barrie Davis, who had nearly been killed when the Me-109
slipped up behind his P-51 during the mission to Galatz, was
ordered to return to Italy aboard a B-17 because his aircraft was
unfit for flying. When Eaker set up a mission for June 11, 1944,
during which the Flying Fortresses would bomb the Focsani
airdrome near Bucharest and continue on to Foggia, Davis was

provided with transportation to Poltava from Piryatin on a Russian C-47. Not only did the fact that he had to return to Italy aboard a bomber instead of his fighter plane scare him but the fact that he had to fly with a Russian pilot to Poltava petrified him. When he arrived at the C-47, he discovered that he would be riding with a conglomeration of Russian passengers, both military and civilian, some carrying live chickens under their arms. He also discovered that the only gun on the aircraft, which was flying unescorted, was a .30-caliber unmanned machine gun. As usual, the Russian pilot took off immediately after starting the engines without warming up or going through the "before takeoff" checklist as American pilots always did. The C-47 got into the air all right, but on the way to Poltava one engine quit and the Russian pilot had to land at a small airfield. He and the copilot took a toolbox from the aircraft and went to work on the bad engine, removing the cowl, and taking out parts without the benefit of a ground mechanic to assist or advise. After about an hour, they started the engine again, pushed the throttle wide open, and when it continued to operate, motioned the passengers back inside. As soon as the cowl was replaced, the pilot took off and completed the flight to Poltava without incident. By this time, Davis was too nervous to even look at the B-17 he was expected to ride to Italy.

A stroke of good luck, as far as Davis was concerned, saved him the ordeal of riding the bomber. Word came to Poltava that one of the 325th Fighter Group pilots had taken ill and would be unable to return to Italy. Davis was to get back to Piryatin immediately so that he could fly the P-51 the next day. By this time it was dark and the only method of transportation available was a jeep. But before he was permitted to make the 75-mile trip, Davis had to wait for two hours until permission was given in Moscow for him to go back to Piryatin. With an American driver, he then headed across country. They were stopped three or four times, at rail crossings and similar places, but after their passes were examined, Davis and his driver were allowed to continue. He arrived at Piryatin a short time before the mission briefing was scheduled, weary but delighted that he did not have to ride the Flying Fortress. However, all the ground-crew men of the 325th Fighter Group that had come into the Soviet Union aboard the B-17s were once again taken from Piryatin to Mirgorod and

Poltava on June 10, 1944, so that they could be flown back to Italy.

Another group of passengers added to the bombers' loading lists were members of a combat camera team that had accompanied the "Frantic Joe" task force from Italy so that a photographic record of the shuttle mission could be made. Lieutenant Edward MacKay, the commander of the unit, took his exposed film with him to his assigned B-17 but as he prepared to load it aboard the aircraft for the flight home the next morning, a Russian officer stopped him. Mackay was abruptly informed that no pictures were permitted to leave Soviet Russia! After arguing with the Russian, MacKay shrugged and turned several cases of film over to him. As it turned out, however, the Russians got unexposed film and MacKay loaded the exposed film aboard the B-17 just as he had planned. At the moment, it appeared that for once an American had outsmarted a Russian but this action eventually turned into a fiasco that had a serious effect on "Operation Frantic."

On the morning of June 11, 1944, the Americans left the Soviet airfields to complete their round-trip shuttle mission. The Periodic Intelligence Report for this mission states:

> Mission Report 11 June 1944. Twenty-two P-51s of the 317th Fighter Squadron, nineteen P-51s of the 318th Fighter Squadron and twenty P-51s of the 319th Fighter Squadron took off from Russian bases at 0710 hours to provide escort for B-17s attacking Focsani airdrome, Rumania. One P-51 crashed on takeoff; eight P-51s returned early. Fifty-two P-51s escorted bombers from 0900 to 1100 hours, 23,000 to 30,000 feet. Twelve enemy aircraft attacked a straggling bomber in the target area and P-51s, engaging them, destroyed three Me-109s and damaged one FW-190. Fifty-two P-51s down at Italian bases 1300 hours. Victories credited to the following:
>
> 1 Me-109 destroyed....Lt. Ferdinand E. Suehle
> 1 Me-109 destroyed....Lt. Richard S. Deakins
> 1 Me-109 destroyed....Lt. Benjamin H. Emmert
> 1 FW-190 damaged....Maj. Herschel H. Green

While escorting the 121 Flying Fortresses as they approached the target area, Sluder noticed one B-17 with an engine out lagging quite a distance below and behind the main body of bombers. His instructions were not to detach segments of the fighter force to protect stragglers, but Sluder tried to keep this B-17 in sight while covering the formation. Suddenly he saw two Luftwaffe fighter planes make a pass at the lone Flying Fortress so he decided to go after the German planes with his flight. Just at that moment an Me-109 slid onto the tail of Sluder's Mustang and he had to cope with the enemy plane until one of the other P-51s drove the German away. As soon as he was in the clear, Sluder started down toward the B-17 again, but he was too late. The big bomber was going down vertically, trailing flames. He saw a couple of parachutes but could not tell how many men survived the holocaust.

Sluder was unaware of it at the time but the B-17 that went down in flames was the bomber carrying MacKay and the pictorial record of "Frantic Joe." It was later learned that MacKay was the only person on the aircraft killed, machine-gunned through the chest. The Flying Fortress crashed with tremendous force, broke apart, and the approximately 500 still photographs MacKay had taken in Soviet Russia were scattered across the countryside. A short time after the crash these pictures, many of them showing the B-17s parked at Poltava and Mirgorod, were picked up by the Germans.

Eaker's task force dropped 1,424 two-hundred-and-fifty-pound general-purpose bombs on the Focsani airdrome with good results. Only the one B-17 was lost. The return to Italy was an occasion for commendation and jubilation. The initial shuttle mission had been conducted in an excellent manner and had deeply impressed the Russians, including Stalin, of the efficiency of the American strategic airmen and their aircraft. Eaker had done an outstanding job getting "Operation Frantic" started and Washington was optimistic about future collaboration between the United States and the Soviet Union.

If Roosevelt, Arnold, or Spaatz anticipated faster action during future negotiations with Stalin, and unquestionably they did, it was a mistake. Four days after Eaker's task force landed back at Foggia, Spaatz was asking Moscow why Stalin had not yet agreed to the expansion plans of the USSTAF he had proposed on June 5, 1944—ten days previously. He repeated his plans, adding additional details. He wanted air bases farther west for use by the B-17s, permission to have 3,375 Americans permanently stationed at the air bases with a comparative increase in Russian personnel to help, and an agreement that about 3,000 airmen could fly into the Soviet Union and out again after varying lengths of stay at the Soviet air bases.

In answer to Arnold's impatient query about the delay in the expansion plans of "Operation Frantic," Harriman tried to explain some of the problems that existed in Moscow despite the optimistic attitude of the Russians now that "Frantic Joe" had been so successful.

> It is true that we have had annoying delays in connection with visas, transport plane clearances, etc., but these delays were caused not by the Red Air Force but by other departments of the Soviet government in breaking down historic inhibitions. Interdepartmental difficulties of this character, where the responsibilities of the departments conflict, are not unknown in Washington.

Yet, in Moscow both Deane and Harriman, the two Americans who had to deal with the top-level Soviet military and party members, were losing some of their optimism. Requests for meetings resulted in the same delays by the Russians; decisions on troubling problems, especially the photo recon corridors, were not made by the Soviets; and all further discussion in regard to bases for American bombers to use in the war against Japan were halted.

On June 15, 1944, the same day Spaatz repeated his request for expansion approval of "Operation Frantic," an incident occurred that plainly indicated all was not well between the two supposed allies. Two American F-5s on a photographic shuttle-mission from Britain to Soviet Russia and using the corridor procedure demanded by the Russians experienced serious trouble en route. Kessler reported the incident to Spaatz and Doolittle the following day, explaining that the two planes had been attacked by Russian fighter aircraft:

> Hoover evaded three Yak fighters after a ten-minute chase and landed. He also experienced Soviet flak. Interrogation shows that pilot was not briefed on contents of JK579 about radio facilities or photos and drawings of bases. Kendall was also subjected to Soviet flak. Consider it necessary that missions adhere closely to timetables submitted. Soviets are confused by invasion markings (stripes instead of star-and-bar). The Yak attack was apparently prompted by such markings and (the markings) should be removed before aircraft enter Russia.

Kessler's letter, while indicating that the American pilots might not have been briefed well enough prior to leaving Britain, and that the strange invasion marking on the aircraft might have confused the Russians, was proof that the photo recon missions were extremely dangerous. The German air force had no aircraft similar to the F-5, so there was no reason for the Russian fighter pilots not to recognize the American planes, especially when they had been warned to be on the alert for two American recon planes en route to the Soviet Union. An incident that occurred the following day, June 16, 1944, clearly indicated that the Russians intended to harass the American photo recon planes any time and anywhere they found them over the Soviet Union. Lieutenant David K. Rowe of the Eastern Command Photo Detachment was shot down on that day and Paul Cullen, who was in charge of the United States reconnaissance program of "Operation Frantic," detailed the incident in a letter to Spaatz:

> Rowe departed Poltava for photo recon of Bialystok and other targets. At 27,000 feet in the vicinity of Kiev, while indicating 185 miles per hour, he observed tracers from the rear and saw two Aircobras closing. Rowe dropped both fuel tanks and at full throttle climbed to 28,000 feet before the flaming F-5 fell out of control. Cannon shot out the throttle quadrant, set the engine on fire, filled cockpit with flame. Sun glasses, oxygen mask and gloves reduced area (of Rowe) seared by flame. Pilot succeeded in bailing out despite holes in chute and cut shroud lines. Immediately picked up (on ground) by Soviets and taken within three hours to a good hospital in Kiev and given excellent medical attention.

Lieutenant Rowe recovered.

The only excuse given by the Russians for the unprovoked attack on Rowe was that "the Red Air Force has a regulation which prohibits photo recon ships from flying over 18,500 feet altitude. Had Rowe not been flying above this altitude he would not have been shot down." United States personnel did not agree with this statement since at no time had the Soviets mentioned the altitude restriction. It was generally believed by the Americans that the Russians did not want Rowe to obtain photographs of the Bialystok area.

Despite this tragic incident that marred the optimistic viewpoint shared by USSTAF personnel after the successful "Frantic Joe," mission, it was generally agreed in Washington, at the

U.S. Military Mission in Moscow, and at Spasso House that the shuttle-mission project was off to an excellent start and the future for "Operation Frantic" and for the use of bases in the Soviet Union from which American B-29s could bomb Japan looked bright. The Fifteenth Air Force, with Eaker leading it, had accomplished its assigned mission with glory. It was now the Eighth Air Force's responsibility to keep "Operation Frantic" moving, and to add to the achievement of the American heavy bombers out of Italy. Spaatz was confident that this veteran air force organization would have no trouble in equalling or exceeding the success of the Fifteenth Air Force.

Unfortunately, in the optimism of the moment, the Luftwaffe was forgotten.

8

"Move the He-111 Aircraft to Minsk!"

COLONEL WILHELM ANTRUP, CO of KG 55 of the Luftwaffe, glanced at the old pine trees concealing his He-111 aircraft and smiled. If it wasn't for the German guards in steel helmets guarding the entrance road and the low structures scattered among the trees, he would have thought he was looking at harmless farm buildings. When he leaned to the right and looked through an opening in the pine trees at row after row of He-111s sitting on the hidden runway, the aircraft that General Rudolf Meister, commanding officer of the IV Fliegerkorps, had ordered flown to Minsk from the Brest-Litowsk-Random area, all thoughts of a peaceful farm disappeared from his mind. His KG 55 and KG 53, the "Legion Kondor" commanded by Colonel Fritz Pockrandt, had been moved to Minsk for a very important reason: to bring the Russian airfields of Poltava, Mirgorod, and Piryatin within range of their aircraft. KG 27, another HE-111-equipped group, and KG 4, composed of He-111s and *Zielmarkierungsstaffel* (target-marking flare planes) were both at secret airfields near Minsk also ready to attack. Antrup silently added up the aircraft available for the operation Meister had planned so carefully:

KG 4:   72 He-111 and 6 Ju-88 (target-marking flare planes)
KG 27: 75 He-111
KG 53: 111 He-111
KG 55: 109 He-111

That would be enough, Antrup told himself. Meister had planned well, but that was to be expected. A second lieutenant by the time he was eighteen years of age, Meister had risen steadily through the ranks to his present position as commanding officer of IV Fliegerkorps. When the Luftwaffe was reestablished in 1939, he had been a lieutenant colonel with the title of Chief of the Education Department in the Ministry of the Air Force. The following year he was promoted to colonel, had nearly died in an airplane crash in 1941, recovered, and was advanced to major general on September 1, 1942, and lieutenant general on March 1, 1943. With this experience it was no wonder he knew exactly what to do when the pictures discovered near the Flying Fortress shot down at Focsani on June 11, 1944, were shown to him—the photos that MacKay had slipped past the Russian officer at Poltava.

The air war on the Russian front had not been particularly successful for Germany, mainly because of poor planning by Hitler. Hitler made his initial preparation for war against the Soviet Union at a time when the Luftwaffe was engaged in a life-or-death struggle with the RAF over Great Britain. Goering himself had tried to change Hitler's mind about the surprise attack on Soviet Russia, with which the Germans had a treaty at the time, but the Führer refused to be deterred. On June 22, 1941, Germany began the eastern campaign against the Russians with a *blitzkrieg* against Russian fighter bases conducted by picked crews of KGs, 2, 3, and 53. At 0130 hours, approximately two hours before the Luftwaffe attack, Stalin tried to warn his military commanders that a German attack was imminent by sending the following message:

> Before dawn on June 22nd all aircraft are to be dispersed on their airfields and carefully camouflaged. All units will come to immediate readiness.

Unfortunately for the Soviet Union, the warning was bogged down along the inefficient Russian communications line and the German air attack came as a complete surprise. Soviet aircraft, sitting on the ground in row after row, went up in flames by the hundreds. This initial Luftwaffe mission indicated that the *blitz-krieg* tactics that had been so successful against Poland in 1939 and the western Allies in 1940 were also going to be successful against the Soviet Union. There was no Russian fighter opposition during this attack and it ended with the biggest victory ever scored in a single day by one air force against another. The Russians lost more than 1,800 planes during the "blitz" while the Germans lost a mere 35! In fact, the results were so incredible that Goering had them double-checked before he would announce the Russian losses to Hitler in Berlin.

However, the Red Air Force was far from being knocked out of the war. At the beginning of the German-Russian hostilities the Russians had about ten times the number of aircraft that the Germans had available and although the Red Air Force suffered enormous losses during the remainder of 1941, it would not admit defeat. On December 11, 1941, Hitler told the German Reichstag that 17,332 Russian aircraft had been destroyed or captured, which, if true, indicated that the Red Air Force had been wiped out. Yet additional Soviet planes were constantly being added to the battle. It was later learned that the Russians had quadrupled their aircraft production during the second half of 1941 and that the total production of new planes for the year was 15,735. No wonder the supply never ran out!

As Antrup checked his He-111s at Minsk three years after the surprise attack of June 22, 1941, he remembered distinctly the futility of his long months fighting the air war on the eastern front. The area that the Luftwaffe had to cover in this combat zone baffled the imagination. For the initial phase of the battle against the Soviet Union, the Luftwaffe had to cover an air space of 1,500,000 square kilometers. Later, a new front was opened north of Leningrad reaching from Lake Ladoga west to the White Sea, past the Barents Sea to Murmansk and Norway. In addition, important war industry targets lay 200 to 400 kilometers east and north of Moscow and in the area of the lower Volga, the Caucasus, the Urals, and Siberia. This huge front had to be covered by four German Luftflotten with a total of 1,945 aircraft, of which approximately only two-thirds were operational at any one time.

When Antrup had been asked by a friend in Berlin why the Luftwaffe had not won the war on the Russian front within a few weeks, his answer had come quickly in the form of questions of his own.

Did the Luftwaffe command consider the climate with its great differences in temperature? Did they know about the gigantic dust clouds above the dirt roads and paths? Did they know about the cloudbursts that make traffic routes impassable within a few minutes, bring the rivers to overflowing, tearing down the bridges? Did they calculate all that? No, no one did. The cry from Berlin was that the victory will be won before winter comes. It wasn't.

During the first days of the German invasion of the Soviet Union the Luftwaffe had complete air superiority. The German army was supported in its rapid advance against the Russian ground troops by constant air attacks at the front and through missions behind the lines against railroad yards and highways used to bring Russian reinforcement to the front lines. The encirclement of the Red Army units near Bialystok—where American lieutenant Rowe was shot down during a recon flight three years later— and Smolensk were made possible through the direct support of the Luftwaffe. The second phase of the German advance, roughly from July 22, 1941, until October 9, 1941, gave the Luftwaffe command a forecast of future events on the eastern front. By this time the German air force planes were distributed along the entire front, so scattered that it was difficult to muster a large enough force against one target to be effective. Primarily, the Luftwaffe supported the German army attack which led to the eventual battle of Briansk and Wjasma, but other operations were also attempted. In the extreme north, the advance on Murmansk was stalled despite German air attacks and the Murmansk railroad continued to operate despite repeated Luftwaffe raids. During this period Luftflotte II, under the command of General Fieldmarshal Albert Kesselring and one Fliegerkorps was transferred to Italy, weakening the German air strength along the Moscow front at the same time that the mud and bitter cold hampered its efficiency.

The next phase of the eastern-front battle lasted until the summer of 1942. On December 6, 1941, a Russian counterattack began in the Moscow area and the weakened German ground troops could not stop the Red Army forces. At the very moment that the Russian counterattack was launched, the Luftwaffe had been hoping for a breathing spell in order to reequip its units, rest its pilots, and prepare for the long winter ahead. As the Red Army troops forced the German forces back, however, the German pilots had to take to the air in every aircraft that would fly, to try to halt the advance. It was a difficult assignment for Antrup and the other pilots and it became even more hazardous when, in February 1942, the Red Army managed to surround a German ground force of 100,000 men at the small town of Demyansk, halfway between Moscow and Leningrad. From February 20 to May 18, Ju-52s of the Luftwaffe supplied the trapped men and flew out the wounded in the world's first large-scale airlift. The operation at Demyansk was a success, but it set a precedent that eventually led to tragedy at Stalingrad.

When the thaw set in during the spring of 1942, the Luftwaffe began to operate more efficiently and the German ground troops managed to contain the Russians, who were bogged down by the mud. From Berlin came Hitler's order to capture the rich oil fields of the Caucasus, but to accomplish this goal it soon became apparent that the Germans had to secure their southern flank by capturing the Crimea, particularly the fortress at Sevastopol. Fliegerkorps VIII, commanded by General von Richthofen, was transferred from the central to the southern front and given the assignment of attacking Sevastopol from the air.

A few days before the beginning of the air attacks on Sevastopol, Antrup, who was now being assigned special tasks on the eastern front because of his long experience in fighting the Russians, was called to the headquarters of Hans Jeschonnek, Luftwaffe Chief of Staff, and ordered to fly back to the Crimea immediately and report to Richthofen. His *War Diary, June-July 1942,* details some of his experiences during this period:

> My old Ju-88 had brought me in nonstop flight from Italy diagonally over the Balkans. Letting down from 5,000 meters I landed at the airport of Evpatoria. Almost tropical heat took away my breath and I was glad that I was wearing only a thin uniform. At the *Flugbereitschaft* I received a Fieseler Storch in order to fly to the staff headquarters of the Commanding General of the VIII Fliegerkorps, who had been informed about my arrival by Jeschonnek. Flying low, I curved into the valley of Tschuruk-su where the Khan's palace Bachtschisarai was located. This was Richthofen's staff headquarters.
>
> Behind his desk, in back of the wide-open window whose narrow curtains waited in vain for a cooling breeze from the Black Sea, Richthofen reminded me of a Khan himself with his narrow, slitted eyes and weathered features. Our conversation was short and formal. He explained to me that the attack against Sevastopol had just started, outlined the assignments of the various Luftwaffe units, and detailed the plans of the air offensive against the city.

He seemed completely in his element in the palace of the Khan giving orders since he was a man who always lived extravagantly. I think this assignment was according to his taste.

I had time for a quick walk around the palace before I left for my duties. The oldest part of this former royal residence showed exactly the strange mixtures of style, the 'one-thing-beside-another' architecture that I had heard so much about but had never seen. An iron gate built by the Italian Novi, and a room built in the eighteenth century that showed late Baroque and had colorful Venetian glass were typical examples. In the yard stood the Fountain of Tears whose legendary story aroused Alexander Pushkin to a romantic poem of love and suffering.

Less than fifty miles from the luxury of Richthofen's staff headquarters palace was the fortress of Sevastopol where the trapped Russian defenders were dying from the bombs dropped by hundreds of German aircraft. Among the pilots who attacked the city was Antrup.

> The next morning I flew to Sevastopol. Altogether there were about 400 Stukas, fighter planes and hunters gathered on the airports around Sevastopol. That means one can count on 200 to 250 airplanes for the attack each day and that is how many we have today. Sevastopol appears from the air like the battle panorama of a painter of war scenes. This early morning the sky is literally full of airplanes that hurry to the city and drop their bombs. Thousands of bombs, altogether more than 2,400 tons of explosive bombs and 23,000 fire bombs have been dropped onto the city and fort. A flight to the enemy doesn't take long—twenty minutes! One had barely climbed to bombing altitude when he is in the target area.

> In impenetrable dust, broken by flashing detonations, the battle area is mostly hidden to the view of the attacking ground troops when the bombers strike again into the narrowing defense ring. In the howling of the Stuka attacks and the whistling of the bombs it seems that even nature holds her breath for a moment. The attacks roll without pause. Blood and dust is the dreadful symbol of Sevastopol.

Sevastopol finally surrendered on July 4, 1942, but after this moment of glory, this zenith of victory in the east, came the descent of the German ground forces and the Luftwaffe . . . although the Nazis did not understand this fact at the time. With their southern flank secure after the fall of the Crimea, the

Germans began an offensive to capture the Caucasus oil fields. By August the lead force of the German units was deep in the Caucasus and on their eastern flank German patrols had reached the outskirts of Stalingrad. Throughout the attack Antrup and other Luftwaffe pilots had provided excellent support for the ground troops, but time ran out for the Luftwaffe at Stalingrad. The Nazi ground troops forced their way deeper and deeper into the city until on November 18, 1942, they were in control of nearly the entire west bank of the Volga. The following day, however, the Russians counterattacked from both the north and the south and five days later the 22 German divisions under the command of General Friedrich Paulus, a total of 330,000 men, were trapped. Paulus decided he could break out of the Russian encirclement if he moved immediately, but Hitler received assurances from Goering that the Luftwaffe could keep the trapped German divisions supplied by air as it had done at Demyansk earlier. These assurances convinced Hitler to order Paulus to stand fast and wait for the Luftwaffe to fly in the required supplies. It was a tragic mistake for the Germans.

From the beginning the Luftwaffe airlift went badly. Newly trained crews, a shortage of aircraft, bad weather, Russian fighters, and accurate antiaircraft fire led to the downfall of the supply-by-air plans of Goering and by January 16, 1943, when the airfield at Pitomnik, the last strip large enough to handle the German transport planes, was lost to the Russians the battle of Stalingrad was lost for the Germans. The formal surrender came on February 2, 1943, when the remaining 91,000 starving survivors of the battle were captured. The Luftwaffe lost nearly 500 aircraft during the siege of Stalingrad and many of their most experienced pilots. Just as destructive for the Luftwaffe was the complete halt in the aircrew training program in the Reich because of a lack of aircraft and instructors, both of which were required for the Stalingrad airlift. In addition, the large amount of fuel required for this operation had caused a serious shortage that now forced a reduction in combat missions on the eastern front.

While the Luftwaffe was suffering this defeat at Stalingrad, Field Marshal Erhard Milch joined Richthofen's headquarters with special powers from Hitler to take over and reorganize the airlift. It was too late. Everything that could be done to save the

German ground troops trapped at Stalingrad had been done. Frustrated and discouraged, Milch wrote in his diary the main points he discussed in late January 1943 with Major General Schmundt, an aide to Hitler, and the Führer himself.

1. I consider it wise if the Führer keeps more distant from single problems of the army command while he, as in the west and south, appoints a special person as chief commander for the eastern front for all three branches of the fighting forces.

2. Intention of the Russians is undoubtedly to retake the Donez area since they depend upon coal. Therefore the order for Army Group Don: Unconditionally hold the Donez area under corresponding flank protection provided by Crimea.

3. Weapons and materiel supply will not be in satisfactory quantity until 1944. Therefore 1943 defense should depend upon strongest build-in into earth, at first with earth works, later concrete barricades and pillboxes, in order to save our own blood and cause the enemy strong losses.

4. In future, forego mobile war in the winter since it is too prone to high losses in men and materiel. Avoid more large encirclement of our troops since air supply, especially in the bad weather of winter, is never completely assured.

Milch made other proposals, according to his war diary, including one that a fighting forces general staff should be established at Hitler's headquarters to help with the planning of future military operations. This suggestion in his diary casts doubt on whether Milch did or did not report his opinions directly to Hitler. It is obvious that if he did, the Führer did not take them seriously since Hitler continued to direct all military operations until the end. Milch, in his diary, states:

Major General Schmundt asked me to bring my opinions personally to the Führer's headquarters after I had fulfilled my tasks. I asked to be allowed to speak freely in quiet discussion instead of before an official gathering. These questions were also discussed later with von Richthofen.

Antrup, a close friend of Jeschonnek, Luftwaffe Chief of Staff, was aware of the controversy and bitterness existing among Milch, Jeschonnek, Goering, Richthofen, and various other high-ranking German air force leaders. After the loss of Paulus' troops at

Stalingrad, Goering tried to shift the blame onto Jeschonnek, and Milch implied that perhaps Richthofen could have done better. While the Luftwaffe high command argued, the Russians soaked up the German ground troops and aircraft like an enormous sponge during the remainder of the winter and spring of 1943. Newly activated German army divisions, reinforced by Luftwaffe field divisions and units of the Waffen-SS, were defeated before they could even establish a defense line in the combat zone. By April 1943 the eastern front had been stabilized along a line extending roughly from Kharkov to Kursk to Orel, with a jutting projection of German troops extending eastward from Orel and a similar projection of Russian troops extending westward from Kursk. Both salients were vulnerable to a pincer movement from the opposing armies . . . and Hitler decided to take advantage of the opportunity to regain some of the prestige his troops had lost at Stalingrad. On April 15, 1943, he issued an order to his generals explaining his intentions:

> This attack is of decisive importance. It must succeed quickly and completely. It must put the initiative for this spring and summer in our hands. All preparations must therefore be made with the greatest care and energy; the best units, the best weapons, the best commanders, and large quantities of ammunition shall be committed in the areas of the main effort. Every commander and every man must be filled with the decisive meaning of this attack. The victory of Kursk must have the effect of a beacon for the entire world.

For this attack, which bore the code name "Operation Citadel," the Luftwaffe gathered as many aircraft as possible. Other fronts were drained and even the reserves from Germany were rushed to the eastern front. Approximately 1,800 planes were assembled for the operation against the Russian salient at Kursk, 1,000 of which were assigned to General Hans Seidemann to support the German Fourth Panzer Army attacking from the south, and 800 supporting the German Ninth Army attacking from the north. The latter group of Luftwaffe aircraft was placed under the command of Major General Paul Deichmann. The pincer operation was scheduled to begin at 0330 hours on the morning of July 5, 1943, at which time the 1,800 aircraft were to be attacking enemy airfields, ground positions, and artillery emplacements.

Antrup and the other Luftwaffe pilots were ready and waiting early on the morning of the scheduled attack. The gathered Luftwaffe planes were based at Mikoyanovka, twenty miles behind the southern front at Byelgorod, and at five airfields around Kharkov. The bomber units had been briefed to take off first and once they were assembled in formation above the air bases, the fighters would take off and join the bombers to escort them to the target areas. As Antrup and the others waited for the signal to taxi to the runway, however, German radio operators monitoring Russian frequencies suddenly heard a large upsurge in the number of messages being exchanged among Red Air Force units. A few minutes later the German radar stations in the Kharkov area reported several large formations of Red Air Force aircraft approaching the airfields where the assembled Luftwaffe bombers and fighters were waiting to take off.

Antrup saw the German fighter planes that were supposed to take to the air after the bombers were airborne taxi past his He-111 and precede him to the runway. Within a few minutes 400 to 500 Russian bombers, fighters, and fighter-bombers and the Luftwaffe fighters were engaged in the largest air battle of World War II. More than one-fourth of the Russian planes were shot down. Very few Luftwaffe planes were even damaged. "Operation Citadel" went off as scheduled, saved from catastrophe by the alert German radar stations and fighter pilots.

Despite this obvious breach of security concerning the German offensive, the first few days of "Operation Citadel" were very successful. The Stukas bombed paths for the tanks to move through, knocked out Russian artillery, and drove the Red Army ground troops to cover. The tank-busting aircraft of the Luftwaffe, the Henschel Hs 129B-2, did an excellent job during the offensive. One unit, the Fourth Gruppe of Schlachtgeschwader Nine commanded by Captain Bruno Meyer, detected a Russian brigade supported by 40 tanks in the open. Using their 30-mm tungsten-cored cannon shells, the German pilots destroyed a half dozen tanks within a matter of minutes and forced the remainder to retreat back toward the Russian lines. Another Luftwaffe unit, their ammunition and bombs gone, so confused a Russian tank force by their low passes overhead that the entire tank force drove into a marsh and was bogged down.

These successes, however, took their toll of the Luftwaffe pilots and aircraft and when on July 11, 1943, the Russians counter-attacked north and east of Orel, the Luftwaffe had to abandon its own attacks on the Russians and defend itself. By July 19, 1943, a Soviet armored unit had blocked the Bryansk-Orel rail-way at Khotinez, shutting off the only reinforcement route for the German armies at Orel. The situation gravely reminded the Luftwaffe leaders of the disaster at Stalingrad, when the Russians had completely encircled the German forces. Once again the dwindling forces of the Luftwaffe were called into action and every plane and pilot in condition to fly moved into the area to open a breech through which the threatened German Ninth and Second Panzer units could escape. Flying as many as six missions a day, Antrup helped prevent a second Stalingrad . . . but it was the last major operation of the Luftwaffe on the eastern front. Once the German ground troops eluded the Russians at Orel they kept retreating steadily and by July 23, 1943, less than three weeks after the opening blow of "Operation Citadel," they were forced back past their starting point. The Luftwaffe was dispersed once again across the entire eastern front, where its strength was steadily sapped as Hitler ordered more and more of its units back to Germany to protect the homeland.

In August 1943, one month before Giles requested his USAAF staff in Washington to study the feasibility of American bombers using Russian air bases for shuttle missions, the Luftwaffe Chief of Staff Jeschonnek realized what Hitler did not understand— that Germany was on a one-way road to defeat. The newly organized Russian armies were advancing steadily; American Lend-Lease aid through Murmansk and other ports was helping these Russians armies to become much better equipped than the German ground troops, who had a scarcity of everything; the Luftwaffe was no longer capable of supplying encircled German ground troops or supporting these same ground troops during offensive action. Goering, also hearing the cry of "Where is the Luftwaffe?" retired to Karinhall, one of his homes, and left Jeschonnek to face the responsibility. Finally, the Chief of Staff could no longer take the pressure; on August 20, 1943, while his staff gathered for the morning's situation discussion, Jeschon-nek retired to his small blockhouse and shot himself.

For all practical purposes the value of the Luftwaffe, as far as any major operation on the eastern front was concerned, ended with the failure of "Operation Citadel." General Gunther Korten, who previously commanded Luftwaffe I on the eastern front and who succeeded Jeschonnek as Luftwaffe Chief of Staff, decided to form "pure" fighter units for the fight on the eastern front and for the defense in the west against the American strategic bombers. He knew that the Soviet Union did not have a strategic bomber force and he was completely unaware that the USAAF was considering using heavy bombers from Soviet air bases. Korten decided that the German fighter planes would aid the Nazi cause much more than tactical bombers supporting German ground troops. However, he maintained a total of about 350 bombers for the battle against the ever-increasing Soviet war industry, which Korten gave credit for the successes of the Red Army ground troops. He decided that through a well-planned and intensive air war against Soviet industrial plants and rail centers he could expect relief from the pressure of the Red Army attacks. A fifty-percent reduction in Soviet electricity output would shut down the most important plants in the Moscow area and along the upper Volga and a similar production loss in Soviet aircraft engine manufacturing would definitely affect the Russian air activities within a few weeks.

Unfortunately, while his basic idea was good, Korten did not consider several important factors such as the ever-changing front lines and the constantly growing Red Air Force. The strength of the Russian air units on November 1, 1943, not counting training planes, was estimated at 23,000 aircraft. The Luftwaffe on this date had a total of 350 bombers consisting of: KG 4, with two groups and one unit of He-111 target-finder planes; KG 27, with two groups of He-111s; KG 53 and 54, with three groups of He-111s each; and KG 3, with one group of Ju-88s.

Despite these odds, Korten still wanted to begin the Russian war industry bombing project. Meister, not so confident, suggested that in order to prove the feasibility of the plan the German aircraft should start by bombing Russian trains and rail centers. Night after night Meister's IV Fliegerkorps concentrated their attacks on the central points of the Russian railroad traffic. Parts of the IV Fliegerkorps, including Antrup's unit, attacked smaller railroad stations. These were especially hard to find but the Germans could not afford to ignore them since the Russian railroad management personnel were extremely skillful. They could shift the rolling stock quickly onto undamaged tracks and keep the trains moving despite Luftwaffe attacks. Antrup and his unit tried various new tactics during the winter of 1943-44 and the spring of 1944, but with little success. Since the Russians would quickly move their trains out of the station area once a Luftwaffe marker plane had dropped a flare and before the German bombers arrived, Antrup decided to have the marker planes also carry bombs and block the exit tracks after they dropped their flares. This was better, but often the bombs from the marker planes went wide of the target and the Soviet trains escaped unharmed. In addition, the weather often changed between the time the Luftwaffe marker planes illuminated the targets and the bombers arrived, sometimes a twenty-minute interval if the plan went awry. Antrup began flying in a wide circle over the target a half-hour prior to the bombing and if the weather did change he would contact the bombers by radio and give them an alternate target.

He also tried sending his bombers out in daylight, but this resulted in heavy losses for the Luftwaffe. The German fighter planes did not have sufficient range to escort the bombers to the target and back and during the time the fighters were not with the Ju-88s and He-111s, the Russian Yaks and Aircobras shot down the bombers in large numbers. Antrup tried adding more fuel tanks to the Me-109s and FW-190s but this slowed the fighters down so much that they could not successfully combat the Russian fighter aircraft.

On June 15, 1944, Antrup was told for the first time that photographs had been obtained from an American Flying Fortress shot down near Foscani several days earlier and that the photographs indicated that B-17s and P-51s of a United States task force had used Russian airfields at Mirgorod, Piryatin, and Poltava. He and his fellow Luftwaffe pilots were disturbed by the information. For the first time during the war, American bombers were in the Soviet Union. Was this a one-attack operation or the beginning of a strong American air fleet in the east? Antrup was aware that the German fighter force was weak in the east. What would Goering do now?

The answer came quickly. "If the American bombers land at Russian air bases in the future," Meister vowed, "we shall attack!"

At that very moment the Eighth Air Force in the British Isles was preparing to fly the second "Operation Frantic" mission to the same three Soviet air bases.

Damaged B17s of "Operation Frantic" task force at Poltava after the Luftwaffe raid.

Two American crewmen were killed when they tried to take cover behind this wall outside the mess tent.

Russian soldiers unloading bombs from a truck at Mirgorod. *(Photo courtesy of James S. Stewart)*

Colonel H. E. Rice, Commanding Officer of the Second Bombardment Group, studies map during the initial "Operation Frantic" mission. *(Photo courtesy of James S. Stewart)*

This B-17 sunk into the soft earth at Mirgorod when the pilot inadvertently got off the steel-matting runway. *(Photo courtesy of James S. Stewart)*

Briefing room of Second Bombardment Group in
Italy as preparations are made for the first Russian
shuttle mission. *(Photo courtesy of James S. Stewart)*

Lieutenant General Ira C. Eaker, Commander of the Mediterranean
Allied Air Forces (center), is welcomed at an American base in the
U.S.S.R. upon completion of the first "shuttle" bombing attack of
German-occupied Europe. In the foreground are: Major General
Alexander R. Perminov, Russian commander at the base; General
Eaker, U.S. Ambassador Averell Harriman; and Captain Henry Ware
of the U.S. Military Mission to Russia. *(U.S. Air Force Photo)*

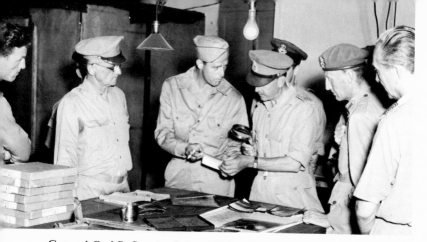

General Carl B. Spaatz, Colonel Elliott Roosevelt, General Alexander, Group Captain Humperies.

"Today there are Americans in Russia—there are a great many Americans in Russia," said Major General John R. Deans, Chief of the U.S. Military Mission to the U.S.S.R., into a Russian microphone as the first contingent of heavy bombers to utilize the new East-West shuttle bombing arrived at American bases in the Soviet Union. To his right are: U.S. Ambassador Averell Harriman, Lieutenant General Ira C. Eaker (background), and Major General Slavin of the Red Army General Staff. (*U.S. Air Force Photo*)

General Eaker and General Walsh talking with a group of Russian soldiers. *(U.S. Air Force Photo)*

First American plane to land at U.S. base in Russia: The P-38 Lightning was the first U.S. Army Air Force "shuttle" plane to land in the U.S.S.R. It was flown on a reconnaissance mission from England by Colonel Paul T. Cullen, who stayed in Russia as Deputy Commander of Operations for the Eastern Command, U.S. Strategic Air Forces in Europe.
(U.S. Air Force Photo)

U.S. flyers in Russia: Lieutenant General Ira C. Eaker, Commander in Chief of the Mediterranean Allied Air Forces, talks to a U.S. fighter pilot after loading the first U.S. shuttle-bombing mission from Italy to the Ukraine. In the background: Major General Robert Walsh and Major General A. R. Perminov, American and Russian commanders of the new U.S. Air Force bases in Russia.
(U.S. Air Force Photo)

This German air force photograph shows congratulations being given to Colonel Antrup and his famous squadron for the Poltava attack. *(Photo courtesy of J. F. Giehl)*

This German air force photo shows the bombs being loaded on the He-lll for the Poltava raid, *(Photo courtesy of J. F. Giehl)*

elwirkungsbildskizze   2.Nachtaufkl.

Flugplatz Poltawa I SU 10375

Karte 1:300 000 Blatt Y50 / Pl.Qu. 35 Ost 40 444

This German air force photograph was taken during the bombing of Poltava on the night of June 21, 1944. *(Photo courtesy of J. F. Giehl)*

9

"Frantic II"

THE EIGHTH AIR FORCE began its participation in "Operation Frantic" on June 21, 1944, on a mission that was to prove historic in many respects. The task force scheduled to continue to fly to Soviet Russia that day after bombing the assigned target was part of the largest American attack ever launched against Berlin. Not only were the American bombers participating in the shuttle-mission project on this day, a project the British were not involved with and did not approve of, but the American airmen were to use a tactic that angered RAF leaders. The British, unlike the Americans, were devoted to area bombing rather than pinpoint precision bombing, and the RAF leaders insisted that Spaatz send his planes along with theirs to Berlin on June 21 on an unprecedented daylight raid to smash the entire city. Spaatz, however, did not believe in terror tactics and after explaining his feelings to Eisenhower and AAF headquarters in Washington, he won his point and was told to direct his own forces only at legitimate military targets in Berlin. Consequently, he assigned only aircraft factories, railroad facilities, and similar impact points in the city as his bombers' targets. Hearing of his determination to strike military targets only, the British withdrew from the June 21 operation. Since Spaatz's plan was not contingent on RAF participation, the field order for the mission went over the teletype as previously planned on the night of June 20 to the 20 combat wings of heavy bombers and 23 fighter groups scheduled for the raid—2,500 American aircraft in all.

Of these 2,500 planes, 163 B-17s and 70 P-51s were assigned to "Frantic II," the second mission of "Operation Frantic." The Thirteenth Combat Bombardment Wing, with headquarters at Horham, had scheduled the Ninety-fifth Bombardment Group, the 100th Bombardment Group, and the 390th Bombardment Group to participate in the shuttle operation, while the Forty-fifth Combat Bombardment Wing, with headquarters at Snetterton Heath, lined up the Ninety-sixth Bombardment Group, the 388th Bombardment Group and the 452d Bombardment Group for the mission. To escort the B-17s to Soviet Russia, Spaatz selected the Fourth Fighter Group and the 352d Fighter Group.

Each of these combat units was composed of experienced, battle-hardened veterans of the air war over Europe. At one time, earlier in the war, Kessler himself had commanded the Ninety-fifth Bombardment Group and he had a special feeling for this unit, knowing that the airmen of the group had learned the techniques of high-altitude bombing the hard way and at the cost of many lives. With the aid of Colonel John Gerhart, one of the original officers assigned to the Eighth Air Force on its activation in January 1942, the group slowly developed into one of the best bombardment units in the European Theater of Operations. At the time of "Frantic II," the Ninety-fifth was commanded by Colonel Karl Truesdell.

If it was possible to have more misfortunes in combat than the Ninety-fifth during its early days—and it was—the 100th Bombardment Group had the dubious honor all to itself. Called the "Bloody 100th," the group earned its nickname with the blood of its own men, not that of the enemy. By June 21, 1944, those crews that were left in the 100th and destined to go to the Soviet Union were tough, shock-proof veterans of aerial combat honed into a sharp flying unit by Colonel Thomas S. Jeffrey, who had been sent to Thorpe Abbotts for that express purpose and had successfully accomplished the task. The 100th Bombardment Group was ready for "Frantic II."

A few miles away, at Framlingham, the 390th Bombardment Group under the command of Colonel Frederick W. Ott was also ready. A steady, dependable combat unit, the 390th had already received two Distinguished Unit Citations for missions to Regensburg and Schweinfurt and had participated in the violent aerial battles of "Big Week," February 20 to 25, 1944. It seemed that anytime the Luftwaffe fighter pilots spotted the Flying Fortresses with the "J" in the square block on the vertical stabilizer, the group markings of the 390th, they gave the formation a wide berth. Spaatz selected this group with no reservations for the second shuttle mission to the Soviet Union.

The bombardment groups of the Forty-fifth Combat Bombardment Wing were outstanding units of the Eighth Air Force, too. The Ninety-sixth Bombardment Group, based at Snetterton Heath, entered combat in May 1943, and had been on most of the important missions after that time until the "Frantic II" operation. Now, under the command of Lieutenant Colonel Robert J. Nolan, the Ninety-sixth was delighted to get the opportunity to add another country to its list—the Soviet Union.

The 388th Bombardment Group had not arrived in Great Britain until the middle of July 1943, but it had made up for lost time by attacking every important target in the USAAF target folder. Under the command of Colonel William B. David, the airmen flying the B-17s with the "H" on the tail had won Distinguished Unit Citations for attacking targets at Hannover, Germany, on August 17, 1943, and Brux, Czechoslovakia, on May 12, 1944. The group was destined to win another unit citation for the mission to the Soviet Union on June 21, 1944, although the crews sleeping in the barracks at Knettishall the night of the 20th were unaware they would be eating their next evening meal at Poltava in the Ukraine.

The 452d Bombardment Group, based at Deopham Green, had opened its combat activities during the air battles of February 1944, a month that was decisive for the entire USAAF. The group suffered heavily during its early operations. The crews of the 452d learned fast, however, and on April 9, 1944, only four months after starting combat operations, the group proved its mettle on a mission to Poznan. Spaatz knew that the groups "had come of age" when he heard about the mission and did not hesitate to select it and its commander Colonel Thetus C. Odom for "Frantic II."

The Fourth Fighter Group, one of the two P-51 units scheduled to fly the second shuttle mission to Soviet Russia, was commanded in June 1944, by the brilliant and gifted Colonel Donald J. Blakeslee. Blakeslee, from Fairport Harbor, Ohio, had directed his group through many aircraft changes—Spitfires, Thunderbolts, Mustangs—and many history-making air battles. While he had as much courage as any fighter pilot in the USAAF, RAF, or Luftwaffe, his most valuable asset was his matchless ability as an air commander. In combat he ruled the sky from the cockpit of his plane, keeping tight control over the 40 to 50 aircraft as they dove, turned, and climbed seeking out the enemy. He moved his planes around in the heavens like men in a chess game, using them in the most effective manner. Not that he ignored the German fighters himself since he took time out from directing long enough to shoot down 15 enemy aircraft, making him an ace three times over. When Spaatz selected Blakeslee to protect the B-17s on the second "Operation Frantic" mission he picked one of the most experienced and reliable fighter group commanders in the Eighth Air Force.

Not that the 352d Fighter Group, under the command of Colonel Joe L. Mason, was a "green" outfit. This unit had been chasing Luftwaffe planes through European skies since September 1943, and in its spare time it attacked submarine pens, V-weapon sites, factories, and other military targets. On May 8, 1944, slightly over a month before its assignment to "Operation Frantic," the 352d had been awarded a Distinguished Unit Citation for routing an attack by a numerically superior force of German interceptors while escorting bombers to targets in Brunswick. This outstanding feat brought them to the attention of Spaatz, who quickly added this group to the units picked to fly to Soviet Russia on the 21st of June.

As task force commander of the Eighth Air Force contingent, Spaatz tapped Colonel Archie J. Old, Jr., the colorful commanding officer of the Forty-fifth Combat Bombardment Wing. Olds had been awarded his pilot's wings in 1932, served at Fort Crockett, Texas, for a year, and then left the service. Not until September 1940 did he return to active duty and then as the assistant armament and chemical officer with the Twenty-ninth Bomb Group at MacDill Field, Florida, an assignment that did not forecast the excitement that was to follow. Two years later, however, he had hit his flying stride. He was then a lieutenant colonel and was commanding officer of the Ninety-sixth Bomb Group, one of the units he would lead to the Soviet Union on "Frantic II." Once he had arrived in the ETO combat zone with the Ninety-sixth, Old began flying missions as though he was afraid the war would end before he got his chance to fight the Luftwaffe. He was on the famous Schweinfurt raid of October 14, 1943, and it was nearly the end of his career. He was wounded in the hand by flak when his aircraft was shot out of formation while it was on the bomb run, but fortunately he was able to get the B-17 back to base safely. He continued to fly combat missions, ignoring his close call and the fact that he was valuable on the ground as a leader as well as in the air. Looking around for a task force commander for "Frantic II," Spaatz did not look any further than Archie Old. He knew that if any officer could make the second shuttle mission a success comparable to the "Frantic Joe" mission led by Eaker, Old was the man.

The 163 Flying Fortresses and 70 P-51s took off from the British airfields early on the morning of June 21, 1944. The weather was bad, with a ceiling over the bomber bases of only 400 feet. Old flew in the lead aircraft of the 388th Bombardment Group which led the entire task force and, as his official report indicates, he had trouble immediately after the 0530 hours take-off:

> After takeoff of lead plane it was found that gas was leaking very badly from around the filler cap on #3 main tank and it was necessary to land immediately following takeoff of the last plane. It was found that the filler cap was not screwed on prop- erly, causing gasoline to syphon. Fifty to seventy-five gallons had been lost but it was decided to take off immediately without re- fueling as assembly routes had been cut short due to the long trip ahead and time was not available to refuel. After climbing through the overcast it was found that the deputy leader had the group assembled and the lead plane was able to assume the proper posi- tion very easily.

The "Frantic II" task force, led by Old after his second take- off, left the English coast at 0707 hours and headed for the Soviet bases, a flight that Old knew would be a total of 1,441 miles for the Flying Fortresses. He had figured the mileage very carefully. The assembly over England would require 99 nautical miles; from the departure point off the English coast, Lowestoft, to the coast of Ruhland was 539 nautical miles; and from Ruh- land to Poltava was an additional 812 nautical miles. Every drop of fuel in the tanks would be required and already Old's aircraft had syphoned away approximately 75 gallons. It was not a comforting thought for the tough colonel but if it bothered him, his expression gave no indication. What did bother him, however, was the fact that 20 of his aircraft had to return to Great

Britain for various reasons, mostly mechanical, before the formation reached the enemy coast. He was not aware of it yet, but five of the P-51s had also aborted the mission.

The main targets for the 2,500 USAAF planes dispatched from Great Britain on June 21, 1944, were aircraft engine factories and marshalling yards in the outskirts of Berlin. Old kept his "Frantic II" task force with the main stream of formations until the planes neared the Nazi capital, then broke away from the other groups. As he did, the Luftwaffe fighters assigned the task of defending Berlin attacked the main group of bombers and overlooked the "Frantic II" formations heading southeast toward the Brabag complex. This industrial complex produced catalysts for the Fischer Tropsch process and two percent of all the petroleum available to the Germans. While the formations attacking Berlin were under concentrated, violent attacks by German fighters, attacks that cost the USAAF 44 bombers, Old's smaller force met only mild opposition. Despite this fact, some of the planes became separated. Twenty-six of the Flying Fortresses bombed a "target of opportunity" at nearby Elsterwerde, while one Flying Fortress hit Podlaska, Poland. Two other B-17s engaged in the only leaflet-dropping activity recorded by the Eastern Command. Old, leading the main task force of "Frantic II" in a bomber that had been seriously damaged by flak as it made landfall over the enemy coast, bombed the Brabag complex with "excellent" results. All the sections of the complex were destroyed or severely damaged except the catalyst plant.

The "Frantic II" task force continued eastward, flying high in the sunny skies, while the remainder of the USAAF bombers turned back toward their home bases in Britain. Near Bjala, Poland, several German fighters attacked Old's Russian-bound bombers but Blakeslee maneuvered his P-51s around the B-17s in such a manner that no bombers were shot down. One American fighter was lost. Old's plane was not hit by the Luftwaffe aircraft but it soon became obvious that he had a serious problem and would be fortunate if he managed to reach Poltava. The flak that had damaged his B-17 as the task force made landfall near Cukhaven had ripped a large hole in the outer right wing panel of the aircraft. At first he had not been too concerned, but later he discovered that he was losing fuel from the right "Tokyo" tanks, the small auxiliary gas tanks that made long-range bombing possible.

"Transfer the fuel from the 'Tokyo' tanks to the main tanks," he ordered.

As the B-17s droned farther eastward, however, Old wondered if his order had come too late. The plane had already syphoned out 50 to 75 gallons of fuel on takeoff when the filler cap on the number 3 main tank had been loose. If much more gas had drained from the damaged "Tokyo" tanks before he noticed the large flak hole, his plane would not reach the Soviet Union.

"Heavy clouds ahead, Colonel."

Old, who had been studying a map on his lap, looked out the cockpit window of the B-17 at the pilot's warning. Directly ahead of the "Frantic II" task force was a solid wall of clouds that extended several thousand feet higher than the formation. Ever since dropping the bombs on the target, Old had been gradually descending as he led the American bombers toward the German-Russian front. This maneuver had saved fuel and increased the airspeed of the planes, but now it appeared that he had made a mistake. If the aircraft had to climb over the towering wall of clouds, hundreds of gallons of precious fuel would be used. He studied the situation and decided he had no choice.

"Start climb," he radioed.

A few hundreds yards to the north, Colonel Jeffrey, commanding officer of the "Bloody Hundredth," heard Old's order and quickly glanced at his fuel gauges. The needles on all main tanks were already getting dangerously close to the red warning line that indicated trouble. In addition, his aircraft and, he was quite certain, the remainder of the group's planes were low on oxygen. It was a hazardous situation for the young colonel from Virginia but Jeffrey specialized in such predicaments. That was the reason he was the commanding officer of the "Bloody Hundredth," the hard-luck group that had a disaster on every mission. By the time the groups were selected for the "Frantic II" mission, however, Jeffrey was satisfied that his unit was as good as any other in the Eighth Air Force. However, he had not thought that the ultimate test would come so soon.

Low on fuel, low on oxygen, and the weather turning bad— these thoughts raced through his mind as he studied the instrument panel in front of him and then stared straight ahead at the wall of clouds. He, like Old, realized that there was no alternative.

"Let's start climbing."

Old led his "Frantic II" task force to 20,000 feet altitude before the B-17s finally broke out into clear sky. Meanwhile, Blakeslee realized that if he wanted to get his fighters onto Russian soil safely he would have to leave the bombers immediately. The P-51s had a limited fuel supply compared to the heavy bombers and the bad weather, added to the aerial battle in Poland, had drained the tanks faster than anticipated. He was aware that one plane of the Fourth Fighter Group had been lost. He did not want to lose any more. With a wave of his hand to Old in the cockpit of the lead B-17, Blakeslee banked his P-51 away from the bomber formations and headed for Piryatin, followed by the remainder of the fighter plane force.

Old leveled off the "Frantic II" task force bomber formations just above the peak of the cloud wall, his altimeter indicating 20,100 feet. As far as he could see ahead of his plane the clouds completely obscured the ground and it was obvious to the veteran air officer that he was going to have difficulty locating the Russian air bases unless the radio homing beacons were operating. When he checked with the radio operator on the aircraft, however, he received only discouraging news.

"The signal comes in strong at intervals," the operator explained, "but most of the time I can't pick it up at all. Evidently it is only being transmitted intermittently."

"Roger. Check our position every chance you get," he told the radio operator.

Old knew that the Soviet officials were not in favor of the American personnel transmitting the homing beacon because they feared that the Luftwaffe pilots would use it to locate military targets inside Russia. It appeared that they were disrupting the transmittal of the signal at a time when the American formation needed it desperately. But there was nothing Old could do about this at the moment. Instructing the lead navigator to concentrate on dead reckoning techniques and to watch for an opening in the solid blanket of clouds beneath the planes, Old led his "Frantic II" task force east. Suddenly, over Poland, he became aware that the task force was not alone.

Shortly after passing Warsaw it was noticed that a German single-engine fighter was keeping pace with the task force, flying just above the low broken clouds, [at] about eleven o'clock. The friendly fighters were contacted and told the position of the enemy fighter.

Although Blakeslee had already led his fighter aircraft away from the formation, when he received the message from Old about the German plane tagging along with the "Frantic II" bombers, he returned to the formation with several of his P-51s. It was a waste of time, as Old explained in his official report.

When our fighters came back to the head of the column, the enemy fighter would duck below the clouds to the deck. Then later it would take up its original position. The German plane kept pace with the task force until bad weather at the Russian front was reached.

Finally, in the late afternoon, Old had no choice but to begin a letdown through the clouds with this force of heavy bombers. According to his navigator they were approaching the vicinity of the Soviet air bases but there was an even more important reason for the immediate descent despite the solid undercast—the emergency radio calls he was receiving from the pilots of the formation.

"Low on fuel. One engine has cut out!"

"Enough gas for ten minutes!"

"Shall we bail out when we exhaust our fuel or try to crash-land in Soviet territory?"

Old's reply to all the calls was a terse: "Stay with the formation. We are approaching our destination."

Farther to the north, Jeffrey had led the "Bloody Hundredth" down through the clouds and was flying over the neat, bunched squares of collective farms at an altitude of 4,000 feet. He, too, was receiving emergency calls from the aircraft in his formation. Finally he received a call that could not be ignored.

"Fuel exhausted! Engines quitting! Shall we bail out?"

Jeffrey looked down at the flat farmlands below and made a quick decision.

"Do not bail out. Repeat, do not bail out. Make an emergency landing on one of the farm fields. Do you understand?"

The answer was immediate, the voice of the pilot confident.

"Roger. Will set this baby down in a Russian farmer's back yard."

A few seconds later the colonel saw one of the B-17s ease away from the formation and begin a slow, controlled descent. He watched the pilot of the Flying Fortress maneuver the big bomber skilfully toward a large field a few miles south of the bomber's planned flight course and saw him set up a downwind leg and a base leg of a landing pattern just as though he was preparing to land back at Thorpe Abbotts on the hard runway.

"Easy, fellow. Take it easy . . . easy . . . easy . . . !"

Jeffrey held his breath during the last few seconds of the emergency landing of the Flying Fortress on the Russian farm, but he had no cause for worry. The B-17 settled on the ground, bounced gently twice, and came to a stop.

"Are you okay?" Jeffrey radioed.

"Not a scratch, not a scratch!"

Eventually seven of the Flying Fortresses of the "Frantic II" task force made emergency landings on Soviet soil before reaching the designated air bases at Poltava, Mirgorod, or Piryatin. The pilots of some of these aircraft located Russian bases other than the three designated air bases provided for the use of the American planes and landed at these airfields rather than on a farmer's field. Overjoyed at finding a suitable runway, the American pilots never gave a thought to the fact that the Russians at these air bases might not welcome them with open arms. After all, the Soviet Union and the United States were allies fighting on the same side against the Axis powers. Why shouldn't one ally help another? Unfortunately, it was not quite that simple and it took all the resourcefulness of the irrepressible Americans to out-maneuver and outbluff the stolid Russians.

As one American pilot headed for a landing at a Soviet air base near Kiev, two Red Air Force fighter planes roared directly toward his plane. He flipped the wing of the big bomber up so the Russian pilots could see the insignia of the USAAF clearly, thinking that this would avoid any "misunderstanding," but the Yaks continued to close on the B-17. As the pilot said later, "Our gunners were always taught to fire at any fighter that came head on at the plane. USAAF fighter pilots knew this and kept their distance but these Russians either weren't aware of the fact or didn't care."

A waist gunner aboard the descending B-17 fired a warning burst at the two Yaks. That was enough. As soon as the Russian pilots saw the .50-caliber tracers crossing in front of their air-craft, they abruptly dove toward the ground. One of the Yaks nearly crashed before he managed to pull his plane out of the steep dive he had put it in. Neither Red Air Force plane came near the B-17 again.

After the American pilot landed, he warned his crew to expect an angry greeting from the Russian personnel at the air base because of the incident. Instead, the crew was met by the com-manding officer of the Red Air Force fighter unit based at the field, who was laughing uproariously. Through an interpreter, he explained that he had not laughed so hard in months as he had when the waist gunner fired at the two planes he had sent up to escort the Flying Fortress to the field.

"Scared rabbits! They ran like scared rabbits!" he bellowed, pointing to two red-faced young Russian pilots standing beside him.

The American pilot tried to apologize for the incident and to explain why his waist gunner had fired, but the Russian colonel would not stop laughing. Just exactly what the Russian Air Force commanding officer had expected the two Russian pilots to do was never explained, but the "Frantic II" crew was glad they had not fired back.

At another Soviet air base near Kiev, a Flying Fortress pilot made a successful landing despite the fact that the plane's fuel tanks were dry. All he needed was enough fuel to fly to Poltava but the sour-faced, rude Russian colonel in charge of the base refused flatly to provide the necessary aviation gas. The American pilot could see by the markings on the fuel drums that it was fuel shipped to the Soviet Union from the United States through Lend-Lease but even when he mentioned this, the Russian colonel just shrugged his shoulders and kept muttering "Nyet!" It appeared that the Americans were in for a long stay at the Russian base or, worse yet, might end up in an internment camp like several other American crews shot down on missions to Poland (other than shuttle missions). This was not good. Suddenly he had an idea. He had a case of American whiskey on board his aircraft to be used at the debriefing sessions in the Soviet Union—the airmen were each given two ounces of whiskey after debriefing if they wanted it—and he wondered if he could "bribe" or influence the stubborn Russian colonel with it. He decided it was worth a try. Within an hour after opening the first bottle of whiskey and sharing it with the Soviet officer, the B-17 was refueled and ready for takeoff. The Russian colonel was so enthused with the Americans by this time he was ready to fly to Poltava with them, but they finally dissuaded him from boarding the B-17.

Fortunately, as Old led his task force farther east under the clouds, the homing beacons at Mirgorod and Poltava began operating steadily and the remainder of the bombers reached the air base safely. Despite their being low on fuel, Old led the B-17s across the field at Poltava in perfect formation, just as Eaker had led the "Frantic Joe" bombers nineteen days earlier on his arrival from Italy. One by one the huge bombers "peeled off" and landed. As soon as the Flying Fortresses were down, the pilots were directed to taxi the bombers to dispersal areas around the main runway. However, since the air base was relatively small, the B-17s ended up parked close together anyway. Fourteen of the Flying Fortresses were parked on the turf at the north end of the air base, while the other fifty-nine that had landed at Poltava were spread out in a gentle arc parallel to the western side of the runway. Three B-17s occupied the only blast-proof revetments on the field. The others were completely in the open.

The Thirteenth Combat Bombardment Wing consisting of the Ninety-fifth, 100th, and 390th Bombardment groups landed at Mirgorod and parked their aircraft in similar manner. Blakeslee's P-51s touched down at Piryatin and were dispersed as much as was possible under the circumstances. Comparing this situation to the dispersal hardstands at their home base in Britain, neither the bomber commanders nor the fighter commanders were happy with the conditions at the Russian airfields, but there was nothing they could do about it. They had been forewarned that Eaker had complained bitterly about the defense setup at the Soviet air bases, and that he did not think the measures taken by the Russians were adequate, but the Eighth Air Force officers had not realized just how dangerous the situation was until they saw it with their own eyes.

Old and his fliers received a welcoming reception from the American and Russian personnel at the air base and then Old was shown to his temporary quarters in the headquarters building at Poltava. Before he went into the room to wash and change clothes, Walsh and Kessler told him that the Russians were giving a dinner in his honor.

"Promptly at 10:00 P.M.," Kessler said. "I'll pick you up."

At the air base everything became quiet as darkness fell across the desolate area. Selected American crewmen remained with the aircraft as guards while the others went to their temporary housing quarters—which turned out to be tents, not houses or barracks. By 10:00 P.M. all work at the field had ended and the Flying Fortresses stood mute in the black night.

High in the black sky Hans Mueller maneuvered his He-177 carefully as he made a slow descent for the hidden German airfield at Minsk. He did not want to make any mistakes now that he had the photographs of the American bombers on the Russian air base at Poltava in his cameras. As his wheels touched down on the runway, Mueller grinned. Within ten minutes the pictures would be in Willi Antrup's hands. Colonel Antrup would know what to do.

10

Disaster at Poltava

THE ANTEROOM of the Luftwaffe headquarters building at Minsk was busy on the afternoon of June 21, 1944. The teletype was chattering incessantly and the military clerks were rushing back and forth throughout the building. It was obvious that an operation was pending, that every man in the building was anticipating an important order. Suddenly a telephone rang and the lieutenant at the desk in the middle of the room answered it immediately. All talking in the room ceased as did the noise of the teletype and the typewriters.

"Yes . . . all right . . . understood . . . at once . . . !"

The lieutenant hung up the telephone and rushed to the now-quiet teletype. By the time he reached the instrument it was chattering again, printing letters that quickly became words that just as quickly formed sentences. As the lieutenant followed the text of the message he glanced several times at the map on the wall. When the teletype stopped, he tore off the message and hurried toward the room of his commanding officer, Colonel Wilhelm Antrup.

As he walked into the office of the commanding officer, Antrup looked up. "What is it? More forms to fill out?"

Antrup feared that the lieutenant had a clerical mess with which he wanted help. He had seen the paper in the man's hand and as far as Antrup was concerned paper work and red tape were worse than fighting American or British airmen.

"No, Colonel. The American bombers have landed at Poltava!"

Antrup's face broke into a smile and he quickly got to his feet. "That is different."

He grabbed the message from the lieutenant's hand and studied it carefully. He read it once, twice, a third time. Finally he patted the lieutenant on the shoulder. "Great! Really great! I can hardly believe our luck!"

Before he could leave his office, Mueller, the reconnaissance pilot who had flown over Poltava at sunset in his He-177, arrived and handed Antrup the photographs he had taken. Antrup studied them as carefully as he had studied the teletype message a few minutes earlier. "This will make it easy for us," he said to the lieutenant. "Very easy."

Antrup hurried to the operations officer and shoved the message and photographs in front of him. "Order all squadrons on immediate alert for 2045 hours. Notify the planes that are in the air to return to the base at once."

After he had made certain that his orders were being carried out, Antrup walked across the grass to the small officer's club where his group commanders were gathered. They had just finished eating and were enjoying their coffee and cigarettes in the lounge room. When Antrup walked into the room, they quickly got to their feet, aware that he would not be in the club unless something special was up.

"I don't like to disturb you," Antrup said, "but as of now all units are on alert for standby preparation at 2045 hours tonight. Please make all necessary arrangements. Instead of the normal patrol flights tonight there is finally something rewarding for you. I will expect you in fifteen minutes at my combat station."

When the group commanders were gathered at the squadron combat station at the appointed time, Antrup acquainted them with the situation, including information on additional B-17s at Mirgorod.

"Tonight you will attack the airfields at Poltava and Mirgorod. It is important that we destroy the American bombers at both fields simultaneously. The target markers and lighters have their exact orders. We will attack from an altitude of 4,000 to 5,000 meters. Sector attack from the northwest at 2400 hours to 0015 hours at both targets. Is that understood?"

The group commanders nodded. There were no questions.

While Antrup checked further on the situation by telephone, the Luftwaffe pilots and crewmen put on their fur-lined flying suits, pulled on their heavy boots and strapped their parachute harnesses tight. By 2015 hours most of German airmen were at their aircraft. In addition to KG 55, Antrup's unit, KG 4, KG 27 and KG 53 had also been alerted for the mission and these units were making similar preparations. At exactly 2045 hours the Luftwaffe pilots and crewmen climbed into their HE-111s and Ju-88s, settled into the crew positions, and waited expectantly for the green, red, white, and blue flares, a different color for each squadron, that would signal time to start engines.

The signals came at 2100 hours and within minutes the air base at Minsk was filled with the noise of the German aircraft moving toward the takeoff runway. Antrup led his unit into the air. As soon as he was airborne, the colonel began a wide circle around the air base so that his wingmen could catch up, and then headed eastward . . . toward Poltava and the American bombers. Fifty miles east of Minsk, the Me-109s and FW-190s assigned to escort the Luftwaffe bombers across the German-Russian front and into Soviet territory joined Antrup's formation and wove a defensive pattern above the bombers.

The colonel was delighted finally to be on an operational mission that had real meaning, one that, if successful, could be evaluated in terms of damage inflicted on the enemy. For weeks all his men had accomplished were night patrol flights, assignments that were frustrating to the veteran Luftwaffe pilots, but flights that were necessary for more reasons than one. Not only were such missions required in order to warn the ground troops of approaching enemy aircraft but because of the weakened condition of the Luftwaffe on the eastern front, the patrol flights were the only type of mission possible. Until this night, there had not been enough Luftwaffe aircraft in one area to launch an attack on the enemy. Only the fact that Meister had decided that the American bombers on the Russian airfields were too good a target to ignore were there so many Ju-88s and He-111s available for the raid on Mirgorod and Poltava. Antrup looked out of the window and checked on the 2,000-kilo bombs hanging under the wings. The bombs were all right. Inside the He-111 there was no conversation between Antrup and his crew. The five men had flown together almost the entire war, could depend upon each other completely, and had no need for words as the German bomber droned eastward above the clouds. Now and then they glanced at each other as they spotted flak guns firing at their plane through holes in the undercast but even then there was nothing to say. The antiaircraft shells would either hit or they would miss, and words wouldn't mean much in either case.

Five minutes after his He-111 crossed the German-Russian front, Antrup saw several Yak fighters heading directly toward his formation. Quickly he picked up his microphone and pressed the button.

"Enemy fighters at two o'clock level."

The Me-109s that were accompanying KG 55 banked sharply toward the oncoming Russian fighters silhouetted by the moonlight and Antrup saw the bright flashes of their cannon as the Luftwaffe pilots attacked. He also saw the guns on the Yak fighters blinking and a Me-109 to his right veered sharply away. It was obvious that the German plane had been hit. Two other Me-109s quickly joined the fray, however, and while the damaged German fighter limped back toward its base, the newcomers blasted the Yak out of the sky in a ball of orange-colored flame. Within ten minutes the Russian attackers had disappeared, either shot down or running for home, and Antrup settled back in his seat and breathed easier. He glanced at his watch. One more hour and they would be over Poltava. . . .

Kessler picked Old up at 10:00 P.M. as he had promised and he, Old, and Walsh went to the dining hall where Perminov had arranged a late dinner in honor of the new "Operation Frantic" task force commander. Old was tired but his change of clothes and the short rest had not only helped him regain his physical strength but had also revived his spirits. He looked forward to the dinner with the Russian commander at Poltava and to renewing his friendship with Kessler, whom he had not seen for several months. Old's enthusiasm was matched by the others and the dinner went very well. The food, by Russian standards, was excellent, there was plenty of vodka and American whiskey, and the conversation was interesting. At 2335 hours, just as Old leaned back in his chair to listen to a joke being told by Kessler, a Russian soldier rushed into the dining room and handed Perminov a message. The Soviet officer read it and looked at Walsh and Kessler.

"German aircraft have crossed the Russian front lines and are headed toward this area."

Walsh nodded. Turning to Old, he said, "This happens quite

often but I think we had better sound the alarm. The German bombers never come this far, but who can tell?" he shrugged his shoulders.

A minute later the air raid alarms sounded and Walsh explained to Old that the sirens had been given to the Russians only a week earlier by the United States through Lend-Lease. Eaker had insisted that the sirens were needed after his visit with the "Frantic Joe" task force.

The three American officers and their Russian hosts resumed their dinner. Outside the dining hall, most of the American crewmen had hurried to the slit trenches provided for protection against possible enemy air raids but a few, accustomed to the German nuisance raids over the British Isles in 1944, stayed in their tents. Others, worn out by the long flight that day from their bases in Great Britain, were sleeping so soundly they didn't even hear the sirens. Kenneth Leininger, a pilot attached to the 337th Squadron of the Ninety-sixth Bombardment Group, was one of the crewmen who did not hear the alarm. A friend awoke him and told him the Germans were coming, but Leininger was so sleepy that he told his friend to "scram" and promptly went back to sleep. Later, he regretted this action.

Twice more the Russian soldier came into the dining room and handed Perminov a message and each time the warning was the same: "German aircraft headed toward Poltava." When the soldier appeared the third time, Perminov glanced at the message, got to his feet, and said, "I think we should go to the slit trenches!"

Old insisted on making a quick check of his crews but once he was certain that the majority of the crewmen had already gone to the slit trenches and had warned the others to do so immediately, he followed Perminov, Kessler, and Walsh to the special trench prepared for the headquarters personnel. Once he was in the trench, Old looked skyward. All he could see were a few stars. There was not an aircraft in sight. . . .

A few miles west of Poltava, Antrup was delighted to see the clouds disappear. He could see the ground clearly and, despite the blackout precautions always enforced by the Russians, it was easy to spot a light here and there below. Even a soldier lighting a cigarette out in the open was plainly visible from his aircraft, as was the momentary glow of a flashlight beam or the shaft of light from a doorway as it was quickly opened and closed as someone entered or departed from a building. Antrup could not locate the Poltava air base but he was not worried. This was the job of the marker aircraft. Yet he knew they were very close to the target area. Very close.

"Pilot to crew, prepare for attack!"

The one-sentence warning was all that was necessary for the veterans flying with him. Once they saw the flares that would be dropped by the marker aircraft to illuminate the target, each of the He-111 crewmen would know exactly what to do and how to do it.

The minutes seemed much longer now to Antrup as his aircraft droned through the black sky still on an eastward course. He looked at his watch several times and silently wondered if he had overshot the Poltava area. Where were the flares? Were the marker planes lost? What was . . .!

"Flare! Flare!"

At exactly 0030—thirty minutes past midnight—the black sky was suddenly pierced by the illumination flares dropped by the Luftwaffe marker aircraft. The marker pilots and navigators had carried out their assignment perfectly. Directly ahead of his He-111, Antrup saw the B-17s of the USAAF lined up on the airfield at Poltava just as clearly as though it were daylight. The sight was surprising, so unbelievable after months of seeing nothing but an occasional Yak in the sky while on patrol, that for a moment Antrup couldn't speak. Never in his life, never during the entire war, had he seen such a target!

"Climb to attack altitude," he ordered, regaining his voice.

As the He-111 slowly gained altitude, Antrup kept staring at the fantastic sight below him, afraid that the B-17s might suddenly disappear before he had a chance to drop his bombs, afraid that he would awaken to find that he was only dreaming. He discovered that it definitely was not a dream, however, when the altimeter needle reached 4,000 meters, the attack altitude, and the Flying Fortresses were still sitting on the Soviet air base as before, unprotected and vulnerable.

"This is going to be like a practice exercise," he muttered. "This will be easy."

It was.

W. L. White, the well-known author and reporter, had arrived at Poltava on the morning of June 21, 1944, after a hectic trip from Moscow with writers from *Izvestia, Red Star,* and *Pravda,* plus several other American reporters. The Russians had told him to be at the Moscow airport sharply at 5:00 A.M. that morning, but when he arrived, White discovered that the flight had been delayed until 9:00 A.M. After a bumpy, erratic flight to Poltava in a Soviet-built Douglas transport, White and Eddy Gilmore, a reporter experienced in the ways of the Russians, arranged for sleeping quarters in the hospital area instead of the Soviet Pullman car reserved for reporters since Gilmore said the railroad car was infested with bedbugs. They unloaded their duffel bags on the beds given to them by a medical officer and then walked around the air base talking with the waiting American and Russian officers. When Old's "Frantic II" task force landed, White interviewed several of the aircrew before he and Gilmore decided to get something to eat at the mess used by the Red Army officers. Halfway to the mess, an antiaircraft gun at the edge of the air base began firing. White looked up and saw a silvery vapor trail high in the sky directly over the base.

"Probably a German recon plane," Gilmore said.

"Do the Luftwaffe bombers follow?" White asked, familiar with USAAF procedures.

"They haven't yet. Probably afraid of the Russian fighters between here and the front."

The dot that was Hans Mueller in his He-177 slowly turned back toward the west, toward Minsk, while the Russian ack-ack bursts trailed his aircraft. He had the photographs he needed.

After eating a dinner of cabbage soup and kasha at the Red Army officer's mess, White wrote a letter home and then joined some other Americans for a sight-seeing trip into Poltava. At 11:30 P.M., after meeting and talking with several Russian citizens in the city and walking through the well-kept park that the Germans had left intact when they retreated, White and his companions piled into their weapons carrier and headed back toward the air base. When they arrived they were informed that an air raid alert had been sounded, and that German aircraft were reported crossing the German-Russian front lines on course for the Poltava area. As White prepared to go to bed in the hospital area he asked the medical officer who had provided them with the sleeping quarters if such alerts were common.

"No, not exactly common, but we had one about a week ago."

"What happened?"

"Nothing. False alarm."

White then asked the question that had bothered Eaker and several of the American officers associated with "Operation Frantic."

"Have you ever seen any Russian night fighters?"

"No. Not one. Evidently the Soviets have them stationed at another base."

This was exactly what Stalin wanted the Americans to believe and by avoiding a direct answer to the informal and formal queries he managed to convince Washington that the Soviet Union had sufficient night fighter squadrons to protect the American bombers while the planes were on Russian soil.

Just after White had put his pajamas on, he heard the Russian antiaircraft guns firing again and he stepped outside his tent to see what was happening. An American officer standing near the tent in the dark muttered, "Can't see what the hell they are firing at up there? They must be jumpy because of that recon plane that overflew the base late this afternoon."

The guns continued to fire. White could tell by the sound of the guns that they were either .50-caliber machine guns or similar weapons, not the heavy guns used by the British or Germans.

"Do you hear any night fighters?" White asked, still concerned over the defense setup at Poltava, more for personal reasons at the moment than military reasons.

Both men listened intently for several seconds and then agreed that they could hear neither bombers nor fighters in the sky. All they could hear was the occasional firing of the Soviet antiaircraft guns.

"Do you know where the slit trenches are?" the officer asked White.

When White replied in the negative, the American officer suggested that he show White where they were since there might not be time to hunt for the slit trenches if an emergency occurred later and he wanted to use them for protection. Rather than take time to change back into his regular clothes, White followed the officer wearing only his lightweight pajamas. They had reached the slit trenches and the officer was pointing out where they began and ended when a brilliant flare suddenly lit up the entire area. As White said later, "That flare was so bright I could even see the little design on my pajamas—which was of no interest to me at the moment at all."

"My God," the officer exclaimed. "There must be German planes up there. Let's get in the trench."

He didn't wait for White to answer. He leaped into the slit trench and White jumped in beside him. In the daylight light of the marker flare, White could see the Flying Fortresses on the air base distinctly, the aircrewmen racing frantically toward the slit trenches, and the air-raid siren screaming in one continuous blast. He also heard one other sound—the deadly whistle of a falling bomb!

Above the air base Antrup maneuvered his He-111 carefully as his bombardier lined up the Flying Fortresses below in his bomb sight. He made only one remark to the bombardier: "Do not bomb the tents!" He watched as the bombardier delicately made last-minute adjustments on his sight, saw the veteran's thumb move slowly toward the small red bomb-release button, and smiled as the thumb pressed the button firmly.

"Bombs are falling!" the bombardier reported calmly.

Antrup immediately banked his He-111 to the left so that he could observe the effect of the high explosives the bombardier had just released. For what seemed an eternity there was no indication that the bombs had even reached the air base but then, just as Antrup was becoming concerned, there was a flash as bright as a streak of lightning, followed by a series of similar flashes. In the illumination of the marker flares still hanging over the air base, the Luftwaffe colonel saw thick black smoke clouds billow up from the field, the origin of which appeared to be directly in the midst of the parked Flying Fortresses of the USAAF.

Pleased with the results of the bombing, Antrup checked the sky for a sign of Russian night fighters. He knew that his bombers had been reported by Russian observers at the front lines since it was impossible to "sneak" 80 Ju-88s and He-111s into enemy territory without being spotted. Antrup anticipated that the Red Air Force would defend their air bases with every resource at their command and he had briefed his crews to be prepared for a violent air battle. Why the Yaks or Aircobras had not yet made an appearance puzzled him.

The colonel continued to circle Poltava as the other Luftwaffe units bombed the Russian air base. He saw Graubner lead his KG 4 bombers over the parked B-17s, maneuvering them into perfect position for bombing, and he grinned widely as the high explosives burst in the midst of the silver Flying Fortresses. Rudi Miller's KG 27 came roaring in next and the attack of this unit was just as accurate and just as devastating. While he waited for Pockrandt to make his bombing pass with his famous "Legion Kondor" outfit, Antrup once again searched the sky for Soviet night fighters. There was not a single Red Air Force plane in the area. He looked at his watch. 0135 hours. He had been over the air base for nearly an hour-and-a-half and the Soviet fighters had not even tried to attack his bombers.

"Incredible!" Antrup muttered.

At that moment the "Legion Kondor" unit—KG 53—crossed above Poltava and dropped their bombs. As Antrup had expected, this veteran outfit matched the accuracy of the other Luftwaffe units that had bombed the American heavy bombers earlier. The air base below was a mass of flames, twisted metal, and exploding fuel dumps. Antrup had never witnessed a more successful mission during his entire combat career . . . and he was aware that more was to come.

On the ground the Americans in the slit trenches were also concerned over the absence of the Red Air Force night fighters, the defending aircraft that Stalin had promised could drive off any Luftwaffe attack. Walsh, Kessler, and Old, huddled in the slit trench, stared at the sky and shook their heads in frustration.

"Those damn bombers have been flying around overhead for more than an hour," Kessler said. "Where the hell is the Red Air Force?"

There was no answer. All the Americans could do was stay low in the slit trenches and watch their valuable task force bombers burn and explode as Antrup and his companions dropped their high-explosive bombs. Another American at the scene that night was Colonel E. D. Gray of the Eighth Air Force and he, too, was amazed at the lack of opposition to the German attackers.

"Not a single Russian fighter up there," he told an American lieutenant beside him in the trench. "I can't understand it."

The lieutenant, a pilot of a B-17 who had just arrived with the

"Frantic II" task force that day, roundly cursed Stalin as another bomb exploded on the base. "I never did trust those damn Russians. Now I know why."

Suddenly, at 0145 hours the attack stopped. The men in the slit trenches cautiously began peering over the sides of the protective ditches, staring at the burning wreckage of their bombers, calling to friends in the darkness to check if there were any injuries, and glancing skyward every few seconds to see if any more Luftwaffe attackers were in the area. As the last of the marker flares died out and darkness once again swept over Poltava, a few of the more adventurous Americans climbed out of the slit trenches and began walking toward the flaming holocaust that had been their Flying Fortresses. Gray joined another officer heading toward the aircraft but he had walked only a few steps when he tripped over an object on the ground. Looking down, he discovered it was an American aircrewman sound asleep. Not even the loud blasts that intermittently sounded above the roaring of the flames as the drums of high-octane gas in the storage dump exploded awakened him. Gray had just about decided to walk on when suddenly he heard a loud noise that he recognized immediately.

"They're coming back!" he yelled to other Americans in the area. "Get back in the trenches." He kicked the sleeping form on the ground. "Get in the trenches, buddy, before you get killed."

The man he kicked, the sleeping pilot from the Ninety-sixth Bombardment Group, Kenneth Leininger, got to his feet and raced to the nearest trench. This action probably saved his life because a moment later the Ju-88s came screaming over Poltava at low level dropping antipersonnel bombs and strafing the area. Two other Americans were not so fortunate. Flight Officer Joseph G. Lukacek, a B-17 copilot, was killed, and Lieutenant Raymond C. Estle, a pilot, was seriously wounded during this second phase of the Luftwaffe attack as they tried to hide behind a brick wall. Estle later died from his wounds. For twenty minutes the German planes crisscrossed the Russian air base while the helpless Americans crouched in the slit trenches, unable to fight back in any way. During this period, not a single Red Air Force fighter plane appeared. Finally, at 0220 hours, Antrup and the Luftwaffe attackers turned westward and headed back toward their bases.

They had not lost a plane and had not encountered an enemy fighter plane.

White, the war correspondent who was huddling in the slit trench in his pajamas, was trembling, partially from the cold, partially from nervousness. During the lull in the attack at 0145 hours he decided to make a run for his tent in hope of getting his uniform. He reached his tent in the hospital area without trouble but soon discovered that his uniform had been torn to pieces by shrapnel that had pierced the walls of his tent. There was a steel helmet in the tent, left there by some former occupant, so in desperation White grabbed it and tried to put it on his head only to discover that it was filled with chocolate bars that had melted during the heat of a summer day and were now frozen solid by the cold of the night. Throwing the helmet away, he started for the door of the tent when he suddenly began to choke from smoke. Looking at his bed, he discovered that the mattress had been set on fire by a white-hot bomb fragment. To save the tent from burning, he dragged the mattress outside into the alley. He took a blanket with him and headed back toward the slit trench. It was fortunate he did so because a few seconds later the Ju-88s began their low-level passes over the airfield. Like the other Americans, White huddled in the trench, wrapped in his blanket, until a sudden bright flash high in the sky attracted his attention.

"Raid's over," the veteran Gilmore said. "That was a magnesium flash bomb used by a reconnaissance plane to photograph the damage. Boy, those guys are going to have a real story to tell Hitler tonight!"

After waiting several minutes and trying to determine whether the explosions still rocking the air base were from the bombs aboard the flaming Flying Fortresses, drums of gasoline at the fuel dump, or more German bombs, White climbed out of the slit trench for a second time and gingerly picked his way toward the headquarters building. Several times Russian personnel warned him that "butterfly" mines were scattered everywhere and that if he stepped on one it was certain death. He tried to stay on the path that led to the headquarters building because it was much easier to see the butterfly mines on it than in the heavy growth at the sides of the path. As he neared the building, he saw Walsh getting into a jeep to check the damage to the task force aircraft. Walsh, too, warned him about the dangerous mines.

Gray was only a short distance away from White in the darkness, a darkness that was tinted pink by the flames of the burning B-17s and which permitted the colonel to check the ground ahead of him as he walked. He, too, was trying to get back to the headquarters building without tramping on a butterfly mine. Suddenly, he changed his mind and decided to try to get down to the flight line in order to assess the damage inflicted on the "Frantic II" bombers by the Luftwaffe. When he reached the perimeter of the parking area he saw a fantastic sight, a sight that revealed both the courage and the incompetence of the Soviets. Squads of Russians, men and women, were trying futilely to extinguish the thermite and gasoline flames with shovels and sticks of wood. Not only were they not getting the fires under control but every time the wing tanks on a Flying Fortress exploded, a number of the Russians were killed or injured! While he had nothing but disgust for the Soviet leaders who had not provided night fighters to defend the air base, Gray had the highest praise for the ordinary Russian soldier and civilian who fought the fires so valiantly that night.

After watching the fires and explosions for several minutes, Gray picked his way to the headquarters building. White was already inside questioning a sergeant about contacting Moscow. The sergeant shook his head.

"All our radio contact with the outside is cut. Even the Red Army radios are knocked out."

Upstairs, White discovered several Soviet officers gathered around a conference table staring at each other, not making any move to go to the airfield to survey the damage. They treated him courteously but all seemed stunned at the events of the night, and did not seem to know what to do.

"Probably waiting for orders from Stalin," another correspondent said. "They can't even take a piss without asking the Kremlin."

Finally, with nothing else to learn at headquarters and with hope of getting further details of the disaster, Gilmore, White, Gray, and several other American correspondents and officers headed for the parking area where the Flying Fortresses—or what was left of them—were located. It took them several minutes to reach the scene because every step was dangerous. They took turns in the lead since the leader had to make certain the path was clear of the butterfly mines. The mines usually glittered in the light of the flames and were fairly easy to see but White knew there could be only one mistake. An American pilot, Art Stennis, had the closest call. His foot was nearly touching the ground when an exploding fuel tank lighted a butterfly mine directly under the sole of his shoe. It took him five minutes before he had nerve enough to move again.

Eventually the group reached the air base, where they joined Kessler, Walsh, and Old, who were staring at the sickening sight. Antrup and his Ju-88s and He-111s had done an excellent job. Where the Flying Fortresses had been sitting more closely, the Luftwaffe had dropped incendiaries of the same type used on London four years earlier. Once the incendiaries started a B-17 burning, the fire quickly spread to the other planes around it. The entire area consisted of gutted Flying Fortresses that looked like huge birds lying on the ground with their backs broken. There was just enough remaining of each bomber so that an observer could identify it as formerly being a B-17, just enough left to break the heart of a crewman who had flown in the plane many times before the fateful trip to Poltava.

In the area where the American heavy bombers had been parked farther apart, Antrup and his wingmen had dropped high explosives. Many of these Flying Fortresses appeared intact until Gray and the others walked closer and saw that the fuselages and wings had hundreds of tiny holes in them, which indicated that the control cables, fuel and oil lines, electrical wiring, and other vital parts of the plane had been destroyed. In addition, the Luftwaffe bombardiers had cratered the runway with huge bombs, making it impossible for any of the Flying Fortresses still flyable to take off anyway.

"Hitler should give each Luftwaffe pilot the Iron Cross," an American lieutenant muttered as he looked at the smoldering debris and bomb-riddled air base. "With diamonds."

The method the Russians were using to clear the air base of the butterfly mines attracted nearly as much attention from the Americans gathered at the flight line as the wreckage of their aircraft. A line of Russians advanced across the field looking for the mines. When they saw one, the leader would call out and the entire line would flatten out on the ground immediately. The leader would crawl forward, inspect the mine, and then retreat to a spot where he, too, had some protection. Finally, he would take a long wooden pole and touch the butterfly mine, which would explode. The Russians would then get to their feet and continue to the next mine. It was a slow, dangerous procedure, much cruder than the American method of using an electric mine detector, but it was effective. Again the Americans admired the courage of the ordinary Russian while they damned the tactics of the Kremlin for causing the disaster.

There was no sleep for anyone at Poltava during the remainder of the morning of June 22, 1944. Exploding fuel tanks, bombs at the storage depots detonating periodically as the flames reached them, and the incessant blasts of the butterfly mines being set off by the Russians kept the air base in an uproar. In the headquarters building, however, it was not these sounds that concerned Kessler, Walsh, and Old. It was the future of "Operation Frantic," the future of Russian-American collaboration. The question uppermost in the minds of many of the Americans as dawn arrived on June 22, 1944, and made the extent of the disaster readily visible was: "Had Stalin doublecrossed the United States, as many had predicted he would?"

11

"Where Was the Red Air Force?"

THE FOLLOWING DAY, while the Americans were still trying to understand the basic reason for the disaster at Poltava, General Meister, commanding officer of the IV Fliegerkorps, sent the following message to all Luftwaffe units involved in the successful mission:

On June 21, 1944, at about 1500 hours, American four-motor bomber planes coming from England occupied Soviet airfields. Despite the fact that the units KG 4, KG 53, KG 55, and KG 27 were not alerted until after 1500 hours these squadrons succeeded in an exemplary way to be prepared in a short time to conduct an annihilating blow against the American units. After an approach under difficult weather conditions and with exemplary cooperation of target finder, target marker and target lighter aircraft, the above units attacked with great success.

On the airfield at Poltava:

    73 Fortresses
     3 Liberators
     4 Lightnings
     4 Douglas
    14 one-motor, type unknown

Destroyed according to photo evaluation:

    41 Fortresses
     1 Lightning
     3 Douglas
     2 one-motor, type unknown
    12 fuel depots

Damage to a greater number of planes can be assumed but is not certain from air pictures. I thank the men of these units and recognize them for their proven bravery.

                                        Meister
                                        General

The German report was very accurate, so accurate that many Americans assumed that the Luftwaffe was receiving information from agents in the Poltava area. The "Damage and Casualty Summary" issued by the Eastern Command a few days later indicated that in some instances Meister underestimated the havoc caused by his bombers that night. The Summary stated:

The following is a summary of damage sustained at Eastern Command, USSTAF, base of Poltava by enemy attack, June 21, 1944.

Aircraft:

	B-17	C-47	F-5
a. Destroyed or damaged beyond economical repair	47	2	1
b. Repairable, over 7 days	11	—	—
c. Repairable, within 7 days	8	—	2

Communications:

    a. 3 channels of Wilcox 96-A transmitter damaged.

    b. 1 receiving RTT antenna damaged.

    c. 1 transmitting Rhombic antenna, RTT down.

    d. 35 miles field wire replaced for radio control circuits.

Airdrome:

    a. 60 bundles steel mat issued for repairs. Repairs completed 0400 hours, June 25, 1944.

Supply:

a. Vehicles	Destroyed	Damaged
2-½ ton, 6x6 cargo	3	—
Tractor, Hi-Speed M-2	1	1
Trailer, Refueling	2	5
Trailer, 40-ft. Crash	—	1
¼ Ton, 4x4 cargo	—	4
2-½ Ton, 6x6 Oil Truck	—	2
C-2 Wrecker	—	1
Tractor, Crane, 6-Ton	—	1
Truck Tractor, 7-½ Ton, 6x6	—	1

    b. Gasoline

100-octane	200,000 gallons

    c. Oil

Aviation 1120	253 gallons

    d. Ammunition

Bomb, H.E. 250-lb (American)	465
Bomb, Incendiary, 100-lb (American)	1,400
Bomb, H.E. 250 kg (Russian)	2

Pins for 250-lb (American)	400
Pins for 250 kg (Russian)	19,000
Flares	40
Cartridge, cal .50, with links	400,000

Note: Above figures estimated to be correct within 20 percent.

It was obvious to Walsh that his Eastern Command was in serious difficulty as far as continuing the shuttle missions was concerned. Not only were the majority of the heavy bombers of "Frantic II" task force destroyed but the supplies and equipment needed to support other shuttle mission task forces, the materiel that had been brought into the Soviet Union during the spring of 1944 under extreme hardship, had been lost as well. The high-octane gasoline loss—200,000 gallons—was a catastrophe because without this fuel the American shuttle-mission bombers could not be refueled once they reached the Soviet Union from either Italy or Britain. Trucks, bombs, cranes, and the other necessary equipment needed to maintain the "Operation Frantic" heavy bombers had been at a minimum. Now, after the disastrous Luftwaffe attack, they were practically nonexistent. It was a serious situation and Walsh was well aware that several important decisions had to be made promptly.

The first decision made during the morning of June 22, 1944, was to disperse the heavy bombers at Mirgorod. During the raid on Poltava several German aircraft had been reported in the vicinity of Mirgorod, but evidently the marker aircraft could not locate the Soviet air base. Walsh and Kessler decided after a conference that there was a strong likelihood that the Germans would try to hit Mirgorod just as they had Poltava. One of the remaining flyable aircraft at Poltava, a Douglas transport, carried a messenger to Mirgorod to explain to Jeffrey what had happened at Poltava and ask him to move the B-17s at Mirgorod back to airfields in the Kharkov area. The transport arrived late the afternoon of the 22nd and within an hour the Flying Fortresses of the Thirteenth Combat Bombardment Wing were lined up for takeoff from the single runway at Mirgorod. Jeffrey's aircraft was near the end of the line and as the pilot swung the heavy bomber around to line up for the takeoff, one wheel tipped a concrete block of the taxi strip and then dropped into the depression. After several attempts to get the B-17 out of the hole failed, Jeffrey gave orders for the pilot to cut the engines and the crew climbed out of the aircraft. There was only one B-17 that had not yet left Mirgorod so Jeffrey decided to get his crew aboard it. When he reached this Flying Fortress, he discovered that it, too, was not flyable.

"The left tire is flat," the pilot explained.

Jeffrey knew that his B-17 was extremely vulnerable to any German attack since it was sitting in the middle of the airfield. He and his crew returned to the plane and tried to jack the wheel out of the hole. This, too, was unsuccessful.

"Looks like we stay here," the colonel muttered. "Let's get back to the trench area. I think we're going to need all the protection we can find tonight."

He was absolutely correct.

At Poltava Walsh, Kessler, and Old had a preliminary meeting concerning the stranded "Operation Frantic" personnel at the Soviet air base. With no aircraft available to fly back to England, arrangements had to be made to get the crewmen home by other means . . . and soon. The crewmen had lost all their clothing and personal belongings aboard the destroyed aircraft. Most of them had nothing but the clothes they were wearing. Walsh immediately contacted Moscow by messenger and asked Harriman to arrange for the evacuation of the approximately 600 Americans by the Air Transport Command (ATC). Since the Soviet officials had a very rigid restriction on the number of ATC aircraft permitted to fly in and out of the Soviet Union, Walsh was apprehensive about obtaining the required permission in a minimum of time. Kessler, however, had other thoughts.

"I believe that this disaster should improve Soviet-American relations," he said. "After all, Stalin should understand that he did not live up to his promise of defending the air bases."

Deane, in Moscow, had the same thoughts. After due consideration he told Harriman that the Russians would probably acquiesce to American requests more promptly now that they had a guilt-complex about the disaster at Poltava. But did Stalin have a guilt-complex? That was the unanswered question. According to the thinking of the Americans familiar with the situation after analyzing the tragedy, the Soviet leaders were definitely to blame for the loss of the "Frantic II" task force at Poltava because of their pledge to the United States that they had the personnel and equipment to protect the air base when it was now obvious that they did not. Walsh had approved an Eastern Command report of the disaster which stated, in part:

> It was known that the Russian military authorities had promised adequate protection of the base from air attack and a definite feeling of security existed among the troops. Russian AA artillery was in evidence all around the airdrome. The artillery was primarily medium-caliber guns. American officers were *not* permitted to examine the weapons and, to date, accurate information as to the number of guns, types and disposition have been withheld.
>
> The dispersal areas for the B-17 aircraft had been restricted to the east half of the flying field because the Russian military authorities insisted that the west side of the field be used exclusively for the dispersal of the Russian fighter aircraft. Approximately 30 Yak-9 and Yak-7 aircraft were dispersed in that area.
>
> A fire truck and two fire trailers were the only direct firefighting equipment available.
>
> Slit trenches were dug near the tent camp to accommodate approximately 300 persons. The total of American personnel present at the time were 370 permanent and 714 transients (crew).
>
> Blackout regulations were enforced during the hours of darkness and were carefully observed by all personnel. Air raid alarms had been installed at strategic points throughout the base area. A warning system had been set up whereby, upon receipt of an air-raid warning, American headquarters and living areas were notified by telephone (or courier) and all alarms were sounded by personnel on duty. Personnel had been previously instructed and had practiced the system.

Another American on the scene, Colonel Gray, concurred that the Soviet defenses were definitely lacking, that the Luftwaffe, except for the inaccurate, sporadic antiaircraft fire from the medium-caliber Russian ground defenses, were practically unmolested. His official report stated in one paragraph:

> There was *no* fighter interception. The bombing appeared well planned, well coordinated and extremely casual. The one or two enemy planes that were coned by searchlights took no evasive action but continued in a normal traffic pattern around the field, unmolested by flak. The number of enemy aircraft was variously reported from 50 to 275 and the Russians claim two shot down though there was no proof of this.

Gray, like many other Americans at Poltava the night of June 21-22, 1944, was suspicious of the Soviet actions during the German air attack. Why did the He-111s he saw coned in the searchlights not take evasive action? Did the Luftwaffe pilots have information that their aircraft would not be attacked by the ground defenses, that the AA fire aimed in their direction would purposely be inaccurate? Or did they have such a low opinion of the skill of the Russian gunners that they considered it unnecessary to take any evasive action? Why had the German aircraft been permitted to roam the skies above Poltava, dropping their bombs and butterfly mines at will, for roughly two hours without a single Russian aircraft being observed by the Americans on the ground?

"In two hours, Stalin could have ordered Yaks in from a dozen air bases in the area—if he had wanted to do so," Kessler said when he talked to Gray.

Consequently, in the minds of the "Operation Frantic" leaders there was little doubt that Stalin had overestimated the strength of his forces and equipment assigned to the defense of Poltava. If this overestimation was an honest error, then he and the other Soviet leaders involved with "Operation Frantic" should and would have a guilt-complex. If, as some Americans believed, the overestimation had been intentional and the canny Soviet leader had wanted the American heavy bombers destroyed to serve his own purposes—and to those harboring this theory there were several obvious purposes such a disaster could serve Stalin—the Russians would *not* have a guilt-complex. Walsh, as Eastern Command commander, felt that he must assume, at least initially, that the overestimation of the defense setup had been unintentional. He issued orders to the American personnel at the three Soviet air bases prohibiting any criticism of the Russian defensive measures. He stressed instead the heroic efforts of Perminov's men and women in attempting to save the bombers.

In Moscow, Novikov, the commander of the Red Air Force, volunteered the opinion to Deane that the German attack on Poltava had been politically motivated, that Hitler wanted to bring the collaboration between the Soviet Union and the United States to a halt and thought he could do so by the air raid. If the Americans accused the Russians of lax defensive measures, and if they downgraded the Soviet pilots and AA gunners because of the tragedy, Stalin would undoubtedly order the American personnel out of the Soviet Union. Deane himself had already presented this point of view in a discussion with Slavin. But he still was not convinced that this answered the ultimate question: Why hadn't the Red Air Force made any attempt to drive off the Luftwaffe bombers during the two hours they attacked Poltava?

Spaatz, discouraged and angry at the loss of so many of the B-17s he needed to support the invasion forces in the west, salvaged one glimmer of hope from the disaster. In a message to Deane he stated that he thought the USSTAF could use the tragedy as leverage on Stalin to improve the "deficiencies" of the operation without any threat of discontinuing the project. He listed the trouble-spots as: target selection, routes to and from the Soviet Union, intelligence matters, supply and transportation questions, number of American personnel permitted into the Soviet Union, and the protection of the bases. Deane and Harriman, studying the message from Spaatz, agreed that if Stalin acquiesced on any or all of the demands made by the USSTAF commander there certainly would not be any question that the Soviet leader felt guilty about the disaster. It was evident that Soviet willingness to collaborate was going to be tested, not only by Spaatz's demands and Arnold's desire for Far Eastern bases from which to bomb Japan but now by the all-important matter of base defense.

As Deane and Harriman prepared for their conference with Stalin and other Soviet leaders to discuss the Poltava tragedy and the future of "Operation Frantic," Old sent a message to the headquarters of the Third Bombardment Division in Great Britain. The last paragraph of his message indicated his feelings about the future of the shuttle missions to Soviet Russia and the defense of the air bases:

> It is not believed heavy bomber operations can be successfully carried out from Russia until adequate defenses are installed consisting of night fighters, AA, and radar. Only two fields are available for the bombers and the enemy can pound them at will with existing Russian defenses. Also, the communications system must be improved for efficient operations and security. Also, it is recommended that pressure be brought to bear on the Russians to relax somewhat their rigid control of flight of American aircraft. Sometimes it takes hours to clear a flight from one field to another. *American fighter pilots were very anxious to take off and attack*

the German bombers (during the Poltava air raid) *but Russian clearances could not be obtained.* German bombers were still over Russian territory at daybreak and the P-51s could have had a field day if they had been permitted to take off. [Emphasis added.]

Why were the P-51s not permitted to take off? This, among other vital questions, was on the agenda for the meeting between Deane and Harriman and the Soviet leaders after the disastrous Luftwaffe raid on Poltava.

While the diplomatic and political meetings were being planned at Poltava and Moscow to thrash out these matters, Jeffrey and the remainder of the "Frantic II" task force faced more immediate problems. The colonel had managed to get all but two of the crews at Mirgorod evacuated, with their aircraft, to Russian air bases farther east. Only his crew and the crew of the B-17 with the flat tire were forced to stay at Mirgorod and, as Jeffrey had anticipated, the German bombers came back to the Ukraine to complete the attack they had begun the previous night. Antrup and his formation had been unable to locate Mirgorod in the darkness of the night of June 21-22, 1944, so all the He-111s and Ju-88s had dropped their bombs on Poltava. On the night of June 22-23, 1944, they returned with only one objective in mind: to destroy the B-17s and related equipment and supplies at Mirgorod.

The German bombers came shortly before midnight and stayed over Mirgorod for two hours, just as they had at Poltava. Once again there was no sign of any Red Air Force fighters. The Luftwaffe marker aircraft dropped their flares, the bombers, completely unmolested, dropped their high explosives on the fuel and bomb dumps, runways, and vehicular equipment on the Russian air base and later made low-level strafing passes over the field. Jeffrey and his companions took cover in the slit trenches and watched helplessly just as the Americans at Poltava had the night before. To the colonel it was incredible to think that the enemy could leisurely bomb and strafe the air base for two hours without being challenged by a single Russian airplane, but seeing was, unfortunately, convincing. He was thankful that the remaining B-17s had been removed from Mirgorod. Otherwise they, too, would have been destroyed.

The toll at Mirgorod was high:

197,000 gallons of 100-octane gasoline
2,500 gallons of 80-octane gasoline
375 gallons of aviation 1120 oil
5,585 gallons of vehicular fuel
A large tonnage of bombs as yet undetermined

The following day, June 23, 1944, Jeffrey returned to his B-17, which was still sitting in the middle of the airfield at Mirgorod with one wheel in the hole caused by the askew cement block. He discovered that while the plane had approximately 50 small shrapnel holes in the fuselage, no control cables or other vital equipment inside the aircraft had been damaged and he decided that, if necessary, he could fly the plane out of Mirgorod. There was still no telephone or radio communications with headquarters, Eastern Command, at Poltava, so the colonel was confused as to exactly what he should do. He felt extremely vulnerable at Mirgorod, however, so he decided that he and his crew should try once again to get the B-17 out of the hole and onto the runway if possible. Taking jacks and long pieces of lumber, they worked for several hours on the mired Flying Fortress and in mid-afternoon finally managed to get the wheel of the plane back on level ground. While they were resting, a C-47 circled the air base, landed, and taxied to the ramp. It was a courier plane from Poltava with orders for any remaining Americans at Mirgorod to evacuate the air base again that night by flying to Kirovograd, a Russian air base south of Mirgorod. The courier had an additional message for Jeffrey from Kessler.

"Unfortunately, there has not been time to notify the Russian antiaircraft units en route that one or more American aircraft will be flying between Mirgorod and Kirovograd today. Since the AA units have orders to fire at every plane in the sky that does not have Red Air Force markings, be extremely careful. You undoubtedly will be fired upon. The Soviet base commander at Kirovograd has not been notified, either."

Late on the afternoon of June 23, 1944, Jeffrey loaded twelve Americans aboard his shrapnel-riddled B-17 including an interpreter who was permanent Russian personnel at Mirgorod, and took off for Kirovograd with some misgivings. Staying low so that the Russian antiaircraft gunners could not anticipate his course, the colonel flew at maximum speed to the Russian air base, arriving shortly before dark. Several Soviet batteries had fired at the Flying Fortress but had missed, a fact that worried Jeffrey concerning the defense of the shuttle bases used by the "Operation Frantic" task forces. He was concerned but pleased because his B-17 had too many holes in it already.

Kirovograd was a Red Air Force operational base. When the Flying Fortress suddenly appeared over it unannounced the Russian pilots raced for their Sturmovik fighters, but Jeffrey had anticipated such action. Quickly dropping the flaps and wheels of the Flying Fortress, the colonel landed before the Red Air Force planes could get into the air to attack. He taxied the plane to the parking area and cut the engines while truckloads of Russian soldiers followed close behind. As he stepped from the B-17, a staff car pulled in front of the bomber and the Soviet commander of the air base got out. It was evident that he was both angry and confused, but before he could speak, the interpreter who had accompanied Jeffrey from Mirgorod explained the situation. As he explained to the Soviet officer that Jeffrey and his crew were from the United States, that the strange aircraft was an American heavy bomber, and that they had been forced to leave Mirgorod because of the Luftwaffe, Jeffrey saw a smile spread across the Russian's face. Suddenly the Soviet commander grasped Jeffrey's hand and shook it as he said something to the American colonel.

"He says that he is very proud to have an American officer at his base," the interpreter explained to Jeffrey, "and he hopes that you enjoy your stay."

The Americans were, in fact, delighted with the attention shown them during their overnight stay at Kirovograd. The Soviet commander gave a dinner for Jeffrey that evening in his private quarters, assigned an old white-haired Russian civilian to tend to the American colonel's needs while he was at the base, and even arranged a tour of the nearby city. The following morning, as Jeffrey was at his aircraft checking to make certain that no one had bothered it during the night, six Russian staff cars drove up to his Flying Fortress and stopped. Several Soviet generals stepped from the cars and asked, through the interpreter, if they might have permission to look at the bomber. They had never seen an American heavy bomber. Jeffrey, when told of the request, gave the visiting Soviet officers a complete tour of the

B-17, explaining the equipment and answering all their questions. The Russians were so delighted that they promptly invited Jeffrey and the interpreter to a mid-afternoon dinner at the divisional headquarters nearby. Jeffrey, with nothing else to do and thinking that he might help improve international relations in a small way by going to the dinner, accepted.

The dinner was austere but the drinks, as usual, were plentiful, and before the meal was half over Jeffrey realized that he was being tested by the Soviets. As his interpreter told him, "They are going to try and drink you under the table, Colonel. I would suggest that we leave as soon as we finish eating. I can think of an excuse and . . ."

Jeffrey shook his head. "Leave? These guys would ridicule every American officer they met if I don't meet their challenge."

He realized that from an objective point of view, his decision to drink with the Russian officers was rather silly, but the time and place and relationship between Soviet Russia and the United States at that moment placed the importance of the drinking bout far out of its normal proportion. He was determined to uphold the honor of the USSTAF, the USAAF, and the United States. The toasts began with wine, advanced to champagne, and by late afternoon had settled down to plain vodka. As the hours passed, the smiles began to fade from the faces of the Russian officers as they watched Jeffrey. The colonel remained steady on his feet and his voice was calm and clear each time he proposed a toast. Toward the end of the dinner he proposed a toast to Great Britain but none of the Soviet officers would join him. He downed his drink alone. He was not quite certain whether they refused to join him because they did not want to drink to Great Britain or because they couldn't drink any more vodka. Getting to his feet, he proposed one more toast.

"Here's to the Soviet Union!"

One officer tried to get to his feet but fell flat on his face on the floor. The others did not even make an attempt to stand. Jeffrey, grinning, downed the vodka and smashed his glass against the wall. From that moment on, the American colonel was the hero of the Russian air base at Kirovograd. Word of his great staying powers spread rapidly and nothing was too good for him.

The following morning an F-5 reconnaissance plane flew to the Soviet air base and told Jeffrey that he was supposed to bring his aircraft and crew back to Mirgorod immediately. The Russian officers who had treated him so royally made farewell speeches and gave him a gift of several bottles of vodka. Jeffrey felt he was leaving lifelong friends behind. He reached Mirgorod to discover that the remaining planes of "Frantic II" were scheduled to leave later that day—June 25, 1944—on a bombing mission that would terminate in Italy. However, it was impossible to load and refuel the 71 B-17s at Mirgorod in time to accomplish the operation during the daylight hours so it was postponed until the following day.

Once again the B-17s were ordered out of Mirgorod and back to Kirovograd. This time, however, Jeffrey's reception by the Russian base commander and Red Army generals who had treated him so well previously, was completely different.

"They acted as though they had never seen me before," the colonel explained later. "They were very formal, very cold. We were restricted to the base and forced to sleep in our aircraft or under the wings. I was glad to get out of there the next morning at 0345 hours."

It was another of the many examples of the unpredictable behavior of the Soviets during World War II.

The surviving 71 Flying Fortresses and the 55 P-51s from Piryatin left the Soviet Union on June 26, 1944, and bombed Drohobycz, Poland. The planes continued southwest to land at Italian bases without loss. The "Weekly Summary" for July 23, 1944, stated, in regard to this raid:

> Although vital installations were not substantially affected as a result of the attack, there was heavy damage and destruction of secondary objectives. One of the distillation units was hit and there was severe damage to a probable wax-treating plant. Fifteen large storage tanks were destroyed.

In Italy the "Frantic II" task force flew one mission with the Fifteenth Air Force and then returned to its bases in the British Isles. It was a discouraged group of USSTAF crewmen who finally reached the airfields in the midlands of England, both those who had come back in their bombers and those who had been ferried home by the ATC after a long and miserable wait at Poltava while the Russians haggled with U.S. authorities about the necessary clearance for American aircraft to evacuate the stranded airmen. The men were so bitter about their treatment in the Soviet Union, not by the civilian population or lower-level military authorities, but by the Kremlin leaders who made the decisions, that it was necessary for the USSTAF to issue a directive pertaining to remarks about the shuttle mission:

> Crews who participated in Frantic mission will be warned not to discuss with anyone, repeat, anyone details of the attack by enemy planes on the base in the Eastern Command. No mention of losses or damage to our aircraft or installations will be discussed except where necessary in connection with official matters.

Partridge

Yet even this directive by the commander of the Third Bombardment Division did not halt the comments by the pilots and crews concerning the shuttle mission disaster and later Spaatz himself had to issue an order pertaining to the same matter.

Restricted
Headquarters
United States Strategic Air Forces in Europe
Office of the Commanding General

000.71   APO 633 U.S. Army
SUBJECT: Interviews regarding Russia

1. It has come to the attention of this headquarters that our good relations with the Russian government and the Russian Air Force may have been endangered by the interviews given to correspondents by personnel returning from visits to Russian bases. While there is much information concerning the Russian operation that may be given safely to the Press and Radio, all personnel should refrain from making statements to correspondents that might be offensive to the Russian government or the Russian people and thereby impair their present cooperation.

2. Unit commanders are to impress upon all officers and men that they are to say nothing critical of the Russians which might endanger our present relations with them.

By command of Lt. Gen. Spaatz

Harris F. Scherer
Colonel, ADG
Adjutant General

It was extremely difficult for the airmen who had been at Poltava the night of the Luftwaffe raid to understand why they were not permitted to say anything critical of the Russians. Considering the fact that the aircraft of two complete bombardment groups had been destroyed without the Red Air Force making an attempt to save them, the directive issued by Spaatz was totally incomprehensible to the pilots and crewmen who had participated in the mission. They did not like it and were convinced that the USAAF was "covering up" a disaster that had been precipitated by the Soviet Union. The fact that only two Americans had been killed was due to the accuracy of the Luftwaffe pilots and bombardiers, not to any defensive measure taken by the Soviet leaders. The consensus among the American combat crews was that the "Frantic II" mission had been useless and, considering the loss of the B-17s, a disaster.

A report filed by Major Reynolds Benson, A-2, Forty-fifth Combat Bombardment Wing on the June 21, 1944, mission summed up the feeling of most of those involved in the operation. He pointed out that actually there was a sparsity of targets within reach of the American heavy bombers when they were based in Soviet Russia and that the vast proportion of targets were closer to Great Britain than to Mirgorod, Piryatin, and Poltava. According to his figures, and they could not be disputed after a careful check was made, the round trip the "Frantic II" task force made to bomb Ruhland via the Soviet Union was longer than if the Flying Fortresses had bombed the targets at Ruhland and returned to Great Britain. He provided evidence that in the area bounded on the north by the fiftieth parallel, on the west by the nineteenth east meridian, and on the southeast roughly by a line from Poltava to the Albania-Montenegrin border, virtually no industrial or war effort targets existed. Railroads, bridges, and rivers, the latter for mining operations, seemed to be the only objectives available.

Much to the chagrin of Spaatz and Arnold, the major explained that all of north Germany, Prussia, and westward to Danzig and Posen could be hit from Great Britain easier than from Soviet Russia. Vienna, Austria, Budapest, Hungary, the Ploesti-Galati-Bucharest triangle, Rumania, Sofia and Constanta, Bulgaria—all targets for the USSTAF—could be reached by the Fifteenth Air Force out of Italy. This left the relatively small area of Poland and the Baltic states—with the progress of the Russian offensive a rapidly diminishing area—that could not be bombed from either Great Britain or Italy. However, although there were targets in this area their proportionate productive capacity was extremely small compared with the vast arsenal of Germany. He asked the question that bothered most opponents of the project: "Would the results which might be obtained by continuing the shuttle missions to Russia be commensurate with the difficulty and length of time required to transfer supplies via Persia to the Russian bases?"

Benson also stated:

> A direct return to home bases in Great Britain and Italy means quick servicing and a high degree of fast maintenance and return to combat of the aircraft which under ordinary battle damage perhaps would be grounded for a long period of time at Russian bases. The present possibility of serious loss on the ground due to enemy action must also be taken into consideration.
>
> Another deterrent to the shuttle project is weather. Prevailing winds aloft preclude a return from Russia direct to the U.K., the time of flight being beyond the safe endurance of B-17s. On any given day weather in Italy suitable for take-off and assembly, over Europe for targets, and in the U.K. for return to bases is seldom satisfactory in all three areas. The Eighth Air Force task force was delayed nine days in Italy waiting for suitable weather conditions over the proposed routes and according to forecasters at the Fifteenth Air Force this synoptic situation was not considered unusual. Thus, protracted delays will inevitably be encountered, tying up a considerable force in an inoperative category.

By late June 1944, as indicated by Benson's report, the comments of the USAAF airmen who had participated in "Frantic II," and the statistics of the losses at Poltava, the logical conclusion seemed to be that the shuttle missions were much too costly for the results achieved. It was evident that the seeds of discontent had been sown at Poltava and that a crisis had been reached in regard to the continuation of "Operation Frantic."

Unfortunately, Washington was not ready to give up on the collaboration attempt between the United States and the Soviet Union. The dream of molding Joseph Stalin into a pliable, agreeable, and cooperative friend of America persisted despite all the evidence available that indicated this was a hopeless goal.

12

The Crisis

THE PENDULUM HAD SWUNG all the way from the elation of Eaker's "Frantic I" ("Frantic Joe") mission to the depression of Old's "Frantic II" operation—within the month of June 1944. After nine months of preliminary negotiations, the miracle of delivering the necessary equipment, supplies and personnel to the Soviet Union in a minimum of time under extreme hardship, and at a cost of millions of dollars, "Operation Frantic" had, within the space of thirty days, turned into a tragic failure in the eyes of many United States military leaders. In addition to the disastrous Luftwaffe attack at Poltava, the overall situation was changing so rapidly on both the eastern and western fronts that the value of the shuttle missions was more questionable than ever. With the invasion of France a reality and the Allied land forces moving farther and farther east, it appeared that heavy bomber bases could soon be established on the Continent if necessary. From such bases the B-17s and B-24s of the USSTAF could reach every Axis target in Europe. On the eastern front the Red Army was moving west so rapidly that the bases at Poltava, Mirgorod, and Piryatin were farther and farther away from the front lines. Long flights over friendly Soviet territory before reaching enemy-held areas did not seem to be justified.

Yet, despite all these factors which clearly indicated that it would be best to abandon "Operation Frantic," Washington refused to do so. President Roosevelt and his military advisors, including the Joint Chiefs of Staff, insisted on showing the Russians that the United States was fighting the Germans with all its will and might and that Washington was prepared to cooperate as closely as possible with the Soviet war effort. President Roosevelt and his close confidant, Harry Hopkins, believed that

"Operation Frantic" would establish a good precedent for friendly collaboration with Stalin after the war ended and were ready to go to great lengths to make certain the United States did everything possible to please the Soviet dictator.

Spaatz refused to risk any additional American heavy bombers on shuttle missions to Soviet air bases unless the Soviet leaders agreed to improve the defenses of the bases. Since he was doubtful that the Red Air Force *could* defend the air bases in an adequate manner, he recommended to Arnold that at least three battalions of American antiaircraft guns and a squadron of radar-equipped night fighters be sent to the Soviet Union. Walsh, upon receiving this suggestion from Spaatz and before passing it on to Deane and Harriman for presentation to Stalin and Molotov, made as thorough an investigation of the existing Russian base defenses as was possible under the security restrictions placed upon him. For the first time he discovered that the Red Air Force had no night fighters, at least as the USAAF understood the term. The USAAF used special planes equipped with radar that operated in conjunction with ground radar stations to seek out the enemy aircraft in the darkness. The Red Air Force had no such planes. It used standard day fighters manned by Russian fliers trained to fly at night. Actually, all this meant was that the Russian pilots were trained to fly by instruments. They had no radar ground stations to vector them on a course to intercept enemy bombers in the darkness, and no radar equipment in the planes to help them locate the enemy bombers when they were close to them. Still, one question bothered the hard-nosed commander of the Eastern Command, and he asked Perminov for an answer.

"At Poltava the German bombers were easily visible in the light of the marker flares and they circled the air base for two hours. Why didn't your fighters intercept them over Poltava even if the Red Air Force planes aren't equipped with radar? They didn't need it that night."

It was a good question, one that was never answered satisfactorily. Perminov stated that Red Air Force fighters had been airborne but that they had been ordered to attack enemy airfields before and during the return of the enemy bombers! When Walsh demanded to know why the Soviets considered bombing the Luftwaffe bases more important than trying to protect the American heavy bombers parked on the air base at Poltava, the Russian had no answer. He merely shrugged his shoulders and walked away.

The commander of the Eastern Command also discovered that while the Russians had a large number of antiaircraft guns most of them were too small and obsolete to be effective against the Luftwaffe. The Soviet gunners had no radar to aid them nor did they work in conjunction with the few searchlight batteries available. It was an "everyone-for-himself" type of defense that resulted in inaccurate and uncoordinated ground fire. Since the enemy attack on Poltava the Soviets had increased the number of antiaircraft guns protecting the three air bases used by the American planes but the number of large guns was still far from adequate. Walsh, after completing his investigation of the base defenses, quickly agreed with Spaatz's suggestion that American units be sent to the Soviet Union for that purpose.

On June 24, 1944, Deane presented the idea to Nikitin in Moscow, stating that the USAAF desired to bring one or more squadrons of American night fighters and their related equipment to the Soviet Union for defense of the air bases used for "Operation Frantic." To Deane's surprise Nikitin agreed that the proposal "made sense." As chief of air operations for the Red Air Force, Nikitin could appreciate the apprehension of Arnold and the other USAAF leaders about the safety of the American aircraft while they were in the Soviet Union—especially after the Poltava disaster. At the same time he proposed bringing in the night fighters, Deane once again brought up the expansion plans he had presented to Nikitin after "Frantic Joe," the mission of June 2, 1944. He reminded the Russian officer that Spaatz wanted air bases farther west for use by the B-17s, permission to have 3,375 Americans permanently stationed in the Soviet Union, and an agreement that approximately 3,000 airmen could fly into the Soviet Union and out again after varying lengths of stay at the Russian air bases. Nikitin said that the expansion plans proposed by Spaatz had been accepted "favorably" by higher authorities and that Deane could expect approval shortly.

When Deane reported Nikitin's response to Spaatz and Arnold, a search began immediately for available American night fighter units to send to the Soviet Union. At the time there seemed to be no doubt that Stalin would approve the plan. Upon inquiry from Spaatz, Eaker agreed to provide a night fighter squadron from the MAAF command. In a letter from Eaker to Spaatz dated June 26, 1944, he explained why he was willing to do so:

> I agree with you 100% that in view of the German reaction we must prepare to defend our Russian bases or abandon the project. My view is that there is no place in Europe now where the hunting is as good as in that area. Our night fighters here have found very few German planes in recent times and our anti-aircraft have no German planes to shoot at. The German reaction to the Frantic project has been stronger than anywhere else in recent times. Walsh advised me yesterday that some 300 German planes have been moved into that area since Frantic was initiated. We all want to destroy the German Air Force—where better than in Russia where the German has indicated his willingness to fight.

The 427th Night Fighter Squadron was selected for the Russian assignment, a unit consisting of twelve specially-equipped P-61s and the associated ground control units required for the night-fighting task. On June 26, 1944, Deane formally submitted his request to the Red Air Force and the General Staff that the 427th be admitted to the Soviet Union. As expected there was no immediate answer, only the reply that the matter would be presented to higher authorities—Stalin—but Deane sensed that the proposal was favorable to those officers at the meeting. He still anticipated no problem, except time, in getting the necessary permission for the night fighter squadron to move to the Soviet Union. On the same day, Harriman met with Stalin to discuss several matters and he also mentioned the idea of bringing a squadron of American night fighters to Russia to help defend the air bases used by the American heavy bombers of "Operation Frantic." Stalin, while nodding his agreement to the idea, immediately inquired whether Harriman was casting reflections on the efforts of the Red Air Force to protect the USAAF planes. Harriman assured him that he was not, but that the United States felt it would help ease the burden of the Red Air Force if the American night fighter squadron was brought to the Soviet Union to "share" the defense duties. This appeased Stalin—for the moment.

After the meetings on the 26th, the long, frustrating wait for an answer from the Kremlin on the proposals began. Despite the fact that the entire "Operation Frantic" had been bogged down since its inception by such delays, the patience of Deane, Walsh, and Harriman was sorely tried each time. While the Americans waited for the Soviet reply, further shuttle missions to the Soviet Union were cancelled. Finally, Spaatz, never a man who enjoyed wasting time, called a conference of all USSTAF officers involved in the planning of "Operation Frantic" to be held at the headquarters of the MAAF, Caserta, Italy, on July 1, 1944. The purpose of the meeting was to discuss both the immediate and long-range future of the shuttle operation. In order to prevent "Operation Frantic" from lapsing completely, Spaatz proposed that the next shuttle mission to the Soviet Union consist of P-38 fighter units. The fighters could bomb a target en route, admittedly with much less high explosive tonnage than that dropped by a task force of Flying Fortresses, and then continue on to the Soviet air bases. While in the Soviet Union the P-38s could defend themselves against any Luftwaffe attack. After their stay in Russia, the fighters could attack another target on their flight back to Italy. In this manner "Operation Frantic" could be kept active until permission was granted by Stalin to admit the American night fighter squadron and its related ground equipment to the Soviet Union. Eaker pointed out that such fighter missions would not result in major damage to any enemy target and would be costly in terms of effectiveness, but he agreed that it was one way to keep the shuttle operation "alive."

Once again Spaatz, always looking toward the future despite the disappointing facts of the present, insisted that the winter expansion plans he had first proposed immediately after the initial "Operation Frantic" mission and that Deane had brought up again on June 26, 1944, during his meeting with Nikitin should stand—except for one change. Now that an American night fighter squadron, its support units, and perhaps three battalions of radar-controlled antiaircraft batteries would be sent to the Soviet Union for defense of the shuttle bases, the personnel permanently stationed in Soviet Russia would number 8,900 instead of the previously proposed 3,375. In addition, bases farther west should be made available to the USSTAF as soon as possible.

On July 10, 1944, when Deane returned to the Soviet Union from Caserta he formally presented the requests to Nikitin while

Harriman explained the new American proposals to Molotov. Walsh, meeting with Red Air Force representatives, detailed the plans Spaatz had proposed and also covered some specific items that were not listed in the formal presentations made by Deane and Harriman. He told the Soviet officers that representatives of the USSTAF wanted three additional dispersal fields for American aircraft coming into the Soviet Union; that the proposed shuttle mission by fighter aircraft would require additional visas for 50 P-38 mechanics; and last, but most troublesome of all, Walsh insisted that American officers involved with "Operation Frantic" should be permitted to survey forward airfields in the Vinnitsa and Kiev areas so that they could select suitable air bases farther west for future Flying Fortress shuttle missions.

This last request seemed routine to Walsh in line with previous proposals by Deane and Harriman in regard to the Soviet Union providing air bases farther west now that the eastern front had moved so rapidly toward Poland. Unfortunately, Walsh had overlooked one fact that Stalin would never overlook—the charge made in 1943 that the Soviet government had murdered 15,000 Polish officers in the Katyn forest. When German troops had discovered the mass grave of the Polish officers, the Polish government-in-exile in London requested an investigation of the German charge by the International Red Cross. Both President Roosevelt and Prime Minister Churchill had attempted to avert a break in relations between Stalin and the Polish government-in-exile over the incident, but it was impossible. Stalin accused the Polish government of working with the Germans to discredit the Soviet Union and severed diplomatic relations with the Polish government-in-exile.

The tragedy of the Katyn forest massacre was still in the news several weeks later when the Germans discovered more mass graves near Vinnitsa, the area where Walsh wanted to investigate sites for new air bases to be used by the American heavy bombers. Between May 22, 1943, and October 4, 1943, more than 9,000 bodies were exhumed from mass graves near Vinnitsa, all clearly executed by the NKVD. Stalin had no intention of permitting a large group of Americans to roam around in the vicinity of Vinnitsa and perhaps unearth many more secrets he wanted buried forever. Rumors came back to Eastern Command that Stalin would never agree to Americans "surveying" Soviet territory, and that his own officers would select any air bases required by the USSTAF for their heavy bombers. Moscow also hinted that the Soviet transportation system could not handle the additional supplies that would be needed for an influx of American permanent personnel such as that suggested by Spaatz, and that the eastern front was fluctuating too much for such an expansion. However, there was no formal reply to the American proposal and there was nothing Deane and Harriman could do but wait. The future of "Operation Frantic" depended entirely upon Stalin's reaction to the proposals for defense of the Russian air bases by American night fighters and possibly American antiaircraft batteries, and the expansion plans, including air bases farther to the west.

As Spaatz had stated during the conference of "Operation Frantic" personnel at Caserta, Italy, early in July, he wanted to keep the shuttle mission project in operation by using fighter aircraft instead of heavy bombers until the air base defense problem had been resolved. Consequently, "Frantic III" was scheduled for the middle of July. Initially, Spaatz planned to use only P-38s but when Moscow continued to delay issuing visas for the P-38 pilots and mechanics and permission for the transport planes required to fly in the equipment for the fighter planes, he and Twining, commander of the Fifteenth Air Force, agreed to use a mixed force of P-38s and P-51s. Selected for the mission were parts of the Fourteenth Fighter Group stationed at Triolo Airfield, Italy; the Thirty-first Fighter Group stationed at San Severo, Italy; and the Eighty-second Fighter Group based at Vincenzo Airfield, Italy. To lead this fighter task force Spaatz chose Brigadier General D. C. Strother, commander of the Fifteenth Fighter Command.

Strother was an experienced combat leader. He was well aware that he had been picked to personally lead the "Frantic III" task force because of the importance of the operation. After the distastrous "Frantic II" shuttle mission, it was his assignment to give "Operation Frantic" renewed life, to accomplish with his smaller fighters what had originally been planned for the huge bombers prior to the Luftwaffe raid on Poltava.

After a delay because of bad weather and an eight-day wait for visas, Strother led 72 P-38s and 41 P-51s from their bases in Italy to the three Soviet air bases. The designated targets en route to the Soviet Union were the Rumanian airfields from which Axis fighters attacked American bombers conducting operations against the oil installations at Ploesti. These airfields, mostly in the Buzau-Zilestia area, were actually more easily available from bases in Italy than on a shuttle mission but "Frantic III" had a twofold purpose. One was, as stated earlier, to keep "Operation Frantic" alive until the heavy bombers could become a part of the shuttle-mission operation again and, secondly, to provide a diversionary attack to draw off enemy fighters while the Fifteenth Air Force bombers dropped their high explosives on the Ploesti oil installations and Balkan communications targets and then returned to their bases in Italy.

"Frantic III" was a moderate success in comparison with the results of Eaker's initial "Operation Frantic" shuttle mission to Russia with the Flying Fortress task force. Strother's fighters destroyed 41 enemy aircraft on the ground, 25 in the air and in addition listed 6 "probables" and 23 enemy planes badly damaged. The bombing results were "good." Five P-38s were lost to enemy action while one was damaged and landed in Soviet territory.

After three days in the Soviet Union, the "Frantic III" fighters still in operation—33 P-38s and 34 P-51s—bombed and strafed an enemy airdrome at Mielec, Poland. This was definitely an Eastern Command target that could not have been reached from Britain or Italy except by the shuttle-mission procedure. The American fighter pilots destroyed 9 enemy planes on the ground, 4 locomotives, and 13 trucks. On the way back to Piryatin one squadron of Mustangs suddenly discovered a "fighter pilot's paradise." The "Intelligence Summary" for June 25, 1944, states:

> At Juroslav, 35 miles east of the target at approximately 1400 hours, the 307th Squadron intercepted a group of Ju-87s engaged in the bombing of Russian battle lines. The squadron bounced the enemy planes and knocked down more than half the group of 30 to 40 aircraft. One Stuka tried to ram. The encounter lasted 20 minutes.

On this mission from the Soviet air bases, Strother's task force destroyed twenty-nine enemy planes in the air, chalked up five more "probables," and destroyed seven on the ground. Four American pilots—Lieutenants Tarant, McElroy, Brooks, and Dideas—each destroyed three enemy aircraft. The Americans suffered no losses. The Red Army troops, who were within 90 miles of Mielec, were particularly pleased with this action.

On July 26, 1944, 55 P-38s and 47 P-51s swept the Bucharest-Ploesti area and then continued back to their bases in Italy. Three days later 14 more of the "Frantic III" task force fighters that had been delayed in the Soviet Union for mechanical reasons returned to Italy. The overall "Frantic III" mission, while not comparable to the "Frantic I" mission, was considered a success and since Spaatz was still reluctant to risk his Flying Fortresses on Soviet air bases, additional "Operation Frantic" fighter missions were placed on the USSTAF agenda.

"Frantic IV" was flown on July 31, 1944, by the Eighty-second Fighter Group out of Vincenzo Airfield, Italy, and the Fifty-second Fighter Group out of Madna Airfield, Italy. It was the second shuttle mission to the Soviet Union for the Eighty-second but it was a much more rugged trip this time. The "Frantic IV" task force ran into bad weather en route and was widely scattered, so much so that operations out of the Soviet air bases were sharply curtailed. The two missions flown while the "Frantic IV" fighters were based in the Soviet Union were against targets previously hit by the Fifteenth Air Force from these bases during the initial "Operation Frantic" mission. This was done partly in response to a Soviet request for the American fighters to bomb the German airdromes in Rumania. A message from Walsh to Spaatz and Eaker on August 2, 1944, explained:

> Conference with Perminov was held today at which the Soviets requested that we concentrate our attack on enemy airdromes just south of Jasi-Akkerman front. Night bombers reported as follows: Chisinan—40; Husi—39; Focsani—30; Buzau—53. There are about 12 other airdromes included in this request. Number of aircraft reported ranges from 5 to 24. This is the first special request by the Soviets for assistance. Suggest that consideration be given to increasing the force of fighter-bombers in order to increase the number of enemy airdromes brought under simultaneous attack.

Spaatz agreed to bomb the targets requested by the Russians and on August 4, 1944, 42 P-38s and 35 P-51s of the "Frantic IV" task force hit Foscani. The American fighter pilots destroyed seven enemy aircraft and damaged six, knocked out three locomotives, and strafed a troop train and six flak batteries. It was a costly mission, however, because five American planes were shot down over enemy territory. One of the pilots shot down was rescued in one of the most dramatic actions recorded during World War II. The official radio report to USSTAF headquarters made a simple announcement of the rescue:

> Lieutenant Richard E. Willsie crash-landed in Rumania with both engines shot out. Flight Officer Richard T. Andrews landed alongside and by discarding their parachutes, both pilots flew to Poltava in Andrews' airplane.

Actually, the rescue was effected in a field near Foscani with Willsie wounded in his head and arm and P-38s circling overhead to cover the rescue from attacking German fighters. One Me-109 was shot down during the rescue. After the two American pilots had crowded into the cockpit of Andrews' P-38, another P-38 pilot strafed Willsie's damaged Lightning and destroyed it before leaving the scene. When Andrews landed at Poltava he taxied to the parking area and cut both engines. The Russian mechanic assigned to his aircraft in conjunction with the USSTAF mechanic jumped onto the wing to help him out. When the Russian saw *two* men climb from the plane, he just shook his head and walked away muttering to himself. Later it was learned that this incident had convinced him that all Americans were "crazy."

On August 6, 1944, the remaining flyable aircraft of the "Frantic IV" task force, 26 P-38s and 27 P-51s, returned to Italy, again by way of the Zilestia target. At the conclusion of this shuttle mission the Eastern Command advised the USSTAF that, balancing losses and battle damage against the relatively unprofitable targets, fighter-bomber attacks were too costly. On August 8, 1944, Kessler radioed Spaatz:

> Dispatch of fighter-bomber force is not recommended since profitable targets from our bases are not available. Strafing attacks are made too costly by battle damage and losses.

It was evident to Arnold, Spaatz, and all other American leaders involved in the overall planning of "Operation Frantic" that the "Frantic III" and "Frantic IV" shuttle missions had not contributed to the basic purposes of the operation as far as the United States was concerned. The basic aims were to prove to the Russians the value of American strategic bombing, to obtain air bases in the Siberian maritime provinces for B-39s to operate against the Japanese, and to improve United States-Soviet relations by collaborating in a military operation. The fighter missions had kept the collaboration attempt active, but only barely. It was obvious that either more American heavy bombers had to be sent to the Soviet Union on shuttle missions or "Operation Frantic" was going to fade out of future military plans. But without Russian approval for the USSTAF to send the night fighter squadron to the Soviet Union to help protect the air bases from further Luftwaffe attacks, it was a calculated risk to schedule any additional Flying Fortress shuttle missions.

It was a risk that Spaatz decided to take on August 6, 1944, the same day the Fifteenth Fighter Command aircraft left Soviet Russia for Italy. He sent 76 B-17s and 64 P-51s of the Eighth Air Force from Great Britain to the Soviet Union, directing them to bomb the Focke-Wulfe aircraft factory at Rahmel, just north of Gdynia, Poland. Spaatz picked the veteran bomber groups, the Ninety-fifth and the 390th, both of which had been on the fateful "Frantic II" mission but had been fortunate enough to land at Mirgorod rather than Poltava. To escort these two groups of Flying Fortresses, he selected the 357th Fighter Group flying out of Leiston, England. The commander of the group, Colonel Donald W. Graham, had celebrated his twenty-seventh birthday on August 5, 1944, and Spaatz jokingly told him the trip to Russia was his birthday present. He was briefed on "Frantic V" on August 4, 1944, and had been extremely busy ever since trying to get his plans in order. He needed more aircraft than usually required for a normal combat mission over Europe and return to Britain and, in addition, he had to select personnel from the maintenance crews to ride with the bombers so that they would help with the maintenance of the 357th aircraft in Russia. By the evening of the fifth, however, Graham had his P-51s ready—64 in all—and his ground crews and spare parts at the Ninety-fifth and 390th bomber bases.

"Frantic V" was mostly routine for both the bomber crews and the fighter pilots. There were no losses and a minimum of casualties and battle damage. The Luftwaffe ignored the task force, evidently not wanting to risk its planes and use its fuel to defend the target, and the only kills were a single FW-190 and a lone Ju-88. The bombing results were listed as "good to excellent" and according to the USSTAF "Weekly Intelligence Summary" for August 20, 1944:

> Two main assembly or repair shops and a hangar were damaged and seven previously damaged stores and dismantling shops were almost completely destroyed. At least fifteen stores-type buildings were demolished and nine or ten others were damaged.

The "Frantic V" task force flew one mission from the Russian air bases the day following their arrival in the Soviet Union. The Flying Fortresses, escorted by Graham's Mustangs, bombed oil refineries in the Trzebinia, Poland, area with "good to excellent" results again. This was an important target that rated a high priority. The refinery complex had an annual capacity of 100,000 tons of crude oil and reconnaissance photographs taken on June 1, 1944, indicated that it was being expanded. Consequently, the damage inflicted on this target by the "Frantic V" task force was important in the overall defeat of the Luftwaffe, one of the few bright spots in the fast-deteriorating "Operation Frantic" collaboration attempt. The Mustangs, flying out of Piryatin, downed three enemy planes. Captain John F. Pugh shot a FW-190 out of the sky, Lieutenant N. T. Nowlin shot down a Me-109 and shared another with Captain John Storch. Two bomber crewmen bailed out over Russian territory but were returned safely by the Russians to Eastern Command headquarters at Poltava. A gunner, Sergeant Donald Simpson was killed, the first American airman killed in air-to-air combat to be buried in Soviet Russia.

It was evident, however, that the Russians were not as friendly to the American airmen as they had been in June when Eaker's first task force landed to begin "Operation Frantic." Cooperation, always lacking to a certain extent, now became almost nonexistent. A report written by Lieutenant Colonel J. B. Browne, A-4 officer of the Sixty-sixth Fighter Wing, who had accompanied the "Frantic V" task force to Soviet Russia aboard a Flying Fortress, clearly indicated the lack of cooperation:

> Our bomber formations arrived in the area of Station #561 (Mirgorod) at 1630 hours but because of limited ground radio facilities and well camouflaged field, landings were not completed until 1830 hours. Every effort was made to transport the fighter spare parts and equipment carried on the bombers to the fighter

field at Station #560 (Piryatin), a distance of about 50 miles. Clearances were not obtained until too late so only 31 fighters could go on the August 7, 1944, mission.

Fortunately, the Soviet defenses were not tested for a second time by the Luftwaffe, probably because the Russian ground troops had advanced so far that the shuttle bases were relatively safe. Spaatz still did not want to take any unnecessary chances, however, so on August 8, 1944, he ordered the "Frantic V" task force back to Britain by way of Italy. Seventy-three B-17s and 55 P-51s proceeded to the American air bases at the Foggia complex, striking again at the Buzau-Ziletsia airdromes with good results. En route to Italy, Graham and his P-51s spotted about 35 enemy planes but only managed to shoot down one Me-109.

It was obvious that the crisis haunting "Operation Frantic" ever since the Poltava disaster had not been solved to any great extent by "Frantic III," "IV," or "V." Cullen, the deputy commander of the Eastern Command under Walsh, made it plain in a report after the completion of "Frantic V" when he said: "USSTAF doctrine holds that shuttle operations are uneconomic. The only justification for the operations is the bringing together of the two forces in the hopes that they will learn to work together."

With the evidence piling up that the Soviets were becoming less cooperative, if that was possible, Deane held two meetings, on August 8 and 10, to discuss the future of "Operation Frantic" and the attempt to collaborate with the Soviets. The principal subjects discussed at the two sessions were (1) "Operation Frantic," (2) proposed ATC routes into Soviet Russia, and (3) "Glacier" operation. A digest of the conference revealed the hopes and the doubts of the American military leaders. On the status of Soviet approval of expanded "Operation Frantic" plans, Deane reported:

> Our latest proposal, under which we would add one additional base and bring in a night fighter squadron, three A/A battalions, an Aviation Engineer Battalion, and other miscellaneous units (total permanent U.S. personnel—8,900) has been approved by the Red Air Staff and the General Staff but is being held up by the Russian Foreign Office. The question of bringing in large numbers of additional U.S. personnel is a touchy one which will probably have to be referred all the way to the top—to Molotov or

Stalin. General Deane is optimistic as to the eventual approval of the program as submitted, and is of the opinion that we should not be too concerned over the present delay. We can continue operating as at present until approval is received and expand our operations next spring.

Deane was not as optimistic as his report indicated but he did believe that the Kremlin would eventually approve a part of the expansion program.

Another part of the report stated that "sufficient steel mat is on hand or en route to permit expanded operations or movement to bases farther west. However, only 300 winter huts of the 1,100 requested have been shipped thus far from the U.S. to bases for winter housing." Deane also explained that the availability of Russian lumber and assistance in erecting additional housing was being investigated but they would not be forthcoming until the answer had been received about the expanded "Operation Frantic" plans. If the Soviets approved the expanded program, Deane was certain that they would give the United States assistance in building additional housing and installations. In his opinion, it was wise to use as much Russian labor as possible despite the fact that many of the local American commanders preferred an all-American show. Deane also said that he believed that the shipment of increased amounts of 100-octane fuel (increased from 6,500 tons to 12,000 tons monthly in anticipation of expanded operations) should continue even if the expansion were delayed. Sufficient storage facilities were available at or near the existing bases.

Since all additional plans for "Operation Frantic" were stalled waiting for the necessary approval from the Kremlin, the officers at the Moscow conference decided to discuss other proposed projects that required Soviet cooperation, projects that would ultimately benefit the United States in its war with Japan. Under the subject of "Proposed ATC Routes into the USSR" the officers reported on the current status of the various routes and future plans:

London-Moscow Route: The proposal under which the British would operate four C-87 aircraft and the Soviets would operate a parallel line with four C-87 aircraft obtained from the U.S. is still under consideration. The ATC has earmarked eight new C-87s for this purpose. However, General Deane is under the impression that the British are losing their earlier enthusiasm for this route. *U.S.-Moscow Northern Route:* We are continuing to press the Soviets for approval of this route, thus far without any results. Colonel Balchen indicated to General Deane that the Swedes will consent to the use of the Stockholm base; further, in the event that Finland capitulates in the near future, he feels optimistic about obtaining her transport facilities in that country. *Cairo-Aleppo Route (Over Turkey):* Unofficially, Molotov has indicated his approval of this route to General Deane. General Smith (ATC) stated that he understood from the State Department that the Turks would probably agree to this route and proposed that the Soviets should be advised that we would like to commence operations as soon as possible. *AL-SIB Route:* General Deane stated that up to recently the Soviets have refused to discuss anything relating to the Japanese and as a result there has been no decision on our proposal to establish an ATC route through Alaska and Siberia. Just before he left he had a lengthy discussion with Marshal Antonov, Deputy Chief of Staff, about Far East matters, including the AL-SIB Route but nothing further has developed in this connection.

The matter of obtaining air bases in the Siberian maritime provinces from which American heavy bombers and fighters could attack targets in Japan, Korea, and Manchuria was undoubtedly one of the basic aims underlying "Operation Frantic." While the Soviet Union was not at war with Japan, it was a foregone conclusion, verified by Stalin, that once Hitler had been subdued, Soviet Russia would join the United States in the fight against the Nipponese. However, with his ground troops and aircraft assigned to the eastern front in an all-out effort to defeat Nazi Germany, Stalin was very careful not to antagonize the Japanese. He did not want a war on two fronts. Consequently, the subject of American bombers and fighters operating against Japan from Soviet air bases was a delicate matter that Harriman and Deane broached periodically to their Soviet counterparts, but about which they had never received a formal answer. At the time of the conference in August 1944, the code name for the operation under which United States heavy bombers and fighters would be based in the Far Eastern Siberian Provinces was "Glacier." In regard to the operation, Deane reported:

Twelve to fourteen air bases have been prepared in the Vladivostok-Komsomolsk area which would be placed at our disposal if the Soviets decide to let us operate from that area. It will be impossible to get a detailed airport map or other pertinent data relating to the Maritime Provinces until the Soviets decide to commit themselves. After that, they will give us everyhing we want which is in their power to give, i.e., billeting, storage facilities, transport facilities, etc.

General Deane indicated, however, that in his opinion the United States Air Force (USAF) should be prepared to use alternate bases, possibly in the Chita area, in the event that it was found that the Russians could not hold their defensive line along the Manchuria-Siberian border. Definitely, he felt that the USAF should not stock the Komsomolsk area until the security of the stores was fairly certain. Deane stated that it would be necessary to ship in all 100-octane aviation fuel from the United States, as the Soviets did not have aviation gasoline of such high-octane content. According to Deane, supplies, subsistence, and incendiary and special-purpose bombs would also have to be provided from the United States.

It was felt that most of these items could be shipped into Siberia under the guise of Lend-Lease, once the Soviets approved the "Glacier" project and took the necessary action to implement it. This secret maneuver was necessary since the Soviet Union definitely did not want Japan to know that it was permitting the United States to use Russian territory to stockpile war materiel for future use against the Nipponese. Deane foresaw no difficulties in getting the necessary items for "Glacier" past the Japanese as the latter had not been stopping any Soviet ships bearing Lend-Lease supplies for weeks. As a matter of fact, the Japanese had been doing everything possible to conciliate the Soviets in order to keep the Russians out of the Far Eastern war.

It was also decided during the two-session conference that the United States should insist that the Soviets take delivery of the B-24 aircraft Stalin had requested and which the USAF had allocated for the Soviets. The B-24s were being offered to the Soviet Union for a purpose. The United States wanted the heavy bombers delivered to the Russians over the Alaska-Siberia (ALSIB) route since this would induce the Soviets to prepare suitable bases along the route which later could be utilized for transferring American heavy bomber groups from the ETO to the Siberian bases. Deane pointed out that compliance with the Soviet proposal to have the B-24s flown in over the southern route and turned over to them at Abadan in Iran would largely nullify the efforts he and Harriman had been making to open up the AL-SIB route. As a matter of fact, in Deane's estimation, the B-24s should be turned over to the Soviets only with the distinct understanding that the USAF was delivering them to build up a Soviet heavy bomber air force in the Far East for operations against Japan. Turning them over to the Soviets at Abadan without such an understanding might negate American efforts toward securing bases in the Siberian maritime provinces. The Soviets, according to Deane, might convert the B-24s into transports and use them for hauling passengers all over the Soviet Union instead of preparing to help in the war against Japan.

In addition, Deane proposed during the conference that as soon as the Soviets indicated that they were prepared to enter the war in the Far East, a joint United States-Soviet Staff should be organized. This staff should have qualified American and Russian officers who could make an immediate reconnaissance of eastern Siberia, particularly the maritime provinces, with a view toward ascertaining the needs of the USAF in that area. He added, however, that until the Russians formally approved the "Glacier" project he did not think the Soviets would permit any survey to be conducted by U.S. Army or Air Force officers, even in civilian guise.

Deane's conference clarified American efforts to collaborate with the Soviet Union in the war against both Germany and Japan. It was evident that the United States had ulterior motives in regard to both "Operation Frantic" and the "Glacier" project, if obtaining help from Soviet Russia to defeat Japan could be considered an ulterior motive. Deane, Harriman, President Roosevelt, and other military and political leaders thought that the subtle approach was the best one to use when asking help from Stalin, and that the blunt, hard-nosed approach would obtain an immediate *nyet* from the Soviet dictator. They thought that Stalin wanted to help the United States, but that the isolation of the Soviet Union from international affairs prior to World War II had aroused a mistrust of other nations in Stalin. If this mistrust could be eliminated, and if Stalin could be convinced that the United States was more than ready to cooperate with the Soviet Union and to help the Russian people in every way possible, then the Soviet dictator would become a staunch friend of the United States and once this happened, he would then be easy to deal with in regard to military and political matters, and postwar relations between the two great countries would be excellent. This was the theory advanced by the American leaders during the hectic months of "Operation Frantic" and it was the theory upon which the conclusions of Deane's August 1944 conference were based.

Only the silence from the Kremlin worried those Americans who believed this theory and the silence, they decided, was only temporary. They were quite certain that the expansion plans for "Operation Frantic" would be approved, that the Soviet Union would soon agree to join in the fight against Japan, that Stalin would permit the American heavy bombers to use the air bases in the Far Eastern Siberian provinces, and that additional air bases would be built along the AL-SIB route so that the American heavy bombers could be transferred from the ETO to Siberia in a minimum of time and with a maximum of safety. The delay in the approval of these proposals, according to those who were convinced the Soviets would fall under the "spell" of President Roosevelt and the United States, was caused by Stalin's considering every detail carefully.

13

The Tragedy of Warsaw

A MONTH PASSED before further shuttle operations, known as "Frantic VI" and "Frantic VII," were undertaken by the USSTAF. This delay was caused largely by the fact that arrangements for these operations became tangled with United States-Soviet negotiations over the expansion of the Eastern Command program and with negotiations for special operations with political implications such as the supply-dropping mission over Warsaw, Poland. Planning for "Frantic VI" started out routinely early in August when Spaatz suggested that Jesau, a suspected assembly plant for the German Me-163 rocket-propelled fighter plane, be bombed by the Eighth Air Force Flying Fortresses en route from Great Britain to the Soviet Union. On August 9, 1944, Walsh informed Perminov about the plans.

> Word has been received from General Doolittle that Frantic VI composed of B-17 and P-51 type airplanes in about the same numbers as Frantic V may be expected on August 10 or soon thereafter. Preliminary plans indicate that the Messerschmitt assembly plant at Jesau airfield near Konigsberg, East Prussia, will be the target.

Unfortunately, because of bad weather on August 10, 1944, Doolittle had to postpone "Frantic VI," and Perminov was so informed that same day. Walsh told Spaatz and Deane the following day that while the Soviets had expressed disappointment over the postponement, he anticipated no difficulty in securing approval of a flight plan for any "Operation Frantic" task force. Walsh, however, did not take into consideration the political implications of such actions in eastern Europe at the time nor the delicately balanced relationship between the United States and the Soviet Union vis-à-vis these political intrigues.

On August 13, 1944, only two days after Walsh had assured him that the Soviets were ready to approve any flight plan for a shuttle-mission task force, Spaatz sent a radio message to Walsh, Deane, and Doolittle which read:

> Dropping armament supplies to the Poles in Warsaw area is planned. We propose to use Frantic VI for this purpose. Force is to be composed of approximately 70 bombers and 100 fighters. Fifty of the bombers will drop supplies and the remainder will bomb an airfield in the immediate Warsaw vicinity. The highest authorities are interested. Please reply fast.

Cullen, Walsh's operations deputy, notified Perminov at 2330 hours on the night of August 14 that Spaatz had proposed "bombing an airfield in the immediate vicinity of Warsaw and to cross the Soviet front at 500 feet at Warsaw or immediately south of the city on the afternoon of August 15 or August 16, 1944." He also requested Perminov to notify him as soon as possible regarding which airfield the Russians preferred the "Frantic VI" task force to bomb. No mention was made at this time about dropping supplies to the Poles in Warsaw.

Twenty hours later, however, Perminov was handed a more complete report on the proposal:

> Frantic VI is planned as a mission of bombing an airfield in the vicinity of Warsaw as a diversionary operation while armament supplies are dropped to the partisans in the Warsaw area. This confirms the information given verbally today.

Walsh had insisted that the more complete report be given the Soviets because he was aware that the Russians were suspicious of any American aircraft task force in the vicinity of Warsaw. As he notified Deane later that same day: "Possible political complications are anticipated."

It was an accurate prediction. The Soviet Foreign Office quickly and bluntly informed Harriman in Moscow that the Soviet Union did *not* concur with using "Frantic VI" to drop supplies to the Poles at Warsaw. Harriman visited Molotov and protested the official decision vigorously, but to no avail. Stalin's secret postwar plans took precedence over any "Operation Frantic" mission or any pretense of United States-Soviet collaboration. The political implications of the Warsaw tragedy and Stalin's actions during the fateful months of August and September 1944 in regard to "Operation Frantic" revealed to those who carefully analyzed the events what the United States should expect in its relations with the Soviet Union *after* World War II ended.

President Roosevelt knew that Stalin and the Soviet Union hoped to exert a powerful influence over all of eastern Europe after the war, but he underestimated the cunning of the Soviet dictator. The first clear indication of Stalin's ruthlessness and a forecast of his postwar intentions came during the Warsaw uprising. While "Operation Frantic" was a minor part of the overall Allied war effort, it was the one and only major collaboration attempt between the United States and the Soviet Union and gave President Roosevelt an opportunity to learn a great deal about Stalin's willingness, or lack of it, to work in conjunction with the United States. Until the Warsaw affair, the answer to Stalin's true attitude toward the United States was clouded and confused. During the Warsaw affair the answer became crystal clear.

During the period of the German-Soviet Nonaggression Pact, before Hitler invaded the Soviet Union, Stalin, having agreed, in effect, with the Nazis to the destruction of the Polish state and the division of its territory between Soviet Russia and Germany, refused to recognize the Polish government-in-exile that had been established in London. In addition, the Soviets deported an estimated one million Poles from the Russian-occupied areas of Poland to the Soviet Union, not because they were causing any trouble, but because they were anticommunist. After Hitler attacked Soviet Russia, however, Stalin found himself in a dangerous situation and in turning for help from the United States and Great Britain agreed to recognize the Polish government-in-exile and grant amnesty to the Poles deported to the Soviet Union. Since the Soviet secret police had already executed nearly 15,000 Polish officers in the Katyn forest, the amnesty came too late but the Allies chose to ignore this fact in an effort to reconcile the Soviet Union and the Polish government-in-exile.

Once the Russian military situation improved, however, Stalin began recanting the concessions he had made to the Poles. He refused to recognize the Polish citizenship of any of the approximately one million Poles he had deported to Russia earlier unless they could prove without a doubt their Polish ethnic origin. Consequently, under this ruling, all Jews, Ukrainians, or other citizens of non-Polish ethnic groups were classified as Soviet citizens. This greatly reduced the number of Poles under the rule of the Polish government-in-exile, which Stalin opposed and intended to replace with his own communist-dominated Polish leadership. By January 1943, Stalin had complete control over all the Poles in Soviet territory and the London-based Polish government-in-exile could not even learn the fate of the deportees, much less help them. When the Katyn forest massacre was discovered by the Germans four months later and the Polish government-in-exile insisted on an investigation by the International Red Cross, Stalin broke off all relations with the London Poles.

President Roosevelt and Prime Minister Churchill, while backing the Polish government-in-exile, thought that they understood Stalin's actions toward the London Poles. Both men thought, at the time, that the Russian dictator was merely maneuvering to make certain that a communist-dominated government would rule Poland after the war. They understood Stalin's desire for such an action, but were convinced that in the end the United States and Great Britain could thwart any actual move in that direction by the Soviets. What they did not understand was that Stalin had a much deeper motive. He was determined to have a "friendly government" in Poland after World War II ended, a government that would repress all evidence of the murderous actions of the Soviet secret police from 1939 to 1941 when thousands of Poles were executed. He wanted all records, archives, and memories of the massacre in Poland destroyed so that the Soviet attempt to control the political destiny of postwar eastern Europe would not be hampered. Unless the London-based Polish government-in-exile was destroyed, past actions such as the Katyn forest massacre might become the core of a propaganda campaign that would greatly reduce Soviet influence in postwar eastern Europe.

Approximately one month after Eaker led the "Frantic Joe" task force of American heavy bombers to the Soviet Union on the first shuttle mission, the Red Army entered an area on the eastern front which even the Soviet government admitted belonged to Poland. However, when Premier Stanislaw Mikolajczyk of the Polish government-in-exile requested permission to move his headquarters to this Polish territory, Stalin rebuffed him. Instead, Stalin gave every indication that he was going to establish the Polish-Communist Committee, known as the "Committee of National Liberation," on the Polish liberated area at Lublin. Time had run out for both the Western governments and the Polish government-in-exile.

President Roosevelt and Prime Minister Churchill both insisted to Mikolajczyk that the Polish premier should go to Moscow for a face-to-face meeting with Stalin in an effort to solve the dilemma. After much pressure from both the United States and Great Britain, Stalin reluctantly agreed to meet with Mikolajczyk, but he played an ace-in-the-hole on July 27, 1944, the very day the Polish premier left London for the Soviet Union. On that day the Soviet dictator announced that the Russian government and the Polish-Communist Committee of National Liberation had signed an agreement permitting the Lublin Poles to assume "full direction of all the affairs of civil administration" in all liberated areas of Poland. Mikolajczyk, after arriving in the Soviet Union, met with Molotov, and the Soviet leader indicated that all of Poland would soon be liberated by the Red Army and that Russian troops were already within ten kilometers of Warsaw and would enter the city on August 6, 1944. The Polish premier was encouraged after his meeting with Molotov by the Russian's friendly attitude despite the fact that no assurances were made that the Polish government-in-exile would have an important role in postwar Poland. Unfortunately, while Mikolajczyk was having dinner at the American embassy with Harriman's deputy, George Kennan, Stalin gave the signal to begin execution of one of the greatest crimes in international history—the tragedy of Warsaw.

Warsaw, a city whose prewar population exceeded 1,200,000, had been under German rule for five years. In July 1944 the citizens saw signs for the first time since 1939 that they might once again be free. They could hear the heavy guns of the Red Army artillery to the east and reports filtered into the city that Russian soldiers had reached the fringes of Praga, a part of Warsaw east of the Vistula River, which divided the city. Every day they could look up and see Red Air Force planes crossing above the city. General Bor-Komorowski, the national commander of the secret Home Army of 40,000 Polish partisans in Warsaw, was confident that the time for the planned uprising in the city was near, and that the Red Army troops would be entering Warsaw proper shortly and would welcome a helping hand in defeating the Nazis by his secret underground fighters. There was only one problem that bothered him. He was in radio communication with the Polish government-in-exile in London, but for some unknown reason he had been unable to establish radio contact with Marshal Rokossovsky, the commander of the Soviet troops on the outskirts of the city. Every message General Bor sent went unanswered. It was a puzzle.

To strengthen his belief that the liberation of Warsaw was at hand, General Bor picked up a radio broadcast from Moscow at 2015 hours on the evening of July 29, 1944, a broadcast in Polish of an appeal made by Molotov and E. Osobka-Morawski of the Lublin Poles which said:

> Poles, the time of liberation is at hand! Poles, to arms! Make every Polish home a stronghold in the fight against the invader! There is not a moment to lose!

The broadcast was one of the planned steps in Stalin's incredible crime.

On the following day, a similar message was monitored in London as the Moscow radio urged the inhabitants of Warsaw to assist the Red Army to cross the Vistula and enter the city. General Bor, still unable to contact the Soviet ground force commander by radio, decided that both messages were authentic; this conclusion was strengthened when, on July 31, 1944, he learned by London radio that Mikolajczyk, the premier of the Polish government-in-exile, had arrived in Moscow to meet with Stalin. He was convinced that this meeting would lead to a direct linkup between his Home Army partisans and the Red Army. He was vitally interested in making contact with the Red Army because he was aware that even if his 40,000 underground fighters managed to gain control of Warsaw from the Nazis, they had only enough food and ammunition to maintain this control for approximately seven days. If they did not have help from the Red Army within that time it could, and probably would, mean disaster for the Home Army. Taking everything into consideration—the two radio broadcasts, the nearness of the Red Army, the Red Air Force planes overhead, and the visit of Mikolajczyk to Moscow—General Bor decided to order his Home Army to attack immediately. He set the zero hour for 1700 hours on August 1, 1944.

General Bor could not conceive that Stalin was so cold-blooded that he would plan a trap for the Poles that would cost the lives of 250,000 men, women, and children. Neither did President Roosevelt nor Prime Minister Churchill.

The underground fighters launched their attack on the German soldiers in Warsaw on schedule and within the first twenty-four hours they captured most of the important buildings in the central sector of the city. The main post office, the water plant, the gas plant, the city's only electric plant, the central railway station, and other buildings were in their hands before darkness fell on August 2, 1944. In addition, General Bor's partisans gained control of the western suburb of Warsaw, Wola, through which any Nazi units moving to reinforce the German ground troops east of the Vistula had to pass. At the end of forty hours of fighting the Home Army had met its objective: it held two-thirds of Warsaw. Now, with the help of the advancing Red Army, it was only a matter of hours until the city would be completely liberated. Both the partisan fighters and the civilians of Warsaw were overjoyed at the events of the past hours. They were rejoicing everywhere. Red and white flags hung from many windows, and the sound of singing and laughing were heard all over the city.

General Bor was worried, however. Since the night of August 1, 1944, no Red Air Force planes had appeared over the city, but even more ominous, the Soviet radio was completely silent on the subject of the Warsaw uprising. The BBC and broadcasts from neutral countries were announcing the news of the uprising within the city and the Red Army ground troops on the outskirts of the city could easily see the Polish flags flying from the capital and other tall buildings of Warsaw. Yet there was not a single word from Moscow pertaining to the uprising, and General Bor did not like it. He sensed, for the first time since the battle within the city began, that something was wrong. Badly wrong. Then, shortly after midnight of August 2, 1944, he learned to his dismay that there certainly *was* something wrong. The Red Army artillery fire, that incessant thudding of Soviet shells hitting German positions in Warsaw, had stopped. Unable to contact the Russians by radio and unable to learn any news from London relevant to the military situation outside Warsaw, General Bor could only wait and pray that his suspicions about the Red military movements were wrong.

They were not.

On the night of August 3, 1944, the Luftwaffe bombed the

positions of the Home Army inside Warsaw, the first time that Warsaw had been bombed since 1939. Despite the fact that Soviet aircraft were based nearby, not a single Red Air Force plane appeared to repulse the German aircraft. With the Red Army artillery suddenly silenced and the complete disappearance of any Red Air Force aircraft over Warsaw, General Bor realized that his Home Army was in a desperate situation. He and his staff had previously estimated that they could hold out a maximum of seven days without aid from the Red Army ground troops. Already three of these days had passed and instead of help being on the way, there was an indication that his Home Army was being abandoned to its fate. His message to London that night emphasized the importance of Mikolajczyk keeping Stalin fully informed of the Warsaw uprising and for the premier to press for Russian aid for the Home Army immediately.

If General Bor had been able to learn the true facts about Mikolajczyk's visit to Moscow he would have been more discouraged. Stalin had summoned the leader of the Polish government-in-exile to the Kremlin and very bluntly told him that unless Mikolajczyk could come to a satisfactory agreement with the Lublin Polish Committee of National Liberation, the Soviet Union would ignore the Polish government-in-exile completely and deal only with the Lublin Poles. Although he knew that the Lublin Poles were puppets of Stalin, the premier had no choice. He agreed to meet with them.

The Lublin Poles arrived the very next day, proof that they had been briefed that such a meeting was in the making. There were three of them: Edward Osobka-Morawski, the same Communist who had signed the radio appeal inciting the Home Army in Warsaw to rise against the Germans; Boleslaw Bierut, a Communist since 1933 and reputed head of the Polish section of the NKVD; and Marshal Rola-Zymierski, a Pole with firm Moscow ties. The Lublin Poles were given an official reception at the Moscow airport, including a personal welcome by Vishinsky, a guard of honor, and a band which played the Polish national anthem. Newspapers described the reception in detail, but absolutely no mention was made of Mikolajczyk or the meeting for which he had traveled to Moscow.

The meeting lasted five days and was a disaster for the London Poles. Mikolajczyk had to agree that the Polish government-in-exile would be reorganized as a compromise between the London and Lublin regimes with the Lublin Poles taking over at least fifty percent of the cabinet posts. In addition, the premier had to agree to an eastern frontier for Poland, known as the "Curzon Line," which he had previously opposed. Just before the conference closed on August 9, 1944, Mikolajczyk received the only good news of the meetings. Stalin assured him that the Soviet Union would give immediate military aid to General Bor's forces in Warsaw.

By this time the Home Army partisans in Warsaw were facing a rising Nazi fury. Wave after wave of Stuka bombers attacked their positions, German artillery hammered them day and night, and German tanks drove them back despite fierce resistance. Food and ammunition were scarce, and medical supplies nearly non-existent. The Royal Air Force, which had been supplying the Home Army for nearly three years, first from its home bases in Great Britain and later from Italy, tried to continue this aerial delivery system after the uprising began but the situation was much different than before. With the sky over Warsaw swarming with Luftwaffe planes, the British pilots discovered that what they once considered a "milk run" was now an extremely dangerous undertaking. A minimum of fifteen heavy bombers loaded with supplies were needed by the Pole underground fighters each day or night and it soon became evident that Air Marshal John Slessor's Special Duties Squadrons in Italy, a unit of MAAF, could not handle the assignment by itself. Slessor, convinced that the round trip of 1,750 miles, much of it over enemy-held territory, and the attempt to drop supplies from low altitude into Warsaw, would result in heavy losses, pressed through both London and Allied officials in Moscow for the Soviets to undertake the job. Both Washington and London approved this approach, but when Stalin balked and piteous appeals for help came from General Bor inside Warsaw, Slessor agreed to try trial flights on the nights of August 8 and 9, 1944.

These two supply missions, flown by a small contingent of the Polish No. 1568 Special Duty Flight based in Italy, were moderately successful, and the efforts to supply the underground fighters in Warsaw by air was increased. Two Liberator squadrons, No. 31 of the South African Air Force and No. 178 of the 205 Group, were diverted from the invasion of southern France to fly the dangerous route to Poland. This time the Germans, in the air and on the ground, were ready and losses were very high. Between August 12 and 17, 1944, the Special Duties Squadrons lost 17 planes out of the 93 dispatched. The No. 31 Squadron alone lost eight aircraft in four nights. After the flight of August 17, 1944, Slessor suspended further supply missions except for a few trips made by Polish volunteers. When the Polish pilots lost four out of nine aircraft in two nights, they, too, abandoned the attempt to supply General Bor.

It was then that Spaatz proposed "Frantic VI" and was turned down by Stalin, for reasons which became obvious later. To emphasize his opposition to aiding the Poles in Warsaw, Stalin, in a meeting with Harriman and Deane on the night of August 15, 1944, refused to allow American *or* British aircraft to land on Soviet territory after dropping supplies to Warsaw. Harriman was extremely angry and in the wee hours of the night sent the following message to President Roosevelt:

> For the first time since coming to Moscow I am gravely concerned by the attitude of the Soviet government in its refusal to permit us to assist the Poles in Warsaw as well as in its own policy of apparent inactivity. If Vishinsky correctly reflects the position of the Soviet government, its refusal is based not on operational difficulties or denial that the resistance exists but on ruthless political considerations.

Harriman was correct. The accuracy of his analysis of the situation was verified when Mikolajczyk, back in London, sent a radio message to Stalin urging the Russian dictator to have the Red Army and Red Air Force attack the Germans. He emphasized that the citizens of Warsaw were being massacred and that they desperately needed help. Instead of a direct reply from Stalin at this time, a statement by the official Soviet news agency, Tass, was broadcast. The broadcast, monitored in both London and by General Bor in Warsaw, sealed the doom of the Warsaw fighters:

> Information from Polish sources on the rising which began in Warsaw on August 1 by order of the Polish emigres in London has recently appeared in various newspapers abroad. The Polish press and radio of the emigre government in London have asserted that the Warsaw insurrectionists were in contact with the Soviet High Command and that this command has sent them no help.

This announcement is either a misunderstanding or a libel against the Soviet High Command.

Tass is in possession of information which shows that the Polish circles in London responsible for the Warsaw uprising made no attempt to coordinate this action with the Soviet High Command. In these circumstances, the only people responsible for the results of the events in Warsaw are the Polish emigre circles in London.

Stalin had twisted the rope tighter around the throats of the Polish government-in-exile in London and placed the entire blame on the massacre taking place in the city of Warsaw upon the London Poles. His puppets, the Lublin Poles, were now in position to take over Poland as soon as the Russians decided to move their military might farther westward.

On August 17, 1944, a furious President Roosevelt personally intervened on behalf of the Warsaw underground fighters and the citizens of the city caught in the middle of the battle between the Home Army and the Nazis. He authorized Harriman to request that the Soviet government reconsider its attitude toward the Polish underground forces and cooperate with Great Britain and the United States in furnishing assistance. Bluntly, he made it clear that the United States intended to help the Home Army in any way possible, with or without the help of the Soviet Union. Harriman met with Molotov to convey President Roosevelt's message. It was a very frustrating and discouraging talk as far as the American ambassador was concerned. Molotov was evasive, noncommittal and, at times, arrogant and discourteous. According to staff members present at the meeting, Harriman, who was always cool and collected in his negotiations with the Russians, was exasperated and made no effort to be tactful. He demanded that Molotov explain why the Soviet government now refused to aid the Polish insurrection when on August 9, 1944, Stalin had personally promised Mikolajczyk that he would. The insolent Molotov merely shrugged and said that after the Polish premier left Moscow, the Soviet government had decided that the Warsaw insurrection was a "purely adventuristic, light-minded affair which was causing many sacrifices." He added that the Soviet leaders did not like the criticism it had received in the western press and radio, especially statements made by the London Poles, and that Russia, in reprisal, intended to abandon the Poles in Warsaw.

This shallow, revenge-seeking reason for not aiding the Poles trapped in Warsaw was hard to believe. Harriman, realizing that Molotov and Stalin were cold-blooded enough to permit hundreds of thousands of Poles to be massacred for just such a reason, demanded to know whether it was true that near the end of July the Soviet radio had encouraged the Poles to begin the uprising and help the Red Army which was advancing on the city to liberate Warsaw. Molotov, upset by the question since he was well aware that the broadcast had been monitored in London and Warsaw, refused to answer. He abruptly ended the meeting by stating that the Soviet government did not wish to associate itself directly or indirectly with the Warsaw "adventure."

On August 19, 1944, Harriman sent the following telegram to the U.S. State Department:

> When the American public understands fully the facts, there will be serious repercussions in the public opinion in the United States towards the Soviet Union and even in its confidence and hopes for the success of post-war collaboration.

Meanwhile, Spaatz again submitted two alternate flight plans to the Eastern Command headquarters at Poltava for Walsh to present to the Soviets for approval, but both were turned down. It was obvious that the Russians felt that the Americans were trying to trick them, that no matter what was designated as the primary target for a "Frantic VI" task force, the American heavy bombers would drop supplies to the partisans in Warsaw. On August 20, 1944, President Roosevelt and Prime Minister Churchill addressed a joint appeal to Stalin, informing the Soviet dictator that they were thinking of the adverse world opinion if the anti-Nazis in Warsaw were abandoned. Both western leaders expressed the hope that all three nations would do everything possible to save as many of the patriots in Warsaw as possible and that the Soviet aircraft would immediately drop supplies and munitions to the partisans. While Stalin stood firm, even after receiving this message from Washington and London, the pressure continued from the western powers, especially by the United States. Gradually the Soviet government began to weaken on the Warsaw issue. As a conciliatory move, Stalin finally approved another "Operation Frantic" mission, although he warned Harriman that no supply drop to the partisans in Warsaw would be permitted during the operation.

"Frantic VI" was flown after the Soviets finally approved the bombing of Chemnitz, Germany, 100 miles south of Berlin. Seventy-five B-17s and 64 P-51s of the Eighth Air Force took part in the mission on September 11, 1944. The American heavy bomber task force consisted of units from the Ninety-sixth Bombardment Group out of Snetterton Heath—the same group that had participated in the second shuttle mission of "Operation Frantic"—and the 452nd Bombardment Group out of Deopham Green. The latter group had also been on the disastrous "Frantic II" mission. The escort fighters were from the Twentieth Fighter Group based at Kings Cliffe, England, and commanded by Colonel Harold J. Rau, who flew a P-51 nicknamed "Gentle Annie."

The mission was a moderate success. The target, the Wandererwerke Small Arms Plant at Chemnitz, was heavily damaged. The roofs of both large machine shops were almost entirely destroyed and at least seven smaller buildings suffered varying degrees of damage and destruction. One B-17 was damaged but managed to land in Soviet territory, while two Mustangs became separated and were forced to make emergency landings. One P-51 pilot who landed at a Russian airfield was detained and not permitted to continue to Piryatin after repairs were made to his fighter, but the second downed American pilot was more fortunate. Forced down at a Soviet airdrome west of Piryatin, Lieutenant Mansher was told that he would have to remain at the airfield until Moscow gave permission for him to join the others. Knowing that this might take a long time, Mansher quickly got a bottle of bourbon out of his Mustang and gave the Russian colonel in charge of the field a drink. By the time the bottle was empty, not only was the American's plane repaired but he and the colonel were the best of friends. Within a matter of hours, Mansher was at Piryatin with the remainder of the Twentieth Fighter Group.

Two days later, on September 13, 1944, 73 Flying Fortresses, escorted by 55 Mustangs bombed the Royal Hungarian Iron and Steel Works and the Mavag Armament Works at Diosgyor, Hungary, and continued to Italy. There were no claims of enemy fighters and there were no losses of American bombers or fighters.

While "Frantic VI" was in progress, Stalin finally reversed himself about aiding the Warsaw insurgents, knowing that it was really too late to save them and that his puppet regime now had the power he wanted it to have before the Red Army liberated the city. On September 12, 1944, after Stalin had agreed to three-power action to help the Poles in Warsaw, Marshall radioed Deane from Washington:

> Condition of Polish patriots in Warsaw is so critical that urgent action is essential in order to take advantage of Soviet agreement for aid. Desire that you, in conference with representatives from Spaatz's headquarters and from the RAF, prepare a plan without delay and secure coordination of Soviet authorities. Plan must take into consideration present location of patriots so as to ensure maximum amount of supplies being dropped to patriots rather than to Germans. Risk to airmen must be kept to a minimum while endeavoring to secure maximum relief of patriots. Spaatz and Portal have been given copy of this message and will send names of representatives to you.

Inside Warsaw General Bor and his trapped Home Army had been waiting for days for American planes to make a large-scale supply drop to them. London had contacted General Bor as soon as the Soviets had given permission for the American bombers and fighters to use the Russian air bases for the long mission to Warsaw, but day after day the flight was postponed. "Frantic VII" was originally planned for September 13, 1944, and had received immediate Soviet approval, but operational problems forced delays. On September 15, 1944, the "Frantic VII" task force actually took off, but had to return to Britain because of bad weather after losing two Mustangs over the Continent. By this time General Bor was so disillusioned that when, at the end of the nine o'clock Polish program broadcast by BBC on the night of September 17, 1944, he heard the melody "One More Mazurka Tonight," the secret signal that there would be an aerial supply drop the next morning, he did not get excited. He had been disappointed too many times before.

Between 1100 hours and noon the following day, a sunny autumn morning in Poland, General Bor heard a loud shout from the people outside his headquarters. He looked out the window and saw the whole sky filled with American Flying Fortresses. The American planes were in perfect formation "as if on parade," and behind them trailed long lines of white dots.

"Parachutes!" he exclaimed.

There was little wonder that General Bor was impressed by the excellent formation of the American heavy bombers over Warsaw that morning: the mission had been assigned to three veteran shuttle mission bombardment groups—the Ninety-fifth, the 390th, and the 100th. This was the third "Operation Frantic" mission for both the Ninety-fifth and the 390th and the second for the 100th Bombardment Group. The bombers were escorted by the 355th Fighter Group from the air base at Steeple Morden, a veteran group that consisted of the 354th, 357th, and 358th Fighter Squadrons. It had been a long mission, having taken the bombers 10 hours and 45 minutes to reach the Russian air bases, but there had been little enemy fighter opposition. Flak, however, shot down one B-17 and damaged several others. One pilot, Lieutenant Paul Hibbard, was killed and two crew members were wounded as the supply drop was made over Warsaw at an altitude of 14,000 feet. The official report of the mission, radioed from Eastern Command to Spaatz on September 18, 1944, read:

> Results largely unobserved. Some crews estimated fifty percent of supplies landed in city. Accuracy can be increased by reducing altitude which is not recommended under circumstances; more practice needed in releasing parachutes and delayed action chutes. Major battle damage to eight aircraft, minor to twenty-seven. Flak generally accurate, intense, both tracking and barrage type. Heavy pall of artillery smoke over city from IP to Warsaw from Russian batteries. Approach was from west to east—led along front lines resulting in flak for entire bomb run. Suggest delayed chutes. Many ripped on release and some failed to open. Others were shot at. White marking strips ineffective. Smoke pots in woods were observed but partially obscured by city smoke. Stationary flares and colored smoke recommended.

On the ground inside Warsaw, General Bor's joy turned to despair as he saw the containers dropping from the Flying Fortresses overhead. The area held by his trapped Home Army was so small that it was impossible to get many of the supply containers within it from an altitude of 14,000 feet. As he watched, most of the supplies fell beyond the reach of the Home Army into areas that the partisans had held only a week before. If the Soviets had permitted the American planes to drop the supplies at that time, there was no doubt that the mission would have been a success. Stalin had won again. He had wanted the drop to be a failure and it was. When the B-17s disappeared from the sky above Warsaw, General Bor turned and walked silently back into his office. He had seen what could have been possible if the Soviets had agreed to aid the Home Army at the beginning of the uprising. Now he knew that for all practical purposes the revolt was over. The Nazis had won because Stalin had permitted them to win.

The Mustangs of the 355th Fighter Group met the B-17s they were scheduled to escort on "Frantic VII" at the Vistula River where it joined the Baltic Sea and flew in a protective formation above the bombers until the supply drop was made over Warsaw. They continued with the Flying Fortresses until they crossed the Russian-German lines. Major E. L. Sluga was CO of the 358th Fighter Squadron on this mission and during a short engagement with several Me-109s lost his element leader in a tragic accident that echoed the tragedy of both the Warsaw uprising and the U.S.-U.S.S.R. collaboration attempt. Shortly after the German fighters came into view over Warsaw, the element leader left Sluga's flight without permission and started after the nearest Me-109. Another flight of Mustangs was dispatched to attack the Luftwaffe planes and as one of the P-51 pilots pursued a German plane, the element leader who had slipped away from Sluga's wing passed between the two aircraft. Just as the element leader crossed in front of the Mustang pilot hot on the tail of the Me-109, the P-51 pilot opened fire. Instead of hitting the German plane, he hit the straying Mustang and shot it down. One other P-51 was lost during the mission and one pilot, Captain Harold J. Hoffman, was wounded by antiaircraft fire but managed to complete the flight to Piryatin.

The following day all the B-17s and P-51s that could fly took off from the Russian air bases, bombed the locomotive repair sheds and transshipment center at Szolnok, Hungary, and continued on to Italy. For most of the American crew members the mission of September 19, 1944, was uneventful and they were delighted to get out of Soviet Russia after a stay of one day. For one man, John S. Bromberg, the flight from Russia to Italy was a fantastic adventure. Bromberg, an ace bombardier, was knocked out of his seat in the nose of the lead Flying Fortress while on the bomb run over Szolnok. He crawled back to the bombsight, however, and managed to drop his bombs on the target before he was forced to bail out of the burning aircraft. As he floated to earth, a convoy of German soldiers used him for target practice and he was hit several times in one foot. Soon after he landed in a cornfield SS men and Hungarian soldiers discovered him, chained his wrists, and, after beating him, dragged him to a nearby truck. He was taken to a farmhouse and put under guard, but not before several women and children struck him with fists and sticks. Later he was locked up in a village cell without windows or lights, bed or chair. Still without receiving any medical attention for his wounds or the beatings he had received after landing, he was taken by trolley and train to Szeged near the Rumanian border on a trip that lasted several hours. Two days later he was moved to Budapest where he was locked in a bare cell with no windows for 20 days. During this time Luftwaffe and SS interrogators tried to get information from him about American bombsights, radar, and aerial cameras but despite a beating by two German officers using rubber hoses, during which he lost consciousness and suffered a broken rib and left collarbone, the tough-minded Bromberg refused to talk. When the Germans finally gave up trying to get information from him, Bromberg was transported to a prisoner-of-war camp in Oberursel and put in a cell without ventilation. A large heater was turned on to make the room unbearably hot. It was then turned off and the room was cooled off until it was unbearably cold. Still he refused to talk.

Again he was put on a train to be transferred to another prisoner interrogation center, but near Fulda a bomb from an American bomber hit nearby, killing two of his guards and knocking Bromberg unconscious. He was put on a stretcher and carried to an infirmary, but when the doctors discovered he was an American he was promptly put back onto the train without medical attention. Eventually, he arrived at a hospital in Obermisfeld which was run by the British under the jurisdiction of German guards where he received his first medical attention since bailing out. When the hospital was liberated by the Eleventh Armored Division six months later, Bromberg went into action with tank and infantry units and on one patrol he killed a German general who tried to shoot him as he entered a house.

While it took Bromberg better than half a year to get back to Britain, the "Frantic VII" crewmen of the other B-17s were back at their home bases within a matter of days. Another "Operation

Frantic" mission was tentatively scheduled to drop more supplies to the partisans in Warsaw using different techniques, but it was too late. General Bor's Home Army surrendered at 0945 hours on the morning of October 5, 1944, and the tragedy of Warsaw ended. The Eastern Command notified the USSTAF of the situation that same day:

> Latest information just supplied by Moscow to local Soviets follows. Many partisans have been evacuated by Russian planes and only a few isolated groups remain in Warsaw. Soviets advise against Frantic VIII as they say Germans will receive supplies.

The Warsaw affair was over. The question in the minds of the political and military leaders in Washington was whether the collaboration attempt between the United States and the Soviet Union was over, too. Had the final "Operation Frantic" mission been flown?

14

"Leave Now!"

DURING AUGUST and part of September the Warsaw uprising and the resulting tragedy occupied the thoughts of most Americans involved with "Operation Frantic." However, there was another undercurrent of controversy threatening the relations between the United States and Soviet Russia during this period. Spaatz had still not received an answer from the Kremlin on the expansion plans he had suggested earlier and not only was he worried, he was angry at the rudeness of the Soviets. On August 5, 1944, shortly after the Warsaw uprising began, Spaatz presented the Russians with an ultimatum.

"Approve the expansion plans by August 14, 1944," he said, "which is the last feasible convoy loading date or the USSTAF will be forced to delay the entire movement of units for expansion for at least thirty days and perhaps longer because of lack of shipping."

Spaatz was irritated by other factors involving U.S.-U.S.S.R. collaboration. The Polish affair had seriously affected the relationship between the Americans and the Russians at Poltava. When the dispute occurred over the Lublin Poles and the London Poles the Soviet displeasure was quickly reflected in the many restrictions immediately placed on all Americans on Soviet soil. American aircraft were grounded without any reason; rescue crews were not permitted to service American planes known to have force-landed in Poland, and injured crewmen were not allowed to be removed to the hospital at Poltava. The seriously ill Americans in the hospital at Poltava normally were transferred to Tehran, where better facilities were available, but after the Polish affair began, the Soviets put an immediate halt to this practice.

Perhaps even more important to the average American soldier stationed at Poltava, Mirgorod, and Piryatin was the fact that

Russian women were no longer permitted to associate with them. Ugly incidents in the villages surrounding the Soviet air bases became more and more frequent. Between July 3 and July 18, 1944, there were 35 incidents involving verbal or physical attacks on off-duty Americans and the Russian girls they were associating with in the city of Poltava. It was noticed that the same man and woman always led the attacks on the couples in Poltava, and an American sergeant fluent in Russian was asked to investigate. When he spotted a small group of Russians led by the suspicious man and woman attacking an American and his girl one afternoon, the sergeant asked two Russian officers standing nearby to intervene. They did, but when the Soviet civilian leading the attack, the strange man who was always accompanied by the same woman during the attacks, displayed a leather-encased identity card, the Russian officers quickly walked away. The man and the woman were NKVD agents acting on orders from the Kremlin!

Moscow propaganda distributed by word of mouth to the Russians working at Eastern Command headquarters in Poltava was that while the United States was currently an ally in all probability the Americans were future enemies of the Soviet Union—so beware. The ill-feeling between the Americans and Russians reached such a pass that on July 15, 1944, Cullen restricted all American personnel to their living and working areas during the hours of darkness and further recommended that if they went into the nearby cities or villages during the day that they go in pairs, not alone. It was also necessary for Cullen to station armed Americans at the storage dumps and warehouses on the three air bases used by the American planes in order to prevent Russian looting.

As the Warsaw tragedy became more and more a focal point of the different attitudes reflected by President Roosevelt and Stalin, the coolness between the Russians and Americans on all levels increased. On August 17, 1944, as Harriman prepared to leave the Kremlin after his futile meeting with Molotov about supplying the Warsaw underground fighters by American heavy bombers on an "Operation Frantic" mission, the irritated, obstinate Russian foreign minister remarked that the "Soviet Union was proposing to revise the question of the Frantic bases." He had the temerity to state that the air bases had been granted for the summer only and the Russians now had an acute need for them and wanted them back!

Harriman, angry about the refusal of the Kremlin to permit the American bombers to supply General Bor's Home Army in Warsaw, snapped, "The air bases were made available for the duration of the war, not just for the summer."

Molotov, sneering at the remark, replied that "Operation Frantic" was not an outstanding success and that the coming winter weather would limit the number of missions possible. However, he said that he was merely warning Harriman that the future use of the air bases was under scrutiny by Stalin and that the matter would be discussed further at a later date. When Harriman insisted that the air bases had been promised to the USSTAF for the duration of the war and, in addition, Stalin had promised other bases for American bombers for use in the war against Japan, Molotov merely shrugged his shoulders and ended the meeting.

It now became evident to even the most fervid Soviet supporters among the American personnel involved in "Operation Frantic" that Stalin had thrown down the gauntlet by issuing a direct challenge to Washington. He was, in effect, saying: We shall take Poland regardless of your desires and there is nothing you can do about it. We no longer want to collaborate with you militarily since we no longer need your help, so take your soldiers out of the Soviet Union. The future of the shuttle missions, and even more important, bases for American heavy bombers in the Siberian Maritime Provinces to use for bombing Japan, seemed bleak.

Slowly but steadily the Soviets dropped even the pretense of collaboration. Visas were delayed or refused to American officers who wanted to visit the "Operation Frantic" bases in Russia; flight regulations were changed for American transports flying between Tehran and Poltava, making them much more restrictive; and American prisoners liberated by the Red Army were mistreated and refused their freedom. Nor would the Kremlin openly say "yes" or "no" to Spaatz's expansion plans. When his deadline of August 14, 1944, passed without an answer and he received Harriman's message three days later about Molotov's threat concerning future use of the Russian air bases, the veteran USAAF officer sensed immediately that "Operation Frantic" was a "thorn in the side" of Stalin that the Russian dictator wanted removed. Stalin, with Soviet military might now in control of the eastern front, was laying his plans for complete Soviet control of eastern and, perhaps, central Europe after the end of the war and he wanted all Americans out of Soviet Russia. He did not want any other nation, especially those the Red Army was liberating as it moved west, to get the impression that the United States had helped the Soviet Union in even a small degree. Nor did he want any Americans in the Soviet Union to keep watch on the actions of the Kremlin or Soviet military units. Stalin intended to play a lone hand in eastern Europe, now that he had the military power to do so, and he wanted no interference, no matter how slight, from the United States.

In the absence of any reply to the shuttle mission queries presented by Deane and Harriman to the Kremlin, and with winter approaching, Washington had to make a decision one way or the other about the future of "Operation Frantic." Harriman finally suggested that in his view, Eastern Command should be reduced for the winter months to a single detachment at Poltava. His idea was that by keeping a small group of Americans at Poltava, "Operation Frantic" would not be abandoned entirely and the option would be left open to try to reactivate the project in the spring. Also, special American bomber missions and reconnaissance flights could still be flown if Soviet permission was granted since the one Russian air base would still be operational. His recommendation was forwarded to Arnold in Washington and on August 28, 1944, Arnold accepted the proposal. Arnold decided to limit the Eastern Command to one base (Poltava) with about 200 permanent American personnel to stay there during the winter months. He further directed that 14,000 tons of steel matting, 300 winter huts, and other items already consigned to the "Operation Frantic" air bases in the U.S.S.R. should be off-loaded in Great Britain or returned from the Soviet Union. Harriman and Deane had suggested that these supplies be stored in Soviet Russia in hope of future operations or to be marked off against Lend-Lease commitments, but Arnold refused. During the next two days Deane submitted Arnold's proposal to the Red Army General Staff and the Red Air Force while Harriman submitted it to Molotov. November 1, 1944, was set as the date of change of the "Operation Frantic" proposal.

A résumé, "Recent Developments in Connection with the Frantic Operation," was prepared by Colonel R. W. Bonnevalle while the United States was waiting for the Soviet reply to Arnold's proposal:

Under the date of 25 August 1944, General Spaatz recommended, in view of the refusal of the Russians to permit entry of the night fighter squadron into the USSR, that this squadron be temporarily assigned to the Twelfth Air Force where it will be valuable in processing the two night fighter squadrons which are to be equipped with P-61 aircraft. This proposal was accepted and the squadron, which is now in North Africa en route to the USSR, will be diverted to the Naples area.

As a result of a further conference between Generals Spaatz, Eaker, Knerr, and Walsh, held at Caserta on 27 August 1944, General Spaatz recommended that we reduce the Frantic operation to one base with approximately 200 U.S. troops to take care of equipment, to continue PRU [Photo Reconnaissance Unit] operations and for any special emergency operations that might be required. (This, in lieu of Molotov's proposal to Ambassador Harriman to close out the Frantic operations entirely). This proposal was accepted in CM-OUT message 88057 dated 28 August 1944. A further message to General Deane requests a speedy decision from the Soviets. If they insist that we cease operations entirely, it will be advisable to close down the Frantic operation before winter sets in in order to avoid winterization problems.

In our CM-OUT message 88057, instructions are given for the diversion of equipment, supplies and materials now en route by water to Murmansk for the Frantic operation. In CM-OUT 25284 dated 4 September 1944, all parties concerned were advised that all pending requisitions relating to the Frantic operation were being cancelled. Further, it was suggested that a review of all Frantic equipment and supplies now in the USSR be made, for the purpose of determining future needs in the USSR, items which should be returned to the ETO or MTO, and items which might be turned over to the Soviets under local Lend-Lease arrangements.

Ambassador Harriman is of the opinion that we should plan to hold in the USSR in storage, a large amount of the supplies now at the bases or en route there, for later use in connection with the Exploration project. ["Exploration," previously "Glacier," is the code name for the project under which bomber and fighter groups would be moved across Europe and Siberia to the Far East for operations against Japan from the Siberian Maritime Provinces.] Under the directive contained in our CM-OUT message 88507 Generals Spaatz, Deane, and Walsh can determine the equipment and supplies now in the USSR which should be reserved for this project.

In UX 67551 dated 4 September 1944 (CM IN 3379), General Spaatz protests against the contemplated assignment of any of the Frantic personnel to the CBI [China, Burma, India] theatre and recommends that all personnel withdrawn from the Frantic bases be returned to the United Kingdom for reassignment duty there. This recommendation was accepted and a reply to this effect is being sent to General Spaatz today.

The summary of the situation by Bonnevalle made it clear that "Operation Frantic" was winding down fast. Any hope of further shuttle missions by American heavy bombers during the winter of 1944-45 was abandoned and the complicated and delicate task of withdrawing United States troops, supplies, and equipment from the Soviet Union began. It was a harrowing procedure, even more frustrating and discouraging than setting up the Russian air bases in the first place. Every move made by Walsh or Kessler at Eastern Command was questioned or halted by Perminov and other Russian officers. Ugly incidents became a daily occurrence, some so serious that it took considerable tact and discipline for Walsh to control the angry Americans under his command.

On September 13, 1944, a Fifteenth Air Force bomber piloted by Lieutenant James D. Ayers was forced down by Russian fighters after bombing the Osweicim Oil Refinery in Poland. As Ayers held the aircraft straight and level over the target for the bombardier to drop the bombs accurately, the plane was hit by antiaircraft. The left inboard engine was knocked out, the aileron controls were shot away, and the gasoline line on the half deck was severed. Before the struggling lieutenant could get the plane back under control it had lost 8,000 feet altitude. Once he did get the bomber under control, Ayers checked his instruments closely and knew that he could not return to his home base, so he took a heading for Rzesvow, Poland, where he knew there was an emergency airstrip in Allied hands. However, the plane continued to lose fuel so that when he spotted a runway near Dembetzen, Poland, the worried pilot made a quick decision. He decided to land immediately—the only choice he really had under the circumstances.

At the time he spotted the runway at Dembetzen, Ayers was still at 15,000 feet altitude. He eased back the four throttles and began a slow descent to get onto the landing strip, but as the altimeter needle dropped past the 3,500 feet mark his earphones crackled.

"Yaks at nine o'clock heading directly toward us!"

Ayers, knowing the fighters were Red Air Force planes, asked his gunners to hold their fire, thinking that once the Russian pilots saw the USAAF insignia on the bomber they would escort his damaged plane down to the runway. Instead, the Yaks began firing as soon as they were within range, setting fire to the gasoline leaking from the half deck, knocking out the hydraulic system, and severing the rest of the controls. At 3,000 feet Ayers gave his crew orders to bail out, but even though they managed to get out of the stricken aircraft, they were still in danger. As the canopies of their parachutes opened, Red Army ground troops opened fire on the descending Americans. Fortunately, none of Ayers' crew was wounded. The Americans were rounded up by the Russian soldiers after they landed and were treated as German prisoners. It took considerable time before they finally managed to convince the Russians that they were Americans and longer yet before they were transported to Poltava.

When Walsh protested this action by the Red Air Force and the Red Army, the Soviet officers ignored him completely. They intimated by their actions that any Americans in territory controlled by the Soviet Union or on Soviet soil could expect such treatment. In September 1944, in a personal message to Harry Hopkins, Averell Harriman expressed some of his sentiments about the way the Russians were acting:

> I am disappointed but not discouraged. The job of getting the Soviet government to play a decent role in international affairs is, however, going to be more difficult than we had hoped. The favorable factors are still the same. Ninety percent of the Russian people want friendship with us and it is to the interest of the Soviet Union to develop it. It is our problem to strengthen the hand of those around Stalin so they can explain that the counselors of a tough policy are leading him into difficulties.

Also at about this time the Soviets began to curtail the intelligence data they had been providing Eastern Command to help with the overall Allied war effort. Cullen, long believing that the Russians were feeding him and other Eastern Command officers misleading information—when it benefited the Soviets to do so—on August 3, 1944, used some data from a Russian intelligence bulletin to refute some statements given to him earlier about the number of Luftwaffe planes on an airdrome the Russians had suggested as a target. Cullen had suspected that the Soviets had hoped to lure the American bombers into a trap by understating the number of German fighters in the area. Once the Russians received his protest, they immediately stopped supplying the Eastern Command with the bulletins that were delivered to Russian military units. Instead, they gave Eastern Command a new type of reconnaissance report that was inconclusive and inaccurate. Russian intelligence officers were irritated that information in their bulletins had been used by Cullen to refute distorted reports sent to Eastern Command and were determined that it would never happen again. Cullen continued to furnish the Soviets reconnaissance photographs taken daily by his aircraft, but he never did find out whether, how, or to what extent this material was used by the Russians in tactical planning or front-line operations.

The conclusion of active operations and the beginning of the wind-down of "Operation Frantic" changed the situation entirely, and for every rebuff or irritation caused by the Russians, the Americans, especially the airmen, began to retaliate. An American pilot who had to make a forced landing at a Polish airfield and accomplished the landing without arousing the anger of the Soviets, refueled his aircraft and took off again as soon as he could. However, he had an extra passenger aboard when he took off—a Polish-American citizen who wanted to get out of Poland. The American airmen gave the dual-citizenship passenger a USAAF uniform and tried to pass him off as a crew member when they landed at Poltava but the Soviets discovered his true identity. Stalin was furious when he heard about the incident.

Until the final October deadline when the Eastern Command 200-man force was confined to the single base at Poltava, many similar incidents occurred. Another B-17 crew tried to "liberate" a Hungarian who wanted to go to the United States; a P-51 pilot chased three Yaks halfway across the Ukraine after one of the Russian pilots made the mistake of firing a burst of gunfire across the front of the Mustang's nose; a Flying Fortress waist gunner emptied his .50-caliber machine gun at a trenchful of Red Army soldiers he saw firing their rifles toward his low-flying bomber as it crossed the eastern front lines; and when an American pilot was refused permission to take off again after landing at a Russian airfield in Poland to repair an engine, he sauntered toward his plane, leaped in, and roared down the runway before the Soviet gunners could get a shot at him. As a final gesture of bravado, the pilot flew across the Soviet field at grass-top level, scattering the frightened Russians in all directions.

On October 5, 1944, a long train pulled out of Poltava headed for Tabriz in Iran; from there a truck caravan rolled across the desert to Cairo, where a ship was waiting bound for Liverpool. All that remained of the adventuresome "Operation Frantic" were the 200 men and a few ancient transport planes at Poltava. For those left behind in the Soviet Union during the winter of 1944-45 while the future of "Operation Frantic" and the entire matter of collaborating with the Soviet Union was discussed in Washington and London, it was a long, miserable period. The terrible Russian winter was unbearable for the Americans, and the Russian personnel were worse. Unpleasant incidents became more and more frequent as the Soviets completely underestimated the fortitude and initiative of the Americans who remained behind. Thinking that because the American personnel on their soil were outnumbered they could harass them at will, the Russians made a serious error. Any Red Air Force sergeant who barked an order at an American enlisted man would usually get a faceful of snow as an answer. When one Soviet officer decided to remove all the butter from the American mess at Poltava despite the fact that the butter was provided by Lend-Lease, he learned a lesson he would never forget. One dark night a young second lieutenant from Texas caught up with the Russian colonel, took a rope that he had brought with him from his ranch near El Paso, and tied the startled and angry colonel to a flagpole. According to reports, he warned the Soviet officer that unless there was butter in the mess the following day, he would hang him by the neck from the flagpole before the week was over. When the colonel, half-frozen, was freed a few hours later, he immediately protested the action to Kessler at Eastern Command headquarters.

"Old Ugly" just shrugged and said, "I like butter, too. Besides, the Texan has already hung ten cattle rustlers. He's too tough for me."

The Soviet colonel, having seen a few American movies, believed Kessler and the butter was restored to the American mess pronto!

The war situation changed so rapidly during the winter months that the importance of "Operation Frantic" lessened. By the time spring of 1945 arrived, Hitler's domain had contracted so much that the bases at Mirgorod, Piryatin, and Poltava were of no real value. Arnold considered pressuring the Russians for air bases in Central Europe or the Balkans as the Red Army approached the west, but Stalin was extremely sensitive over his tenuous control of these areas. He wanted to gain complete and permanent control after the war and he did not want any American planes or personnel in the areas to interfere. When Arnold mentioned the matter, Deane replied:

> Harriman feels that no approach should be made regarding air bases in Poland until or unless we are prepared to deal with the Lublin Poles. Consequently, he believes that this question should be cleared with the State Department before we make any approach to the Soviet government in Moscow. Under the armistice terms for Rumania, the Soviet command will exercise control on behalf of the United Nations and undoubtedly the introduction of the AAF would involve considerable difficulty which might well be avoided.

As Deane suggested, Arnold contacted the State Department and the Eastern Division of the State Department informed him that it ". . . believed this to be an unwise move politically." Arnold insisted that he wanted the bases anyway so that he could move Eaker's MAAF to Central Europe to shorten the war. He wanted permission to send 2,000 men to two air bases and on January 5, 1945, a formal request was made to Moscow. As usual, there was no answer. At Yalta, however, the question was brought up again by Harriman, and Stalin agreed "in principle" to give the United States two bases in the Vienna-Budapest area. Once again the negotiations stalled, just as they had for the original "Operation Frantic" bases, the main dispute being over the control of the bases. Stalin insisted that Soviet officers would be in command while Arnold insisted that any base from which American aircraft were operating and which was supplied by United States materiel and personnel must be commanded by American officers.

While this stalemate dragged on, Washington also reviewed the value of air bases in the Siberian maritime provinces, one of the initial reasons for having begun "Operation Frantic." Arnold and Spaatz had both been determined to obtain Soviet air bases in Siberia for use by their heavy bombers in the air war against Japan. However, the war situation in the Pacific had changed considerably, too, since that original intent. Less than two weeks after "Frantic I" ("Frantic Joe") took place, U.S. Marines had invaded Saipan, one of the Marianas Islands in the Pacific. This began an "island-hopping" operation by United States military forces in the Pacific that moved so quickly during the remainder of 1944 and the first six months of 1945 that even Washington was surprised. Guam, Tinian, New Guinea, Biak, Morotai, Palau, Okinawa, Taiwan, Leyte, Luzon, and Iwo Jima were secured and provided "stepping stones" for the USAAF for the preparation of its final assault against the Japanese home islands. Using these islands as bases for operations or as refueling stops, the Pacific Ocean was no longer the obstacle to air operations that it had been earlier because of the great distances between Allied bases and the target areas. On November 24, 1944, one month after the Eastern Command was reduced to a single Russian air base at Poltava, B-29 Superfortresses made their first attack on Tokyo from bases in the Marianas Islands. Consequently, the need for Soviet air bases in Far Eastern Siberia was no longer critical. The secured islands in the Pacific Ocean were just as suitable, and since these island bases were under United States control, the frustrating negotiations always associated with any collaboration attempt with the Soviets could be avoided. Time, valuable time, could be saved.

In 1944 there was another factor, a secret factor that only a few individuals in the United States knew about, that made any aid by the Soviet Union in defeating Japan questionable. Based on a letter that President Roosevelt had received from Dr. Albert Einstein six years earlier, the "Manhattan Project" to develop an atomic bomb was nearing the test period. If, as the experts working on the project under the direction of Major General Leslie R. Groves believed, the new bomb was a success there would be no need of help from the Soviet Union to defeat Japan. In fact, after seeing what Soviet Russia was doing in eastern and central Europe —seizing control of liberated country after liberated country so that in the postwar period the Soviet Union would be the dominant power in a large part of Europe, Washington did not want Stalin's token help. If the Soviet Union entered the Pacific war just before it ended, it would give Stalin an excuse to stake a Soviet claim to countries in the Far East territories.

Taking into consideration both the overall war situation in Europe and the Pacific and the development of the new bomb, Washington decided to keep a low profile as far as "Operation Frantic" was concerned. Arnold did not want to cancel the project entirely until he knew for certain that the atomic bomb would be successful and that he would not need air bases in the Siberian maritime provinces for his B-29s, but he no longer pressed for Soviet air bases in Poland or the Balkans. While this decision was under consideration, Stalin had relented somewhat and had permitted an American party under Eaker's leadership to inspect three bases at Oradea, Sokodor, and Bekescsaba. Eaker did not think any of the three were suitable. On April 19, 1945, the Joint Chiefs of Staff, however, decided to notify the Soviet Union formally that the United States no longer desired bases in the Soviet Union and the following message was sent to Eisenhower and Spaatz under that dateline:

Joint Chiefs of Staff have approved the following:

a. That the Soviet authorities be informed that because of the advanced stage of the European war we consider it inadvisable to take advantage of their agreement to provide the United States air bases in the Budapest area.

b. That we abstain from Tactical Air Operations in support of Soviet ground forces except upon their specific request from the Soviet authorities.

c. That we request the Soviet authorities to repair our stranded aircraft and evacuate them and our stranded air crews to a central point in the Balkans where they will be turned over to us for onshipment to Italy; and that if this is agreed, we inform the Soviet authorities that we shall no longer require the air base at Poltava and, at the same time, express our gratitude for the hospitality they have extended to us in connection with the Frantic bases.

d. That we abandon all efforts to introduce United States personnel into the USSR or USSR-controlled territory except on matters essential to the United States in the prosecution of the present war; and that all projects involving American missions to Russia be cleared by an agency of the Joint Chiefs of Staff. Exception to the foregoing will be made for such projects as the Naval survey party for the Gdynia area and the United States bombing survey teams.

This message from General George Marshall clearly indicated American disillusionment with the attempts to collaborate with the Soviet Union and the desire to culminate any further attempts prior to the end of the Japanese war so that Stalin would not be able to make a land-grab as he had in eastern Europe. Stalin, however, immediately understood the aim and intent of the Joint Chiefs of Staff and decided that he would now try to hold the United States to the agreements made during "Operation Frantic." When the need for air bases in the Siberian maritime provinces seemed vital to American planners, Deane and Harriman, with Washington's approval, had agreed to certain terms with Stalin for such bases. They had agreed that the United States would send the Soviet Union about one million tons of supplies as a reserve stockpile for the Red Army when it finally attacked the Japanese in Manchuria. These supplies were to reach the Soviet Union not later than June 1945, and were to be in addition to the American supplies sent to the Soviet Union for use in the war against Hitler. The United States immediately set about fulfilling this supply commitment in late 1944, wanting the materiel to reach the Soviet Union by the deadline but Stalin, once he was certain of getting the materiel, began to stall about providing the Siberian air bases. When the Joint Chiefs of Staff decided that the bases were no longer needed, the flow of supplies was halted and Stalin was furious. The main targets of his anger were the Americans at Poltava who were assigned to the evacuation of the base. The deadline for removing all American personnel, equipment, and supplies from the Soviet air base was May 1945, but it soon became obvious that harassment by the Soviets would make it necessary to extend the deadline. Major General Edmund W. Hill had replaced Walsh as head of the Air Division of the U.S. Military Mission to Moscow after Washington decided to disband the Eastern Command. He met with the usual Russian harassment and eventually he asked Harriman to be relieved of the assignment because he believed that he could be of greater use elsewhere. Harriman, reluctant to lose Hill, finally agreed to the change. The Soviets, however, were uncooperative with Hill until the very end.

When his orders came to leave the Soviet Union, Hill requested that the plane Spaatz had made available to him to facilitate his travel in the Soviet Union (but which the Russians had denied entrance to Soviet territory) be cleared to Moscow from Cairo, where it was grounded at the time. This request was denied. Harriman then offered Hill the use of his aircraft, but again Moscow objected. Molotov stated that Harriman's plane was for the use of the ambassador only. Hill then suggested that he fly out of Moscow on the regularly scheduled shuttle flight to Poltava, knowing that once he reached Poltava he could board one of the transport planes evacuating personnel and supplies from the air base to Cairo. Denied. He then requested rail transportation. Denied. A virtual captive in Moscow, Hill asked Harriman to meet with Molotov again to resolve the problem of his leaving the Soviet Union. At the meeting, Molotov told Harriman that the general could leave by "commercial" airline, which did not exist in the Soviet Union at the time. Harriman realized that it was a pretense, of course, but he agreed to this proposal in the hope that Hill could finally make his way to another country where he could get adequate transportation to the United States. The "commercial" airliner turned out to be an American Lend-Lease C-47 used to haul freight. An overstuffed chair had been installed in the freight section for Hill, the only seat on the plane except in the cockpit.

The C-47 was scheduled to fly from Moscow to Tehran, but instead landed at Baku on the Caspian Sea. At Baku, Hill went into the air terminal to try to get something to eat, only to discover that ham and eggs would cost him $42.00 at the artificially-pegged rate of exchange. He decided to go hungry until he reached Tehran. While he was waiting for the C-47 to take off again, a Russian civilian who could speak some English came over to him and stated that the Soviet authorities wanted to see him in another room to open his baggage for inspection. Hill, thinking his bags were still on the C-47, went into the other room to explain, but was shocked to see his bags already in the room. He was told to unlock his bags but refused, stating that he was traveling under diplomatic immunity. They forced his secretary to open his bags, however, and the Soviets searched them very closely, even making a page-by-page study of his paperback novels. Hill, angry, told the Russians that he considered the search harassment and that if they continued he would recommend that all Russians traveling in the United States zones of occupation be given the same treatment. The Russians immediately said that the examination was over and that Hill's secretary could lock his bags.

When the American general returned to the flight line he discovered that his bags had been loaded onto a different C-47; he had to lie stretched out on top of the baggage all the way to Tehran.

This rudeness was later compounded when he received a letter from the U.S. War Department informing him that the Soviet Union had sent a bill to the U.S. State Department for more than $25,000 to pay for Hill's travel from Moscow to Tehran. The U.S. War Department wanted his comments on the bill. Understandably, the general's comments were strong and emphasized that the bill should not be paid under any circumstance.

During December 1944, before Washington definitely decided that the United States needed no help from the Soviet Union to defeat Japan, a tall, slender, salty-speaking ex-airmail pilot by the name of William L. Ritchie arrived in Moscow on a secret mission. Brigadier General Ritchie was a personal representative of General Arnold at the time and was in the Soviet Union with several other American military officers to brief the Soviets on American plans for the war against Japan. Ritchie and his associates were there to state, not negotiate. Russian officers had to agree; they were not given any opportunity to do otherwise. As spring approached and it became evident that, because of the atomic bomb development and the overall war situation, no help was desired from the Soviets in defeating Japan and Washington decided to end "Operation Frantic." Ritchie was asked if he would replace the departing Hill. He was well-known in United States military circles for his toughness and stubbornness in dealing with the Soviets, and circumstances at Poltava definitely required such an officer during the spring of 1945.

Ritchie arrived at Poltava for an inspection on May 30, 1945, and within a matter of hours he realized that there was a "secret war" going on at the air base between the Russians and the Americans about which the outside world knew nothing. One of his first actions was to review the evacuation plans Deane had transmitted to Spaatz on May 16, 1945:

Referring to your message of 15th of May and in view of our conversation in Berlin, the following plan for the evacuation of Poltava is being implemented:

1. Personnel

   a. Twenty-two officers and 162 enlisted men assigned to Escom will be evacuated by air direct to Cairo for return as individuals to U.S.

   b. One officer and 20 enlisted men on TD [temporary duty] from 15th AF will be returned by air to the 15th AF via Cairo.

   c. Three officers and 6 enlisted men (crews for your three-C-47s) will be returned to the 302nd Transport Wing, USSTAF, with their aircraft upon completion of evacuation.

   d. Two officers and 4 enlisted men, combat crews from 15th AF now detained as principal and witnesses to a fatal auto accident at Poltava will be returned to 15th AF by air as soon as case is cleared up and prior to final closure of case.

2. Equipment

   a. By rail to Moscow such equipment, subsistence, and PX stores as are needed in Moscow, amounting to approximately 15 cars.

   b. By air direct to Cairo approximately 15 C-46 loads of special Air Corps supply items, special signal equipment including classified radar and crypto equipment and some medical, ordnance and special service items.

   c. Remainder of equipment and installation including the fixed radio transmitter will be turned over to the Soviets on Lend-Lease or salvage.

Soviets have agreed to direct flights between Poltava and Cairo for the accomplishment of the evacuation. Cairo has been requested to clear flights over Turkey. Evacuation by air will begin as soon as confirmation of this clearance has been received, probably by 17 May.

It did not take Ritchie long to realize that the Soviets had no intention of keeping to their agreement with Deane concerning the evacuation of Poltava. One of the first "rules" the Russians tried to set up after Ritchie's arrival was that only Red Air Force pilots and crews could fly American aircraft still in the Soviet

Union, including Ritchie's C-47. The general absolutely refused to abide by the order, well aware that during "Operation Frantic" the Soviets had already "appropriated" 62 American aircraft. He knew that if he permitted a Red Air Force crew to take off in an American plane from Poltava that would be the last he would see of it. Ritchie's refusal to abide by the order left the Soviets only one choice—shoot down any American aircraft that left Poltava manned by an American crew. They did not have the nerve. The salty Ritchie later spotted a B-29 on an airfield near Moscow and wanted to hijack it, but Harriman, wanting to avoid an international problem, stopped him.

Since Ritchie could remove only such equipment and material that was flyable from Poltava it soon became obvious that millions of dollars worth of American supplies would be left behind for the Russians to use, including the three air bases that American money and skilled labor had rebuilt. Yet even this windfall did not appease the Russians. When a warehouse full of food was given to the Soviets, Ritchie was harassed because there were ten cans fewer peaches than they expected despite the fact that the warehouse contained thousands of cans of peaches! The discrepancy was reported to Moscow. Thousands of gallons of 100-octane gas had to be left at the air base, but when Ritchie requested 50 gallons for his automobile in Moscow, he was told that he could take 300 gallons, or none. Since he did not have a large enough container to hold 300 gallons, the general told his driver to fill six 50-gallon drums, but the Soviets would not permit it. The driver had to take the 300 gallons of gasoline in one container or not at all. Consequently, Ritchie did not get any gasoline for his automobile.

One of the most delicate problems the general had to settle was the charge against an American lieutenant who had accidently killed a Russian woman in an automobile accident near Poltava. The lieutenant was not permitted to leave the Soviet Union until he stood trial for the woman's "murder." Ritchie was determined that no American officer was going to be left behind when "Operation Frantic" ended. When a Soviet trial board found the lieutenant guilty and sentenced him to two years at hard labor, Ritchie was prepared to load the officer on his C-47 and shoot his way out of the Soviet Union, if necessary. Aware of the general's anger, the Russians immediately reopened the case, suspended the sentence, and handed the lieutenant over to Ritchie, who had him aboard the next American plane heading for Cairo.

One technique the tough-minded general developed to perfection in his dealings with the Soviets during the evacuation of the personnel, flyable equipment, and supplies from Poltava enabled him to completely outsmart even Stalin several times. When a problem existed, Ritchie would set a definite date for receiving an answer from the Soviets, explaining in writing that if no answer was received by that time he would do as he wanted to solve the problem. He was well aware that the Russians did not like ultimatums and would never meet them. They always had the "I'll show those Americans" attitude. Arnold had promised the Soviets a number of B-24 aircraft, but the Russians haggled about training crews, equipment, and how they should be delivered. Ritchie sent an ultimatum letter to the Red Air Force setting a date by which the B-24s had to be accepted. As usual, the Red Air Force staff ignored the ultimatum and Ritchie, at midnight of the date set, promptly sent a letter to the Soviets cancelling the deal. Later, he referred all Soviet protests to his ultimatum letter.

When he was in the midst of evacuating Poltava, Ritchie discovered a warehouse full of all types of secret weapons and equipment used in undercover, behind-the-lines assignments by the OSS (Office of Strategic Services—U.S. precursor of the CIA). Upon investigating he learned that it was equipment that had remained in the Soviet Union when a deal between the OSS and the NKVD failed to materialize. He wanted to get rid of the highly explosive secret weapons but he did not want the Soviets to get their hands on the equipment, so he resorted to his ultimatum procedure. Ritchie sent an official letter to the Russians stating a time and date for the Soviets to remove the equipment from the warehouse. The ultimatum was not met, but the general knew he was being watched closely by the NKVD, who wanted the secret weapons, but did not want to "lose face" by meeting an American officer's ultimatum. Ritchie took a truck to the warehouse at midnight of the deadline date but, much to the surprise of the Russian driver, who was an NKVD agent, he did not load any of the secret materiel on it. Instead, Ritchie took a long drive in the empty truck through the countryside, followed all the way by several carloads of NKVD agents. Meanwhile, an American sergeant loaded all the OSS devices into another truck, took them to a nearby river, and dumped them into the water through a hole in the ice. The Soviets were furious, but Ritchie calmly referred them to his ultimatum letter.

In retaliation for Ritchie's unrelenting battle against their harassment, the Soviets refused to permit the cargo planes carrying equipment and personnel out of Poltava to fly to Cairo via Ankara, which was much faster. They notified the general that American transport planes would have to fly by way of Baku and Tehran to Cairo. This was a hardship because transport planes were scarce, many of them being used in the Pacific Theater of Operations as the war against Japan required more and more aircraft. After Harriman interceded, the Soviets relented to the extent of permitting one cargo plane a day fly to Cairo via Ankara if the loading list, route, altitude, and flight time were given the Soviet authorities twenty-four hours in advance. Despite following this procedure very carefully, one of the American C-46s was forced down by Yak fighters on the second day. Ritchie was so angry he halted all evacuation movement and demanded a written agreement signed by the Foreign Office before he would continue the evacuation of Poltava. For an entire week, the Russians and the general were in a stalemate, but when the Kremlin finally decided that Ritchie meant exactly what he said, the agreement was executed and a copy was given him.

By June 22, 1945, the general was prepared to close down all American operations at Poltava and officially end "Operation Frantic." Two aircraft were loaded and waiting for clearance— one to carry Ritchie and his staff, the other to haul out the files containing the documents relating to the project that was being terminated. Since there was going to be a big victory parade in Moscow's Red Square the next day, Stalin wanted Deane, Harriman, and Ritchie to be present and visible to the press so that he could use their presence to impress the rest of the world that the Americans appreciated the Soviet Union's victory over the Nazis. However, when it came time to take off from Poltava for Moscow, Ritchie discovered that *his* aircraft had been cleared by the Russians for the flight but that the second aircraft, the one carrying the files, was not. The general refused to go. He immediately called Deane in Moscow and explained the situation. It was decided that unless both planes were cleared to fly to Moscow none of the Americans would appear at the victory parade the following day. The Kremlin was notified, but there was no reply. Ritchie sat in his plane all morning, through lunch, and until—at 1430 hours in the afternoon—Stalin decided that the presence of the Americans at the victory parade in Red Square the following day was more important than confiscating the United States files pertaining to "Operation Frantic."

The two transport planes carrying the last Americans from Poltava and the files touched down at the Moscow airport at 1830 hours on the evening of June 22, 1945, and "Operation Frantic" was only a memory.

It was ironic that Poltava was officially closed as far as "Operation Frantic" was concerned one year to the day after the disastrous raid by the Luftwaffe that had been its death knell.

15

The Indictment

WAS "OPERATION FRANTIC" a success?
A study of the statistics of the project is interesting. Seven task forces, four from the Eighth Air Force in Great Britain and three from the Fifteenth Air Force in Italy, made the long, hazardous flight to the Soviet air bases. These task forces carried out a total of eighteen bombing and strafing missions, not including the Warsaw supply mission. Seven of the missions were West-Target-East shuttle missions to Soviet Russia, eight were East-Target-West shuttle missions from Soviet Russia to Italy, and three were East-Target-East missions in which the Soviet airfields were used for both takeoff and return.

The total number of bombers and fighters coming in on these missions to Eastern Command bases was 1,030, consisting of 529 Flying Fortresses, 106 Lightnings, and 395 Mustangs. These planes completed a total of 2,207 sorties to or from Soviet bases, of which 1,122 were bomber sorties, 414 were fighter sweeps, and 671 were fighter escort sorties. The bombers hit twelve different targets besides hitting one target of opportunity in force. They dropped a total of 1,955 tons of bombs with results that were rated "good" in all cases except two "fair" and two "excellent." The fighters strafed three additional targets and three that had been hit by the bombers.

The number of photographic reconnaissance sorties from or to the Eastern Command bases totalled 117, and 174 targets were photographed. Of the 117 sorties, 33 came from Italy, 29 returned to Italy, six came from Great Britain, and 49 were East-Target-East photographic sorties which both originated and terminated at the Soviet bases.

In air-to-air combat, the fighters, together with escorted bombers, destroyed at least 100 enemy aircraft, probably destroyed

20, and damaged 48. In addition, the six strafing missions on the eastern front destroyed 60 enemy aircraft on the ground, probably destroyed seven, and damaged fifteen trucks, four tank cars, and two buses, besides damaging additional transportation equipment and strafing numerous enemy airdrome installations, one troop train, and six flak batteries.

In the course of "Operation Frantic," the following battle losses were incurred by the USAAF: five Flying Fortresses and seventeen Mustangs or Lightnings lost in combat; two killed, ten wounded, and 41 missing in action; 43 Flying Fortresses, two C-47s, and one Lightning were destroyed by German air attacks and two Americans were killed and fourteen wounded by the Luftwaffe attack.

The statistics, however, do not answer the question about the success or failure of "Operation Frantic" because the project had other purposes which were of more importance than the bombing of enemy targets. Since some of these purposes involved subtle intrigue, measuring the percentage of success or failure is extremely difficult. As for the targets bombed, for example, nearly all of them could have been reached without utilizing the Soviet airfields and with less effort, so it is evident that, based on bomb damage inflicted on the targets originally scheduled to be attacked by the USAAF, "Operation Frantic" was a failure. Stalin did not permit the Flying Fortresses to bomb the targets Spaatz considered important, so Spaatz had to compromise and attack those targets his planes were allowed to attack. Nor was the aim achieved of forcing the Luftwaffe to send additional fighter units to the east just as the cross-Channel invasion was scheduled in the west. Some of the high-ranking Germans considered the shuttle missions a propaganda stunt, and Field Marshal Wilhelm Keitel stated that he was convinced that the entire affair was an attempt to demonstrate to the Germans how closely the Americans and the Russians were collaborating. Instead of causing panic among the German leaders, "Operation Frantic" provided the Luftwaffe with an excellent opportunity to conduct one of its most successful missions against the USAAF during the entire war—the disaster at Poltava. Whether the Soviet Union was a party to this tragedy or not has been argued ever since.

Since the Luftwaffe attack on Poltava on the night of June 21, 1944, sounded the death knell of "Operation Frantic," an analysis of this incident in light of postwar Soviet international behavior is important. At the time the Soviets were criticized by the Americans for not providing adequate protection for the "Operation Frantic" air bases. They were not criticized formally by the United States, but in Washington and London such leaders as Arnold, Spaatz, Churchill, Eaker, and others were puzzled and angry that not a single Red Air Force fighter plane appeared over Poltava that night to attack the German bombers. Antrup and the other Luftwaffe pilots circled over the air base and the surrounding area from 0030 hours until 0220 hours, dropping their high explosive bombs, anti-personnel bombs, and strafing at will without one Red Air Force night fighter challenging them. To make matters more confusing, the Russians refused to permit the American Mustang pilots of the Eighth Air Force who had landed at Piryatin that day to take off and attack the Luftwaffe planes. Immediately after this USAAF disaster, an investigation was undertaken by a board of American officers. Their conclusion was that the Soviets had underestimated the defense needs of the air bases and had also underestimated the strength of the Luftwaffe in the area. Later, however, as "Operation Frantic" encountered more and more "Kremlin trouble," some Americans began to wonder whether these were the only reasons for the Poltava disaster— or if they were the true reasons at all.

The initial "Operation Frantic" mission on June 2, 1944, flown by the Fifteenth Air Force out of Italy, had been an outstanding beginning for the project. Worldwide publicity about the USAAF heavy bombers using Soviet bases was achieved and despite the fact that the Soviet authorities, including Stalin, seemed overjoyed with the results of this first shuttle mission, it appears that the Kremlin had second thoughts about the entire project a few days later. Stalin was already preparing for postwar domination over as much of Europe as possible while Roosevelt and Churchill, while certainly not ignoring postwar matters, in 1944 were concentrating on the defeat of Hitler. When it became apparent to Stalin that other nations, including those he wanted to control after the end of the war, were getting the impression that the USAAF was in the Soviet Union to help Russia defeat the Germans on the eastern front he had a change of heart about "Operation Frantic." With his Red Army moving into Poland and pushing the Nazi forces back, Stalin was confident that the Soviet

Union could now defeat the Germans without the help they so desperately needed and had received during the earlier years of the war from the United States. He decided that he wanted the USAAF out of the Soviet Union as soon as possible despite the auspicious beginning of "Operation Frantic."

The Soviets knew that they could not merely notify President Roosevelt they no longer desired Americans on their soil and would he please withdraw the "Operation Frantic" personnel as soon as possible. Such a crude move would create a mistrust in 1944 that might affect later Soviet political moves. Stalin did not want to show his hand over "Operation Frantic." He wanted the United States to "trust" the Soviet Union until he could position his forces so that there would be no doubt about Soviet control of most of the liberated countries in eastern Europe after the war ended. If the United States began actively to oppose the Soviet Union in 1944, there was the possibility that his postwar plans for eastern Europe might be thwarted. It was too early in the game to play this hand. Nor could he force the Americans to leave Soviet Russia and abandon the shuttle-mission project in the immediate future merely by placing obstacles in the path of the "Operation Frantic" leaders. Under orders from President Roosevelt, Deane, Walsh, Kessler, Spaatz, Harriman, and other "Frantic" military and diplomatic personnel were constantly compromising and backing down in the face of the strict regulations, flat refusals, harassing tactics, and rude treatment of the Soviet officers with whom they had to negotiate or the Kremlin party leaders who often made the final decisions. As Harriman stated later: "From a political viewpoint, President Roosevelt was determined that he could use a wartime friendliness with Stalin to develop a successful postwar relationship. Before he died he realized that his hopes had not been fully achieved."

In June 1944, however, when the Soviet leader told the Americans at Poltava or Washington or London that they could bomb only the targets the Red Air Force selected; that their reconnaissance planes could fly only at certain times, at certain altitudes, in certain corridors; that only a limited number of mechanics and ground personnel could be admitted to the Soviet Union . . . the Americans nodded agreement, and sometimes added "Thank you." Consequently, Stalin, who wanted the Americans out of the Soviet Union as quickly as possible, but did not want Washington to think the Kremlin had forced them out deliberately, had one remaining alternative that offered an answer to the problem. The answer was the Luftwaffe. If the German air force destroyed one of the "Frantic" task forces there was a possibility that the United States might decide that the cost of "Operation Frantic" was too high for the results achieved and would withdraw their forces from the Soviet Union at their own instigation. Since the American heavy bombers were always escorted by a strong force of Mustang fighters en route to and out of the Soviet Union, it was obvious that the Luftwaffe could not destroy a "Frantic" task force in the air. Their best opportunity would be to attack the American planes on the ground and at night.

Were the Germans tipped off by the Soviets that on the night of June 21, 1944, 73 Flying Fortresses of the Forty-fifth Combat Bombardment Wing of the Eighth Air Force would be parked on the air base at Poltava? There are many indications that this information was given to the Germans by either the Soviets or by German sympathizers alerted by Moscow to deliver the information. For some reason never officially revealed, several of the Luftwaffe aircraft that participated in the Poltava mission were moved east to positions nearer the Soviet air base several hours before the "Frantic II" task force led by Old left the other bombers of the Eighth Air Force and continued toward the Soviet Union. There was no way that the Luftwaffe could tell that another shuttle mission was in progress that early the morning of June 21, 1944, unless someone had alerted them to the fact. A German report on the mission by Hans-Detlef Herhudt von Rohden states:

> About 1000 hours on the morning of June 21, 1944, the Chief of Staff of IV Fliegerkorps in the Brest-Litovsk area received an emergency telephone call from Air Fleet Six headquarters. Fifteen minutes later the Commanding General told his staff that a strong unit of U.S. heavy bombers was flying to Russia. Immediately plans are made to attack. At 1500 hours the Commanding Officer issued the mission order: 'Tonight you are to attack the airfields of Poltava and Mirgorod. It is important to destroy simultaneously the U.S. bombers.'

According to this authoritative German report on file in the German Air Force Archives, General Rudolf Meister, commanding officer of IV Fliegerkorps, gave the attack order to bomb

Poltava and Mirgorod the night of June 21, 1944, before Old had even landed his task force in the Soviet Union! Since, as far as the Germans knew, many other Soviet air bases in the Ukraine *could have* been used by the American heavy bombers, it is obvious that Meister had been informed that Poltava and Mirgorod were the destinations of the "Frantic II" bombers.

Another strange incident occurred during the shuttle mission while the American heavy bombers were en route to the Soviet air bases, one that was accepted as a fact of war at the time. As Old stated in his report to the Third Bombardment Division after the attack:

> Shortly after passing Warsaw it was noticed that a German single-engine fighter was keeping pace with the task force, flying just above the low broken clouds, about eleven o'clock.

Many of the crewmen aboard the Flying Fortresses testified later that the lone Me-109 seemed to have a charmed existence. When the American heavy bombers crossed the eastern front, the German ground defenses fired barrage after barrage at the aircraft but were careful to avoid firing near the Me-109. This was understandable; the German gunners obviously did not want to shoot down a German plane. However, when the bombers continued eastward and flew above the Red Army units, the Russian gunners also fired at the American task force although they had been alerted in advance that the Flying Fortresses would be flying over their front lines. Even more surprising was the fact that the Russian gunners avoided firing at the German fighter, too! It was as though the gunners had been warned not to harass the Me-109! Fortunately, the Red Army gunners did not damage any of the B-17s either, but it was because of their lack of accuracy, not their lack of effort.

The Me-109 continually radioed position reports of the "Frantic II" task force to Luftwaffe ground stations until bad weather over the Soviet Union forced the pilot to return to his base. By this time, Mueller in the He-177 reconnaissance aircraft was on his way to the Ukraine to take the photographs of the B-17s on the Soviet air bases which Antrup and his pilots used later that night to destroy Old's task force at Poltava. The only reason that Mirgorod was not bombed the night of June 21, 1944, as planned, was the fact that one of the Luftwaffe flight leaders made a navigational error and ended up over Poltava rather than Mirgorod. With fuel at a minimum, this group of German aircraft also bombed Poltava.

Once the attack began, the puzzling questions asked by every American at the scene that night was: "Where is the Red Air Force?" Why didn't the Russians send up their fighters during the nearly two hours the Luftwaffe spent over Poltava bombing and strafing the American planes? Were there no aircraft available? To listen to some military and political leaders at the time was to be convinced that the Soviet Union really did not have much air power and did not use the planes they had very often or very effectively. This mistaken opinion was, to some extent, understandable because of the fact that the Soviets were so secretive that they rarely confided in American military leaders. Most Americans were hazy about Red Air Force activities in 1944 simply because there was no way to learn the true facts. Later studies have proved, however, that by 1944 the Russians had a very strong air force and used it extensively and efficiently— when they so desired.

After the Red Army recaptured Kiev, the stage was set for a rapid Russian advance westward. Two and one-half weeks after the Normandy assault in the west, the Soviet summer offensive began and it was supported by more than 70 air divisions! This was the same month—June—the Luftwaffe bombed Poltava, and Poltava was within an hour's flying distance of the jumping-off place for the Red Army offensive! No planes to defend Poltava? Ridiculous. The 70 air divisions consisted of more than 7,000 planes. By June of 1944 the Red Air Force had new Yak fighters capable of speeds greater than 360 miles per hour and equal in performance to the latest model Me-109. La-7 fighters and IL-10s, which were remodeled IL-2s, were available. It is now known that during this period the performance of the Red Air Force, including the defense units, was finer than ever before. Stalin made certain that the units assigned to defend the Soviet air bases and cities received new aircraft types. While the defense units consisted of a much smaller number of planes and pilots than the ground support units, they were well trained and more than a match for the German pilots on the eastern front in 1944. This is proved by the fact that 68 percent of all German aircraft downed by the Russian defense systems in 1944 were accounted for by fighter pilots—twice as many as were downed by gunners on the ground.

The excuse that no Red Air Force fighters appeared over Poltava during the Luftwaffe attack because the Russians had no night fighters has no basis either. Night fighter training had begun in the Red Air Force as early as 1942, and while the Soviet pilots had no radar to rely on, they were experts in engaging German aircraft caught in the illumination of ground searchlights. There were many searchlights that fateful night at Poltava, but *no* Red Air Force fighters.

The answer to the question: "Where is the Red Air Force?" is obvious: It was on the ground, where it had been ordered to stay! Political objectives coveted by Stalin dictated that the "Frantic II" task force be destroyed by the Luftwaffe and the fact that only the American heavy bombers parked at Poltava were attacked that night was no fault of the Russian dictator. It was due to the previously mentioned error in navigation by a Luftwaffe fight leader. Either through a shrewd, calculated negligence or by outright complicity with the Germans, Stalin took the initial step in achieving his aim of getting the USAAF out of the Soviet Union.

Further proof of the Stalin plot at Poltava was the Soviet refusal to permit the American fighter pilots who had landed at Piryatin to take off and engage the German bombers during the German air raid. Old, in his message to the Third Bombardment Division after the Poltava attack mentioned this strange fact:

American fighter pilots were very anxious to take off and attack the German bombers but Russian clearances could not be obtained.

The Mustangs of the Fourth and 352nd Fighter Groups had been refueled after the "Frantic II" task force arrived from Britain and were ready to go. So were the pilots. Fliers such as Blakeslee, who already had fifteen German fighters to his credit, would have disrupted the German attack despite the fact that they had no ground radar facilities to vector them to the enemy aircraft. They did not need radar. The sky over Poltava was brightly illuminated by the flares dropped by the Luftwaffe marker planes and by the Russian searchlights that flooded the sky with light. The Ju-88s and He-111s were readily visible to the naked eye and would have made fine targets for the veteran American fighter

pilots . . . but the Soviets, not wanting the enemy attack interrupted, refused permission for the Mustangs to take off!

Even after the Poltava tragedy, President Roosevelt, Harry
Hopkins, and other politicians, diplomats, and military leaders
believed that Stalin was making an effort to collaborate with the
United States. They were convinced that Poltava had been an
unfortunate incident that could not be blamed directly on the
Soviets, although they admitted that the Red Air Force and Red
Army had insisted from the beginning of "Operation Frantic"
that they could and would defend the bases used by the American
heavy bombers. "Give Stalin another chance," was the theme and
the same American "compromising and backing down" conduct
was followed during negotiations in the weeks after the Luftwaffe
raid. When the Russians asked for something, they got it. An
oxygen system for their high-altitude photographic reconnaissance
planes was added to the Norden bombsight and automatic pilot
they had already received from the USAAF. Night fighters and
the related radar equipment to direct the night fighters from the
ground was offered to the Red Air Force, including American
personnel to train the Russian pilots and radar operators. The
Russians were never satisfied. In July and August 1944, the Soviets
requested and were given information on American signal and
radar equipment used at Eastern Command headquarters and it
was not until after the Warsaw affair that the USAAF finally
became wary. At that time the secret United States cryptographic
sites and radio range stations were made out of bounds to Russian
personnel, but it was too late. By then the Soviets had learned all
they wanted to know about the equipment, just as they had already learned all they wanted to know about the B-17s and
P-51s used on the shuttle missions. They demanded and accepted
copies of every photograph taken by the American reconnaissance
planes, but in return gave the USAAF no photographs of German
targets. They "appropriated" USAAF aircraft and never returned
them . . . and Washington advised Eastern Command to "overlook" such actions in hope of winning Stalin's favor.

Deane was becoming more and more disillusioned as the weeks
passed but he had to follow the "compromise" approach with the
Soviets that President Roosevelt advocated. One of the most
discouraging and tragic problems he tried to negotiate successfully with the Soviets was the repatriation of prisoners of war.

Since Germany had a policy of keeping her war prisoners as far from the countries of which they were nationals as possible, the majority of American prisoners of war were in camps in eastern Germany, Poland, or the Balkans. Many of these prisoners were USAAF crewmen, some of whom had been shot down on the shuttle missions. It certainly seemed logical and humane that the Russians, as they freed these American prisoners, would turn them over to the United States for prompt return home. Deane, being the senior military officer in the Soviet Union, made a formal request to the Red Army General staff that this procedure be followed, and was assured that such instructions would be issued to the advancing armies. The general immediately sent a request to Great Britain for medical supplies, several luxury items, and new clothing. He also requested the Persian Gulf Command to have a store of such needed supplies ready for air delivery to points inside liberated areas when required. The American hospital facilities at Poltava were enlarged and arrangements were made to fly seriously ill liberated prisoners to the hospital as soon as they were released. In addition, Deane organized a group of officers and enlisted men who had had special training to make contact with the freed Americans. All was in readiness, but the Soviets, in one of the most inhumane actions between allies during the entire war, refused to give Deane any information on American prisoners of war. Numerous meetings were held and numerous agreements were signed, but the Russians did not honor any of them. The Americans not only had to survive the Germans; they also had to survive the treatment given them by the Russians who were, supposedly, allies.

On February 17, 1945, while the Eastern Command was still headquartered at Poltava, three American officers arrived in Moscow after walking and hitchhiking across Poland and western Russia. Captain Ernest M. Gruenberg, Second Lieutenant Frank H. Colley, and Second Lieutenant John N. Dimmling, Jr., had escaped from the Germans a month earlier near Szubin, Poland. As they moved eastward behind Russian lines, they soon discovered that the Soviets were putting Americans who had escaped from the Nazis into "camps" where they were kept as though they were still prisoners of war. The trio of officers was detained at such a camp near Wegheim, near Exin, Poland, but escaped. Moving eastward toward Moscow, they hid from the Russians, seeking shelter from Polish farmers and peasants. By some miracle the NKVD did not apprehend the three American officers and they reached Deane's office to report on the condition of other American prisoners who had been "liberated" by the Soviets.

Armed with the information from the three officers, Deane confronted the Soviets again and demanded the release of the Americans. It took a personal appeal from President Roosevelt to Stalin and continuous and relentless pressure by Harriman on the Soviet Foreign Office before a trickle of Americans were turned free. It was a sordid affair that was a further indication that the Soviet leaders intended to harass the United States in every manner possible. Poltava and the prisoner-of-war controversy should have convinced even the most staunch Soviet supporter among the Americans that Stalin was on a course that would lead to serious difficulty for the United States after the war ended; unfortunately it did not.

The Warsaw tragedy of August and September 1944, was the most obvious clue to Stalin's postwar intentions. Stalin did not even try to hide his motives during this affair. After radioing encouragement to the underground fighters inside the city to begin the uprising, he failed to help them with the Red Air Force or the Red Army. He then refused to permit the American heavy bombers of "Operation Frantic" to help General Bor and his Home Army. Instead, Stalin left them to die in Warsaw at the hands of the Nazis so that his handpicked Lublin Poles would gain control of Poland. It was one of the most traitorous deeds in history. Yet, unbelievably, many government military American leaders still thought Stalin could be trusted. Despite the fact that Stalin plainly indicated by his actions that he intended to have Poland under Soviet control regardless of what the United States or Great Britain wanted, men such as Marshall, Eisenhower, and Roosevelt still thought the United States could get along with the Soviet Union after the war. Washington thought that when Stalin said he wanted a "friendly government" in Poland or in the Balkans or in some other eastern European nation he meant a government with which the United States and Soviet Russia would not have undue trouble; Stalin actually meant a communist government he could control!

One man who was not duped was George F. Kennan, Harriman's deputy. He felt that this was the time to have an eye-to-eye showdown with the Soviet leaders, to confront them with the choice of either collaborating with the United States to establish truly independent governments in eastern Europe, or relinquishing all further American support and fighting the rest of the war on its own. He argued that the United States no longer owed Soviet Russia or Stalin anything and that, in his opinion, we had never owed them anything. The cross-Channel invasion was a reality, American troops were on the European continent in force, and all of the Soviet Union had been liberated. The stakes now were non-Soviet territories that had been captured by the Germans. If Stalin, as indicated by his actions during the Warsaw crisis, did not want these countries to make their own choice of government, then the United States should sever all military relations with the Soviets. The military and political leaders should have listened to Kennan and read his September 1944 essay, *Russia—Seven Years Later,* in which he emphasized that as long as Stalin and the men around him ruled the Soviet Union, western statesmen would be in a precarious position in conducting relations with Soviet Russia. "Men of good will from abroad," he stated, "will have no assurance that their efforts on behalf of better relations with Russia will not lead to tragedy instead of to the results they are seeking."

As the winter of 1944-45 wore on and "Operation Frantic" was reduced to the 200 Americans at Eastern Command headquarters at Poltava, the ruthless ambitions of Stalin and the men around him became more and more evident. The Kremlin promptly concluded armistice agreements with the Finns, the Rumanians, and the Bulgarians as these territories were "liberated." The terms were always dictated by the Soviets and the "booty" of these countries, such as American-owned oil fields in Rumania, soon came under Soviet control. Even when a tripartite control commission was established to govern the countries freed from Nazi occupation, the Soviets refused to cooperate with the representatives of the United States and Great Britain. They would withhold information from their British and American colleagues, completely ignore their suggestions, and bring in the NKVD to isolate the allied officers from the citizens of the area as though they were dangerous enemies. As the winter months passed, the United States lost most of its prestige and all of its influence in aiding the liberated countries of eastern Europe to choose their own rulers and form of government.

The Yalta conference of the Big Three in February 1945 was Stalin's ultimate victory: Soviet domination of postwar eastern Europe. The conference was a continuation of Stalin's subterfuge. Many agreements—or what passed as agreements—were reached by the ailing President Roosevelt, Prime Minister Churchill, and Marshal Stalin. They agreed on plans to occupy Germany once Hitler was defeated and confirmed the new westward shift of Poland's boundaries. They agreed to set up an interim government in Poland, bringing in the London Poles, the free Poles from within Poland, and the Lublin Poles, to hold a "free and unfettered" election, and, in addition, Stalin agreed that all the other countries of eastern Europe would have the right to hold free elections and that the three governments would work together to assure such elections. Stalin also made a secret promise that the Soviet Union would declare war on Japan within three months after Germany's surrender. In return for this promise, the Soviet Union was promised the Kurile Islands and the southern part of Sakhalin Island, which Japan controlled, as well as other concessions.

Both Roosevelt and Churchill returned from Yalta convinced that they had finally reached several firm agreements with Stalin and that at last, there was a mutual understanding between the Soviet Union and the western allies. Churchill, in addressing the House of Commons, stated:

> The Crimean Conference leaves the Allies more closely united than before, both in the military and the political sphere. Most solemn declarations have been made by Marshal Stalin and the Soviet Union that the sovereign independence of Poland is to be maintained and this decision is now joined in both by Great Britain and the United States.

President Roosevelt, only weeks away from death, addressed a joint session of both Houses of Congress and declared:

> One outstanding example of joint action by the three major Allied powers in the liberated areas was the solution reached on Poland.

The actual results were vastly different from what either Roosevelt or Churchill expected, although by this time they should have been aware of Stalin's true character. Within weeks it became evident that Stalin had no intention of honoring the so-called Yalta agreements. He never permitted free elections to be held in Poland as he had promised, and the country remained under Soviet control. He enslaved millions of people in eastern Europe, using the Yalta "agreements" as an excuse. He did not declare war on Japan until after the first atomic bomb had been dropped on Hiroshima. He then quickly seized Manchuria and North Korea.

Before he died on April 12, 1945, President Roosevelt was aware that Stalin was breaking his Yalta promises. On April 1, 1945, less than two weeks before his death, he forwarded a message to Harriman in Moscow to be given to Stalin. In the communication Roosevelt said:

> I cannot conceal from you the concern with which I view the developments of events of mutual interest since our fruitful meeting at Yalta. The decisions we reached there were good ones and have for the most part been welcomed with enthusiasm by the peoples of the world who saw in our ability to find a common basis of understanding the best pledge for a secure and peaceful world after this war. So far there has been a discouraging lack of progress made in the carrying out, which the world expects, of the political decisions which we reached at the conference particularly those relating to the Polish question.

By the time "Operation Frantic" was formally ended and Ritchie gave the orders for the remaining two American transport planes to fly out of Poltava in June 1945, it was obvious that Stalin had no intention of keeping the Yalta agreements. The lessons of the months of tactful approaches and protracted negotiations by the Americans involved with the shuttle-mission project that had resulted in no Soviet concessions had not been heeded by President Roosevelt and his staff at Yalta, and the free world paid the price in the postwar years. "Operation Frantic" was, mistakenly, considered a "minor" secret operation by American military and political leaders. Consequently, these same individuals, who had the responsibility of guiding the United States through the difficult years after World War II, overlooked the lessons learned at Poltava and Moscow during the project. If they had understood that Stalin and his cohorts in the Kremlin intended to treat the United States in the postwar years exactly as they had during "Operation Frantic," that they had no intention of collaborating with the American leaders except when the Soviet

Union would benefit, postwar relations with the Soviet Union would have been handled much differently by Washington than they were. The concessions, compromises, and half-measures that weakened the United States and strengthened the Soviet Union during the postwar years would have been avoided.

This "backing down" by the Americans never stopped throughout the entire lifetime of "Operation Frantic" and there is little doubt that this lack of firmness affected the postwar relations between the United States and the Soviet Union. Stalin used "Operation Frantic" to probe the Americans to see what manner of men they were and to test their mettle. He used the project not only to obtain military secrets but to "feel out" the world he had shut himself and Russia out of during the first thirty years of the Russian Revolution. Unfortunately, conscientious officers such as Deane, Spaatz, and Kessler thought that by agreeing with the Russians they would eventually win them over and that the Soviets would cooperate to a much greater extent. This was an error in judgment that was not based on any lack of courage by the Americans involved, but on a lack of understanding of the Russians.

The disaster at Poltava was a disaster for the entire free world . . . but no one realized it until it was too late.

Appendix

Eastern Command Fact Book

compiled by
Major General Robert L. Walsh

SUMMARY OF BOMBER OPERATIONS

Part I

DATE	AIR FORCE	BOMBERS DISPATCHED	NOT BOMBING AND EARLY RET.	BOMBERS ATTACKING	TARGET	BOMBS DROPPED		RESULTS
						GENERAL PURPOSE	INCENDIARY	
JUNE								
2	15th	130	0	130	Debreczen	1030 x 500	—	Good
6	15th	112	7	104	Galati A/D	1234 x 250	1026 x 100	Good
				1	Ftr A/D nearby	16 x 250	—	Unknown
11	15th	129	8	121	Focsani	1424 x 250	—	Good
21	8th	163	20	114	Rhuland	777 x 500	295 x 100	Good
				1	Podlaska	8 x 500	—	Unknown
				26	Elsterwerda	6 x 500	946 x 100	Good
				2	Dropped leaflets			
26	8th	72	1	71	Drohobycz	1125 x 250	—	Good
JULY								
No Bomber operations during July								
AUGUST								
6	8th	78	2	76	Rahmel	446 x 500	—	Excellent
7	8th	57	2	55	Trzebinia	828 x 250	—	Excellent
8	8th	73	0	75	Buzau A/D	526 x 250	—	Good
					Zilistea A/D	560 x 250	—	Good
SEPTEMBER								
11	8th	75	0	75	Chemnitz	345 x 500	241 x 500	Fair
13	8th	74	1					
18	8th	110	3	107	Warsaw	Dropped Supplies		Fair
19	8th	93	1					

SUMMARY OF BOMBER OPERATIONS

Part II

DATE	BOMBERS LANDING AT BASES	BOMBERS DOWN IN SOVIET TERR.	BOMBERS LOST				CASUALTIES			CLAIMS		
			ENEMY AIRCRAFT	FLAK	ACC.	UNKN.	K.I.A.	W.I.A.	M.I.A.	DEST.	PROB.	DAMG.
JUNE												
2	129	—	—	—	—	1	—	—	11	—	—	—
6	112	—	—	—	—	—	—	—	—	2	3	1
11	to Italy	—	—	—	—	1	—	—	10	2	—	—
21	137	7	—	1	—	—	—	7	10	1	1	3
26	to Italy	—	—	—	—	—	—	—	—	—	—	—
JULY No bomber operations during July.												
AUGUST												
6	75	1	—	—	—	—	—	1	—	—	2	2
7	57	—	—	—	—	—	1	—	—	1	—	—
8	to Italy	—	—	—	—	—	—	—	—	—	—	—
SEPTEMBER												
11	74	1	—	—	—	—	—	—	—	—	—	—
13	to Italy											
18	105	1	—	—	—	1	1	2	10	4	1	—
19	to Italy											

SUMMARY OF FIGHTER OPERATIONS

Part I

DATE	AIR FORCE	FIGHTERS DISPATCHED	ABORTIVE	FIGHTERS ATTACKING	TARGET	FIGHTERS LANDING AT BASES	FIGHTERS DOWN IN SOVIET TERRITORY	FIGHTERS LOST
JUNE								
2	15th	69	5	64	Debreczen — Escort	64	—	—
6	15th	47	5	42	Galati — Escort	45	—	2
11	15th	59	7	52	Foscani — Escort	To Italy	—	1
21	8th	70	5	65	Rhuland — Escort	63	1	1
26	8th	58	3	55	Drohobycz — Escort	To Italy	—	—
JULY								
22	15th	119	—	119	Buzau & Zilistea A/Ds	113	1	5
25	15th	78	11	67	Mielec A/D	78	—	—
26	15th	102	4	98	Bucharest-Ploesti area	To Italy	—	2
29	15th	14	—	—	Kecskmet	To Italy	—	—
AUGUST								
4	15th	77	—	77	Focsani A/D's	65	7	5
6	15th	60	7	53	Zilistea area	To Italy	—	—
6	8th	64	—	64	Rahmel — Escort	64	—	—
7	8th	39	10	29	Traebinia — Escort	39	—	—
8	8th	67	12	55	Buzau and Zilistea A/D's	To Italy	—	1
SEPTEMBER								
11	8th	64	—	64	Chemnitz	61	2	1
13	8th	62	—			To Italy	—	—
18	8th	73	9	64	Warsaw — Escort	71	—	2
19	8th	62	7			To Italy	—	—

SUMMARY OF FIGHTER OPERATIONS

Part II

DATE	CASUALTIES			CLAIMS			FIGHTER STRAFING
	K.I.A.	M.I.A.	W.I.A.	DEST.	PROB.	DAMG.	
JUNE							
2	—	—	—	—	—	—	Escort of Bombers
6	—	2	—	6	—	—	Escort of Bombers
11	—	1	—	3	—	1	Escort of Bombers
21	—	1	—	6	—	2	Escort of Bombers
26	—	—	—	—	—	—	Escort of Bombers
JULY							
22	—	5	—	15	6	12	A/C on ground 41-0-11, dest. 6 locomotives, 2 trucks, 3 RR tank cars. damg. 4 trucks.
25	—	—	—	29	5	7	A/C on ground 9-7-2, dest. 4 locomotives, 13 trucks, 2 buses, 1 staff car.
26	—	2	—	20	—	5	A/C on ground 6-0-1
29	—	—	—	—	—	—	No encounters.
AUGUST							
4	—	4	—	3	—	7	A/C on ground 4-0-1, dest. 3 locomotives and 1 tank car. Strafed 1 troop train, 1 truck with troops, 6 flak batteries, and hangers and buildings
6	—	—	—	—	—	—	Nil
6	—	—	—	—	2	2	Escort of Bombers
7	—	—	—	3	—	—	Escort of Bombers
8	—	1	—	1	—	—	Escort of Bombers
SEPTEMBER							
11	—	—	—	—	—	—	Escort of Bombers
13							
18	—	2	—	4	—	5	Escort of Bombers—0-0-1 A/C on Ground
19							

SUMMARY OF PHOTO AND WEATHER RECONNAISSANCE MISSIONS
JUNE 1944

40 F-5 aircraft were dispatched from Eastern Command
* 32 F-5s returned to Eastern Command
8 F-5s continued to Italy.
8 F-5 aircraft were dispatched from Italy and Britain and landed at Eastern Command.
20 of the above missions landed in Eastern Command after successfully photographing enemy installations.
* 1 F-5 was shot down in Russian territory by a Russian fighter on 26 June. The pilot, Lieutenant Rowe, was injured.

SUMMARY OF PHOTO AND WEATHER RECONNAISSANCE MISSIONS
JULY 1944

45 F-5 Aircraft were dispatched from Eastern Command
36 F-5s returned to Eastern Command
9 F-5s continued to Italy
13 F-5 Aircraft were dispatched from Italy and landed at Eastern Command.
29 of the above missions landed in Eastern Command after successfully photographing enemy installations.
There were no losses or casualties during the month.

SUMMARY OF PHOTO AND WEATHER RECONNAISSANCE MISSIONS
AUGUST 1944

23 F-5 aircraft were dispatched from Eastern Command
12 F-5s returned to Eastern Command
11 F-5s continued to Italy
9 F-5s were dispatched from Italy and landed in Eastern Command.
18 of the above missions landed in Eastern Command after successfully photographing enemy installations.
There were no losses or casualties during the month.

THE FOLLOWING CONVERSION FACTORS ARE MAXIMUM CAPACITIES
PER AIRCRAFT FOR EACH ITEM OF SUPPLY LISTED IN THE
DAILY OPERATIONAL SUPPLY STATUS REPORT

	B-17	P-38	P-51
Gasoline (100-Octane)	2,780 gals	756 gals	510 gals
Oil (1120 Ac)	45 gals	26 gals	12 gals
Oxygen	660 cu ft	42 cu ft	42 cu ft
Ammunition (.50-cal)	7,450 rounds	1,200 rounds	1,600 rounds
Ammunition (20-mm)	—	150 rounds	—
Bombs			
250 lb, G.P.	16		
250 kg, G.P.	12		
100 lb, I.B.	42		
Belly Tanks			
50 gal	—	—	2
75 gal	—	—	2
108 gal	—	—	2
165 gal	—	2	—

DAILY OPERATIONAL SUPPLY STATUS

QUANTITIES ON HAND

As of 2000 hours 1 October 1944

ITEM	UNIT	STA. 559	STA. 560	STA. 561	COMMAND TOTAL
Gasoline (100-octane)	gals	646,625	463,404	1,146,104	2,256,133
Oil (1120 Ac)	gals	114,227	12,555	36,837	163,619
Oxygen	cu ft	43,950	1,717	50,622	96,289
H. E. Bombs:					
250-lb	rds	0	0	384	384
250-kg (Russian)	rds	14,364	0	14,364	28,728
Incendiaries:					
100-lb	rds	11,676	3,780	9,828	25,284
500-lb Clusters	rds	1,344	0	1,344	2,688
Ammunition:					
.50-cal	rds	1,022,455	863,605	521,255	2,407,315
20-mm	rds	12,950	0	20,040	32,990
Jettisonable Tanks:					
50 gal	ea.				
75 gal ⎱ P-51s	ea.		136		136
108 gal ⎰	ea.		90		90
165 gal P-38s	ea.	227		369	596

EFFECTIVE STRENGTH

STATION	B-17 COMPLETE LOADS	B-17 LIMITING FACTOR	P-38 COMPLETE LOADS	P-38 LIMITING FACTOR	P-51 COMPLETE LOADS	P-51 LIMITING FACTOR
559	66	Oxygen	86	20-mm Ammo	0	Belly Tanks
560	0	H.E. Bombs	0	Belly Tanks	41	Oxygen
561	76	Oxygen	133	20-mm Ammo	0	Belly Tanks
Command	142		219		41	

NOTE:
1. For each type of supply the number of maximum aircraft loads equivalent to the quantity on hand is calculated. The least number of maximum loads equals the number of complete loads available, and the corresponding type of supply is the limiting factor.
2. In each case a single stock of supplies is presented in terms of use by three different types of aircraft. Complete loads for these different types represent *alternative* uses.

Statistical Control
Eastern Command

MAINTENANCE REPORT

WEEKLY SUMMARY OF AIRCRAFT REPAIR

Station No. COMMAND TOTAL
As of 1700 hrs Saturday

Week Ending 30 September 1944

	BATTLE DAMAGE		NON-BATTLE DAMAGE		
	BOMBERS	FIGHTERS	BOMBERS	FIGHTERS	CARGO
A No. A/C undergoing repair at beginning of week.	2	0	0	0	0
B No. A/C received for repairs during week.	16	1	0	0	0
C No. A/C repaired (completed) during week.	13	1	0	0	0
D No. A/C undergoing repair at end of week.	5	0	0	0	0
E Total A/C repaired to date.	61	34	19	200	11
F No. A/C salvaged during week.*	1	0	0	0	0
G No. A/C salvaged to date.	44	1	0	5	2

NOTE 1.—Lines "A" plus "B" minus "C" should equal "D."

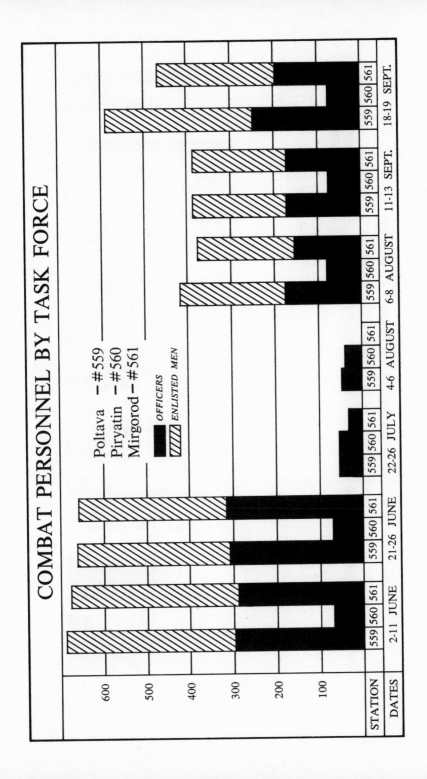

COMBAT PERSONNEL BY TASK FORCE

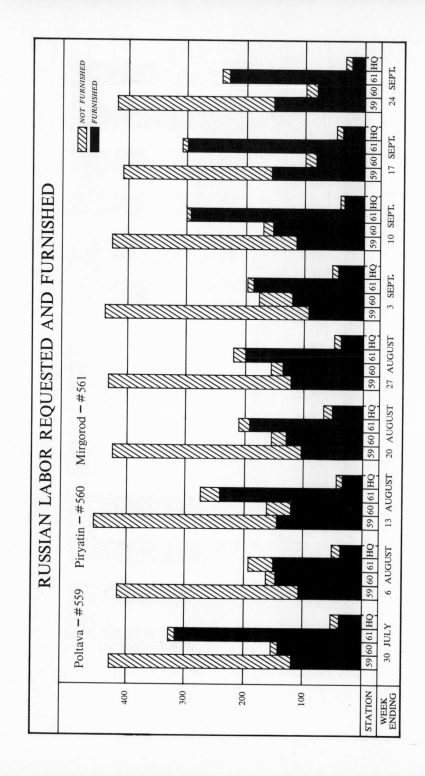

RUSSIAN LABOR REQUESTED AND FURNISHED

Poltava – #559   Piryatin – #560   Mirgorod – #561

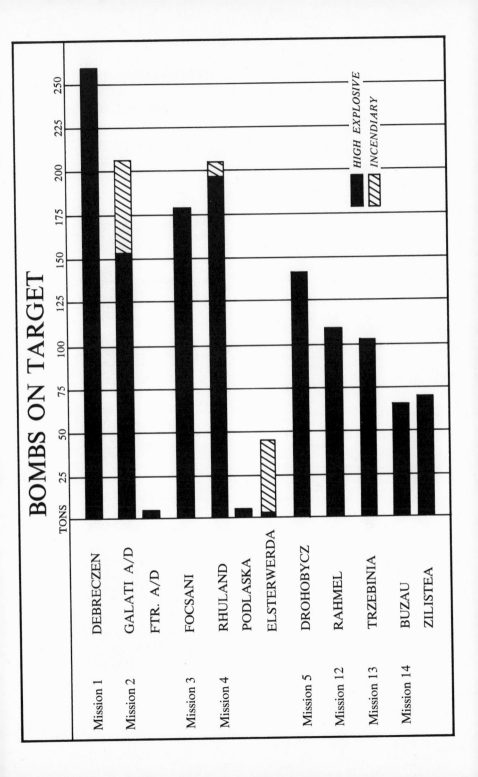

BOMBS ON TARGET

HIGH EXPLOSIVE
INCENDIARY

TONS 25 50 75 100 125 150 175 200 225 250

Mission 1   DEBRECZEN
Mission 2   GALATI A/D
             FTR. A/D
Mission 3   FOCSANI
Mission 4   RHULAND
             PODLASKA
             ELSTERWERDA
Mission 5   DROHOBYCZ
Mission 12   RAHMEL
Mission 13   TRZEBINIA
Mission 14   BUZAU
             ZILISTEA

Bibliography

BOOKS AND ARTICLES

Baumbach, Werner. *The Life and Death of the Luftwaffe.* Translated by Frederick Holt. New York: Coward-McCann, Inc., 1960.

Bekker, Cajus. *The Luftwaffe War Diaries.* Translated and edited by Frank Ziegler. New York: Doubleday & Company, 1968.

Bor-Komorowski, Lieutenant General T. "The Unconquerables." *Reader's Digest,* February 1946.

Churchill, Winston S. *Triumph and Tragedy.* Boston: Houghton Mifflin Company, 1953.

Craven, Wesley Frank, and Cate, James Lea. *The Army Air Forces in World War II, vol. 2, Europe: Torch to Pointblank, August 1942 to December 1943.* Chicago: The University of Chicago Press, 1949, and vol. 3, *Europe: Argument to V-E Day, January 1944 to May 1945.* Chicago: The University of Chicago Press, 1951.

Deane, John R. *The Strange Alliance: The Story of Our Efforts at Wartime Co-operation with Russia.* New York: The Viking Press, 1947.

Dennett, Raymond, and Johnson, Joseph E. *Negotiating with the Russians.* Boston: World Peace Foundation, 1951.

DuPre, Colonel Flint O., USAFR. *U.S. Air Force Biographical Dictionary.* New York: Franklin Watts, Inc., 1965.

Esposito, Brigadier Gen. Vincent J., USA (Ret.). *A Concise History of World War II.* New York: Frederick A. Praeger, Inc., 1964.

Feis, Herbert. *Churchill-Roosevelt-Stalin.* Princeton: Princeton University Press, 1957.

Fischer, Louis. *Men and Politics: An Autobiography.* New York: Duell, Sloan & Pearce, 1946.

Freeman, Roger A. *The Mighty Eighth: Units, Men and Machines.* New York: Doubleday & Company, 1970.

Gurney, Gene. *Five Down and Glory.* New York: Ballantine Books, Inc., 1958.

Harriman, Averell W. *America and Russia in a Changing World: A Half Century of Personal Observation.* New York: Doubleday & Company, Inc., 1971.

Henderson, Captain David B., ed. *The 95th Bombardment Group H, USAF.* Privately Printed. Cincinnati: The 95th Group Photographic Section, 1945.

Hicks, Dr. Edmund. "Soviet Sojourn." *The Air Power Historian,* January 1964.

Jablonski, Edward. *Flying Fortress.* New York: Doubleday & Company, Inc., 1965.

Jensen, Oliver, Ed. *America and Russia.* New York: Simon and Schuster, 1962.

Kennan, George F. *Memoirs 1925-1950.* Boston: Little, Brown and Company, Atlantic Monthly Press, 1967.

Kilmarx, Robert A. *A History of Soviet Air Power.* New York: Frederick A. Praeger, 1962.

Lane, Arthur Bliss. *I Saw Poland Betrayed.* New York: The Bobbs-Merrill Company, 1948.

Maurer, Maurer, ed. *Air Force Combat Units of World War II.* Washington: USAF Historical Division, 1960.

McDowell, Ernest R., and Hess, William N. *Checkertail Clan: The 325th Fighter Group in North Africa and Italy.* Fallbrook: Aero Publishers, Inc., 1969.

McFarland, Marvin W. "Air Power and the Warsaw Uprising." *Air Power Historian,* October 1956.

Mackintosh, Malcolm. *Juggernaut: A History of the Soviet Armed Forces.* New York: The Macmillan Company, 1967.

Mirchuk, I., ed. *Ukraine and Its People.* Munich: Ukrainian Free University Press, 1949.

Olmstead, Merle C. *The Yoxford Boys: The 357th Fighter Group on Escort over Europe and Russia.* Fallbrook: Aero Publishers, Inc., 1971.

Price, Alfred. *Pictorial History of the Luftwaffe 1933-1945.* London: Ian Allan, Ltd., 1969.

Rust, Kenn C. "Black Night at Poltava." *RAF Flying Review,* vol. XIV, No. 11, 1959.

Saunders, Hilary St. George. *Royal Air Force 1939-1945,* vol. 3, *The Fight is Won.* London: Her Majesty's Stationery Office, 1954.

Toliver, Colonel Raymond F., and Constable, Trevor J. *Fighter Aces.* New York: The Macmillan Company, 1965.

Wedemeyer, Albert C. *Wedemeyer Reports.* New York: Holt and Company, 1958.

White, W. L. *Report on the Russians.* New York: Harcourt, Brace and Company, 1945.

ARCHIVES, REPORTS, AND MANUSCRIPT COLLECTIONS

The following reports were obtained from the *USAF Historical Archives,* Maxwell AFB, Alabama.

Benson, Major Reynolds. *Operation Frantic.* 527.476, 1944.

Bonnevalle, Colonel R. W. *Recent Developements in Connection with the Frantic Operation.* 522.161, 1943-44.

Browne, Colonel J. B. *Notes on Frantic V.* 520.476, 1944.

Deane, Major General John R. *Digest of Conference Held with General Deane on 8th and 10th August, 1944.* 522.161-5, 1943-44.

—— *Spring Frantic Operations.* 519.476-3, 1945.

End of Frantic—Messages. 522.1621-1, 1945.

Frantic VI. 519.476-1 and 527.476B, 1944.

Giles, Major General Barney M. *Employment of Heavy Bombers from Airports in Russia.* 522.161-5, 1943-44.

Gray, Colonel E. D. *Experience at Poltava.* 522.161-5, 1944.

History of the Eastern Command. 522.01-1, 1944.

Lewis, Major D. M. *Narrative: Frantic VII.* 1944.

MAAF Historical Report on Project Frantic. 622.430-6, 1945.

Marshall, General George C. *Evacuation of Poltava.* 522.161-5, 1945.

Old, Colonel Archie J., Jr. *Report of Frantic II.* WG-45-SU-OP, 1944.

Scherer, Colonel Harris F. *Interviews Regarding Russia.* 527.476, January to July 1944.

Spaatz, Lieutenant General Carl. *USSTAF Mission to Russia.* 522.161-5, 1943-44. *Shuttle Bombing Operations to Russia.* 522.161-5, 1943-44.

Strategy and Russia. 522.01-2, 1944.

Supply Routes Considered for Frantic. 522.161-5, 1943-44.

Visit by Mission of USSTAF Officers Relative to Frantic Project. 522.161-5, 1943-44.

White, Brigadier General Thomas D. *Summary of Attached Board Proceedings on Enemy Bombing of Poltava, 22 June 1944.* 522.161-5, 1943-44.

The following reports were obtained from the *Luftwaffe Archives, Bundesarchiv-Militararchiv,* Freiburg, Federal Republic of Germany.

Gundelach, I. G. *History of the Kampfgeschwader General Wever 4.*

Meister, General Rudolf. *Commendation to Luftwaffe Pilots on Poltava Mission,* 1944.

Minsk-Flugplatz der Kampfgeschwader KG 53 und 55.

Rohden, Hans-Detlef Herhudt Von. *Letzter Grosseinsatz Deutscher Bomber Im Osten.* Europaische Sicherheit, 1951.

Zantke, Ziegfried. *140 Viermots Blieben in Poltawa,* 1953.

Additional reports and manuscripts include:

Antrup, Colonel Wilhelm. *Personal Account of the Luftwaffe Attack on Poltava.* Neubiberg: Unpublished.

Davis, Barrie. *Recollections: Mission to Russia 1944.* Zebulon: Unpublished.

Eastern Command Report. Dayton, Ohio: U.S. Air Force Museum Archives.

Hogg, Roy. *To Russia in a Mustang.* Springfield: Unpublished.

Julian, Thomas Anthony. *Operation Frantic and the Search for American-Soviet Collaboration, 1941-1944.* Thesis. Syracuse: Syracuse University, 1967.

Macdonald, Donald J. *My Shot Down Story.* German Prisoner-of-War Camp: Unpublished, 1944.

Sluder, Colonel Chester L. *Participation in Operation Frantic by 325th Fighter Group, 2-11 June 1944.* Albuquerque: Unpublished.

The History of Frantic 26 October 1943-15 June 1944. Dayton, Ohio: U.S. Air Force Museum Archives.

Walsh, Major General Robert L. *Eastern Command Fact Book.* USAF Academy: The Academy Library.

Index

Index